Why Noise Matters

Why Noise Matters

A Worldwide Perspective on the Problems, Policies and Solutions

John Stewart

with Arline L. Bronzaft, Francis McManus, Nigel Rodgers and Val Weedon

publishing for a sustainable future

London • New York

First published 2011
by Earthscan
2 Park Square, Milton Park, Abingdon, Oxon OX14 4RN

Simultaneously published in the USA and Canada
by Earthscan
711 Third Avenue, New York, NY 10017

Earthscan is an imprint of the Taylor & Francis Group, an informa business

For more information on Earthscan publications, see www.earthscan.co.uk or write to earthinfo@earthscan.co.uk
Earthscan publishes in association with the International Institute for Environment and Development

British Library Cataloguing in Publication Data
A catalogue record for this book is available from the British Library

Library of Congress Cataloging in Publication Data
Stewart, John.
  Why noise matters : a worldwide perspective on the problems, policies, and solutions / John Stewart with Arline Bronzaft ... [et al.].
    p. cm.
  ISBN 978-1-84971-256-9 (hardback) — ISBN 978-1-84971-257-6 (pbk.) 1. Noise pollution. I. Bronzaft, Arline L. II. Title.
  TD892.S75 2011
  363.74—dc22   2011003939

ISBN: 978-1-84971-256-9 hardback
ISBN: 978-1-84971-257-6 paperback

Typeset in Minion and Myriad by Composition and Design Services
Cover design by Rob Watts

MIX
Paper from
responsible sources
FSC
www.fsc.org FSC® C004839

Printed and bound in Great Britain by
TJ International Ltd, Padstow, Cornwall

Contents

List of contributors   *vi*

List of figures, tables and boxes   *vii*

List of acronyms and abbreviations   *viii*

Pre-introduction   *x*

Introduction   1

1.   Why Noise Matters   5

2.   Noise: Widespread and Worldwide   22

3.   Hear Me Now! Noise Can Harm Your Health!   47
    Arline L. Bronzaft

4.   Noise: The Neglected Green Issue of Our Age?   62

5.   Noise in the Workplace   79

6.   Transport Noise   94

7.   Neighbour/Neighbourhood Noise   108
    Val Weedon

8.   Piped Music: The Music You Cannot Turn Off   119
    Nigel Rodgers

9.   Noise and the Law   131
    Francis McManus

10. Making Change Happen   162

Index   *167*

List of Contributors

John Stewart is one of the UK's leading campaigners. In 2008 he was voted the country's most effective environmentalist by the *Independent on Sunday*. He currently chairs the UK Noise Association and headed up the coalition which defeated plans for a third runway at Heathrow Airport.

Arline L. Bronzaft, Ph.D. is a Professor Emerita of Lehman College, City University of New York and an Expert Witness on Noise Impacts. She serves on the Mayor's GrowNYC, chairing its noise committee, and was also named to this volunteer position by the three previous Mayors. Dr. Bronzaft conducts research, writes and lectures on the adverse effects of noise on our mental and physical well-being. She has written broadly on noise including chapters in environmental books and encyclopedias, published articles in academic journals, and writings for the more popular press. She is frequently quoted in the media in the United States and abroad. In 2007, she assisted in the updating of the New York City Noise Code.

Francis McManus is Professor of Law at Edinburgh Napier University where he specialises in environmental law and the law of delict. He has published widely and has a particular interest in noise law.

Nigel Rodgers is the founder of Pipedown, the Campaign for Freedom from Piped Music, and a writer on history, art and philosophy. Among his recent books, co-authored with Mel Thompson, are *Philosophers Behaving Badly* (Peter Owen) and *Understand Existentialism* (Teach Yourself/Hodder.)

Val Weedon, the President of the UK Noise Association, is a leading campaigning journalist, author and lobbyist. She was awarded an MBE in 1997 for her campaigning work with the Right to Peace and Quiet Campaign, which she founded in 1991. Her work has been published widely in newspapers, magazines and journals. Val's book *The Quiet Guide* was published in April 2007. She also contributes features to the online music and lifestyle magazine *Zani*.

List of Figures, Tables and Boxes

Figures

6.1 Number of people exposed to road and rail traffic noise
   in 25 EU countries in 2000   95
6.2 Percentage of people annoyed as a function of noise
   exposure of dwellings (Lden in dB(A))   95

Tables

1.1 Sound levels and human response   16
1.2 Physical symptoms of exposure to noise at very low frequencies   18
5.1 Construction site equipment   85

Boxes

1.1 Val Weedon   7
1.2 Andrew Martin   8
1.3 The intensity of the hum   19
1.4 A small sample of press cuttings collected from UK newspapers
   over the past 25 years about the hum   20
2.1 Managing environmental noise in India   34
2.2 Sensitivity to low-frequency noise   41
4.1 Bernie Krause   69
4.2 Noise in US National Parks   74
5.1 Teenage work noise led to deafness   82
5.2 Ferry workers warned about hearing risks   83
5.3 The construction industry   85
6.1 The importance of slow   98
6.2 Escaping traffic noise   99
6.3 The way aircraft noise is measured   103
7.1 The limits of mediation   115

List of Acronyms and Abbreviations

ASBO	Anti-Social Behaviour Order
ASOC	Antarctic and Southern Ocean Coalition
CAA	Civil Aviation Authority
CAMRA	Campaign for Real Ale
CDA	Continuous Descent Approach
CWU	Communication Workers' Union
Defra	Department for Environment, Food and Rural Affairs
DNL	Day-Night Average Sound Level
EC	European Commission
ECHR	European Convention of Human Rights
EES	Environment Effects Statement
END	Environmental Noise Directive
EPD	Environmental Protection Department
ESIA	Ear Science Institute Australia
EU	European Union
FAA	Federal Aviation Administration
FEHRL	Forum of European National Highway Research Laboratories
FICAN	Federal Interagency Committee
GDP	gross domestic product
HACAN	Heathrow Association for the Control of Aircraft Noise
HSE	Health and Safety Executive
IMO	International Maritime Organization
IPCC	Intergovernmental Panel on Climate Change
ISVR	Institute of Sound and Vibration Research
MoD	Ministry of Defence
MPA	Maritime Protection Area
NAS	Noise Abatement Society
NHS	National Health Service
NICU	neonatal intensive care unit
NPS	National Park Service
NRDC	Natural Resources Defense Council
ONAC	Office of Noise Abatement and Control
PIL	Public Interest Litigation
RMT	National Union of Rail, Maritime and Transport Workers
RNID	Royal National Institute for the Deaf

RPQC	Right to Peace and Quiet Campaign
TPS	Town Planning Scheme
UN	United Nations
UNESCO	United Nations Educational, Scientific and Cultural Organization
US EPA	US Environmental Protection Agency
VAD	vibroacoustic disease
VPP	Victoria Planning Provisions
WHO	World Health Organization
WTO	World Trade Organization

Pre-introduction

A number of books have been written about noise. They have ranged from technical manuals and academic textbooks to handy guides on what individuals can do when faced with a noise problem.

Our book aims to be different. It looks at noise worldwide. It asks hard questions of politicians and decision-makers about their failure to tackle noise. It explores why noise, despite posing a real threat to the planet's natural sound systems, has not become an issue for the environmental movement. It examines noise in the work place. It looks at the links between noise, the consumer society, people's aspirations and globalization. It suggests practical solutions to noise problems for both the richer nations and the global south, involving the public and private sectors.

Most chapters refer to the UK but also look beyond it. The aim is to present an international perspective on noise. Where chapters do concentrate on particular countries – for example, the law chapter (Chapter 9) focuses on the UK, the US and Australia, and the chapters on neighbour noise and piped music (Chapters 7 and 8) largely describe the situation in the UK – it is in the belief that an in-depth look at the issue in selected countries will point the way to solutions which can be applied more widely.

The book was the brainchild of John Stewart who has written the majority of the chapters and has edited it. Experts in their field have written particular chapters: Dr Arline L. Bronzaft, one of America's most respected noise experts, has written the health chapter (Chapter 3) and has contributed sections on the American experience to Chapters 2 and 9. Francis McManus, professor of law at Edinburgh Napier University, has written the chapter on noise law (Chapter 9). Val Weedon MBE, the leading noise campaigner of her generation in the UK, has written the neighbour noise chapter (Chapter 7). Nigel Rodgers, the secretary of Pipedown, has penned the chapter on piped music (Chapter 8).

We would also like to thank Henry Thoresby for his thoughtful contributions to the book, Juliet Solomon for her guidance and inspiration in getting the project off the ground in the first place and Binnie Holligan for her help with the legal research.

Introduction

I t was an embarrassing moment. We were in a café drawing up plans to write this book. An old friend spotted us and came across to chat. He asked us what we were up to. When we told him we were putting together a book about noise, an embarrassed smile came across his face. 'Noise?' he asked. 'Yes, noise,' we replied in a whisper.

To admit you regard noise as a problem can be like owning up to the fact you once spotted trains or buses. It is seen as quaint, old-fashioned, not part of the modern world. To write a book about it is not something you mention even to your best friends!

Noise, however, is the pollutant which disturbs more people in their daily lives than any other. The picture is consistent across the globe. In Rio de Janeiro, noise regularly tops the list of complaints (Schafer, 1998). In New York, noise is consistently the number one issue on the city's helpline. In Europe, 450 million people, that is 65 per cent of the total population, are exposed daily to noise levels which the World Health Organization (WHO) regards as unacceptable (Berglund et al, 2000). In factories, down mines and on construction sites, noise remains a significant problem, particularly in the poorer countries.

Moreover, noise is threatening the planet's natural sound systems in much the same way as climate change is threatening runaway global warming. It is esti-mated that over the past 40 years a third of the planet's ecosystems have become aurally 'extinct' (Hull, 2007) and that underwater noise has doubled for each of the past five decades (McDonald et al, 2006). Yet, there is no mass movement pushing for action to tackle global noise pollution and few governments have put it anywhere near the top of their political agenda. For most, noise remains 'the forgotten pollutant'.

In this book we try to make sense of this apparent contradiction: noise is a problem everywhere, with a demonstrable impact on our health and quality of life, and on our planet, yet few governments have anything like a coherent strategy in place to deal with it; and, for the green movement, it is rarely an issue. This lack of interest from environmentalists is possibly a by-product of the way society has failed to prioritize noise. But it may also reflect a lack of real knowledge within the green movement of how seriously noise is threatening the planet as well as depriving people of the chance to enjoy the peace and quiet of the natural world.

So why do most governments – with some notable exceptions such as Hong Kong and China – fail to tackle noise?

Pressure from big business plays a role. Companies in many industries – from aviation to tyre manufacture – have fought hard against tighter noise regulation. The globalized market, too, can work against efforts to tackle noise. It creates pressure to produce goods as cheaply as possible, meaning many employers fail to invest in noise-reducing devices, particularly in the industrializing countries, where 75 per cent of the world's workforce is employed. Perhaps more fundamentally, globalization depends upon cheap, long-distance transport to function. Aircraft and ships, both of which generate a lot of noise, have become the workhorses of the global economy. However, the pressure is not all one way: countries such as India would argue it is globalization that has forced it to take noise more seriously. To compete in the globalized market, it has had to manufacturer quieter products in order to meet the higher standards required by industrialized countries.

It is too simple to lay all the blame at the door of big business and globalization. As the consumer society has become established, ordinary people have embraced noise in a quite unexpected way. In Chapter 1 we explain the phenomenon: 'There are fascinating signs, most obvious in the richer countries of the world where the consumer society has become embedded, that a growing number of people not only accept noise but see it as something positive because it is associated with the consumer goods they value. It is not noise that disturbs them, but silence. It seems that attitudes towards noise are being shaped and changed by the consumer society.'

This book explores the competing pressures that these new attitudes are putting on governments. There are two worlds colliding: the people who broadly enjoy the noise of the consumer society; and their fellow citizens who are increasingly disturbed by it. We cite as a case study the Labour Government of Tony Blair and Gordon Brown, which was so wedded to rampant consumerism that it utterly failed to see the need to tackle noise, thus leaving many to live with the misery of their noise problem.

The book also looks at the question of noise and social justice. We show that, while noise can and does affect rich and poor alike, it is poorer communities across the globe that are most exposed to it and, as a rule, have the least opportunity to do anything about it. If governments fail to tackle noise, the biggest impact will be on low-income and vulnerable people. The worst affected of all will be poor communities in the poor world: there is no double-glazing in the shanty towns.

Solutions

The book, though, is as much about solutions as problems. What is so frustrating is that solutions to many noise problems exist but are not being implemented or sometimes even sought. For example, it is estimated that, with the right measures in place, annoyance caused by traffic could be cut by 70 per cent (den Boer and Schroten, 2007). There is also considerable scope for reducing noise from ships and trains. In factories and on construction sites there are a wide range of things that can be done to cut the noise from the machinery. A lot of neighbour noise problems could be eliminated through better sound insulation between properties and the adoption of a much tougher attitude towards noisemakers. Piped music could simply be switched off! And, in fact, should be in places like hospitals where patients have little option but to endure something they may positively hate. As one patient, ending his days in hospital, said: 'Heaven please hear me and let my end come without music or TV!' There is also a growing body of case law in many countries that can assist with noise problems.

Of course, some problems will be more intractable. Aircraft noise, despite some technological improvements, will be with us for many years to come. High-speed trains may continue to be noisy for the foreseeable future. Wind turbines, badly located, can cause real problems, a fact the green movement needs to recognize. In the understandable rush to develop renewable energy, many environmentalists have become as dismissive of the noise problems from wind turbines as their opponents, the climate deniers, are of climate change. Are they in danger of becoming 'the noise deniers'?

More widely – and this is a theme which runs through the book – the gains from improved technology may be cancelled out if the people of the world, particularly those in richer countries, continue to use ever more cars, planes and ships and if ever more goods are carried across the globe. Hong Kong, for example, is spending millions of pounds on noise reduction measures merely to stand still because of the number of new cars pouring onto its streets each year. It may require a different lifestyle for many of us, and a more localized economic system, if we are to conquer noise. Not dissimilar, perhaps, to the measures the green movement advocates for tackling climate change.

But there will be no real progress in dealing with noise unless government attitudes towards it change. Although useful steps can be taken at a local authority or regional level, the evidence shows that it is only when national governments take noise seriously that significant progress is made. The most startling examples, which we cite in some detail, are China and Hong Kong. Some years ago both countries – then independent of each other – took the decision that noise was a growing problem and put in place a national strategy to deal with it. Although both places remain very noisy, significant progress has been made. For example, in China, despite a huge increase in the number of vehicles on its streets, the average noise from traffic in Beijing went down from 77 decibels in 1976 to 69 decibels in 2004. In contrast, the good progress the US was making in tackling noise stopped in its tracks when Ronald Reagan scrapped a national noise programme, arguing it was best dealt with at a more local level.

Perhaps most frustrating of all is the fact that it would not cost a fortune to tackle noise. We explain in the book that we do not envisage all the costs falling on the state. It has an important role in developing a broad strategy and setting an effective, overarching regulatory framework but governments are never good at micromanaging the economy. When they try to do so, it tends to lead to sterility and bureaucracy.

The private sector has a role to play. At the most basic level, private firms need to find money to pay for the installation of effective noise protection measures in their factories and on their construction sites. Although there has been noticeable progress in cutting workplace noise in the industrialized world over the past few decades, often as a result of trade union pressure, it is a very different picture in the industrializing world: we cite harrowing stories of young children deafened for life as a result of prolonged exposure to very high noise levels. That needs to change.

More positively, a properly incentivized private sector can help drive the market for quieter products. With the right regulatory framework in place, it can provide some of the creative energy necessary for innovation. That would bring a new generation of quieter products onto the market-place, with the additional advantage that the costs of developing them would fall on the private sector and, indirectly, on its customers, not on the state and the taxpayer. Moreover, where the state did need to pay for noise improvements, it could expect to get at least some of the money back in the reduced health and other costs associated with noise. In short, costs are far from an insurmountable barrier, although this book does recognize that they will be a much bigger problem in poorer countries where it suggests a step-by-step approach be adopted.

This book is about change. About how to make change happen. In the last chapter we outline practical steps that can be taken. We conclude that change is eminently possible. It is the one thing we want to make a noise about.

References

Berglund, B., Lindvall, T., Schwela, D. and Goh, K. (2000) *Guidelines for Community Noise*, World Health Organization, Geneva

den Boer, L. and Schroten, A. (2007) *Traffic Noise Reduction in Europe*, CE Delft, Netherlands

Hull, J. (2007) The noises of nature', *New York Times*, 18th February

McDonald, M. A., Hildebrand, J. A. and Wiggins, S. M. (2006) 'Increases in deep ocean ambient noise in the Northeast Pacific west of San Nicolas Island, California', *Journal of the Acoustical Society of America*, vol 120, no 2, pp711–718

Schafer, R. (1998) *The Book of Noise*, Arcana, Canada

CHAPTER 1

Why Noise Matters

*Some people are tormented by noise, while many
of their fellow citizens revel in the noisy lifestyle
they have embraced as part of the consumer society.*

Sound is all around us, and has been since we were conceived. The womb is full of sounds. The foetus hears its mother's voice and her movement, breathing and digestive processes. Its 'hearing' is less with the ears, which are filled with fluid, than through vibrations in the skull (Menon, 2004). So sound is natural. It gives meaning to our lives. We use it to communicate, to celebrate and to mourn. It can warn of danger. It has been central to humans, mammals and animals down through the ages.

Sound adds to the enjoyment of life. Whether it is relaxing beside a babbling brook, listening to a favourite piece of music or cheering on your football team from the terraces, sound brings pleasure. It can also be inspirational. Great oratory, fine music or the sound of voices raised in song can have a powerful emotional effect on people.

Sassoon put it like this in his poem *Everyone Sang*:

*Everyone suddenly burst out singing;
And I was filled with such delight
As prisoned birds must find in freedom,
Winging wildly across the white
Orchards and dark-green fields; on – on – and out of sight.*

*Everyone's voice was suddenly lifted;
And beauty came like the setting sun:
My heart was shaken with tears; and horror
Drifted away ... O, but Everyone
Was a bird; and the song was wordless; the singing will never be done.*

Sound has been used – and at times abused – to inspire armies, to create revolutionary movements and to drive sportsmen and women to new heights of achievement. A competition was even launched in the UK in 2006 for the loudest and most passionate football supporters! The sound levels were scientifically measured at every Coca-Cola Football League match in the country during the opening two weekends of the season. The competition was won by the Colchester United supporters, with a decibel level of 128.5!

Sound becomes *noise*

So when does sound become noise? There is no simple answer to that question. There is no clear dividing line. There is no point at which an increase in decibel levels automatically turns sound into noise (see boxes on how noise is measured). One person's sound can be another person's noise. The beat of the background music in a department store, for example, is enjoyed by some shoppers but drives others to distraction.

The way we react to sound, to noise, is influenced by a number of factors. Acousticians estimate that about one in ten people are particularly noise-sensitive. Typically, these people will become 10 per cent more annoyed by noise than the general population, according to the German psychologist, Rainer Guski (1999). All of us, though, are likely to become more annoyed if we believe the noise may be harming our health or putting us in danger. We can get very annoyed too – even desperate – if we feel we have no control over the noise or we cannot stop it getting worse. We can be particularly disturbed when our neighbourhood suddenly becomes noisy – such as the introduction of a new flight path overhead. Generally, we are less annoyed if we feel there may be benefits linked to the noise: such as jobs or economic regeneration. We are also less annoyed if we believe the authorities are doing everything they can to mitigate the effects of it. But none of these variables should be used to downplay the fact that noise is a pollutant which can do serious damage. The relationship between noise and health is explored further in Chapter 3.

When noise really disturbs

When noise – any noise – becomes really disturbing, it can dominate every aspect of our lives. It always seems to be there, an ever-present shadow, darting, taunting, tantalizing, forever just out of reach. The desire to get rid of the offending noise by almost any means possible can become overwhelming. People spend their waking – and sleeping – hours fantasizing about how to stop it. They dream of poisoning the barking dog, of shooting down the roaring jet, of smashing the neighbour's stereo or of derailing the latest lorry that thunders past. Murder – or suicide – is just the end-point of that process. It is not surprising that from time to time people will say they have been driven to murder because of the noise they have endured. And it is not known how many suicides can be attributed to noise. Too often these acts are dismissed as the extreme reactions of odd-balls who cannot cope with the modern world. But anybody who has had a serious noise problem will understand the feelings

---

BOX 1.1   Val Weedon

Little did Val think she would become the UK's leading anti-noise campaigner when as a teenager she worked for the Small Faces rock band in Carnaby Street at the height of their fame in the swinging London of the 1960s. She liked the pop music of the era. Her regular haunt was the Marquee in Soho. The noise problem that was to change Val's life didn't start until 20 years later. By then she was living with her two children in a house in the Thamesmead council estate in South London. She had been there for about 12 years. She was a broadcaster on the local radio station, deeply involved with the community and on friendly terms with her neighbours. She jumped at the chance to buy her house. And then a new neighbour moved in next door and the music started. It was so loud that Val and her husband Phil could hear the lyrics through the wall. They asked the neighbour to turn it down, which at first she did, but then it was back at the same volume. 'We couldn't relax or watch television and I kept bursting into tears at work,' says Val. 'It turned into a full-scale battle. We threatened to take her to court but she just sent a note back saying "good luck to you". All the council did was to send us a leaflet about taking our own action.' In the end Val sold up. 'I had to give some of my right-to-buy discount back but we were so desperate we had no option. We are permanently sensitized now and, if we hear that bass, those feelings of panic return.' After her experience, Val set up the Peace and Quiet Campaign to assist noise sufferers. At its height in the 1990s it had thousands of members. She received an MBE for her work. She then founded and became the coordinator of the UK Noise Association. But she says the noise experience will never leave her. 'We now live in Kent. We have had to take out a large mortgage to buy a detached house because, if we were attached to anybody, I would live in fear that a new neighbour might start playing their music excessively loud and our nightmare would return.'

---

that lead to murder. *The Washington Post* (1994) quotes Pamela Parker Shine, who had been a noise inspector for eight years in Montgomery County, US, as saying: 'I have never seen anything that affects people like noise does. When someone gets woken up at three in the morning, they really can lose it. And I can't say I blame them.' Again, there is more on this in Chapter 3.

Although only a small number of people resort to suicide or murder, many lives are changed forever by noise problems. See, for example, Val Weedon (Box 1.1) and Andrew Martin (Box 1.2), but Val and Andrew are not alone. When sound, which is essential to living, is abused, it can suck the life out of people.

The changing sound of noise

Noise, of course, is not new. It has been with us down through the ages. Emily Thompson in her fascinating book, *The Soundscape of Modernity* (2004), quotes the Buddhist scriptures which listed the 'ten great noises in a great city' in 500 BC as 'elephants, horses, chariots, drums, tabors, lutes, song, cymbals, gongs and people crying "Eat ye, and drink"!' We only have to read accounts

---

BOX 1.2 Andrew Martin

Andrew Martin is a successful author and journalist. He admits that noise has become an obsession. He takes up the story: 'I well remember the fatal conversation of ten years ago that started it all ... My landlord-to-be, a very pleasant straight-up-and-down fellow, said, "The only slight drawback with the room is that the man next door keeps a couple of dogs in his backyard and they bark sometimes. Is that going to bother you?" "Shouldn't do," I said, "I like dogs." I learnt a lot over the following year. I learnt, for example, that the best earplugs have the brand name Quies and you can buy them from most independent chemists, but not Boots. I learnt that you can create benign abstract noise by tuning your radio to the spaces between stations; that electrical fans by Cianni have a consoling rattle when switched to their highest speed and that this will drown out two dogs, even as they give voice to the hysteria understandably called for by the arrival of the milkman. The two dogs spent as much time barking as they spent not barking. They would bark whenever anyone walked down the street or when any car passed, or just because they hadn't barked for a while. I developed a plan for eliminating the two dogs. Their lives seemed so miserable, I reasoned, that if I killed them, I would be doing us all a favour. My plan was to freeze a poisonous powder of some kind into an ice cube and then lob the ice cube into the dogs' drinking bucket, which was directly below my window. What would be the reaction of the dog owner? Would he arrange for an autopsy to be conducted? I had never complained directly to the owner because that would remove the option of doing away with his dogs, but would suspicion fall on me in any case because I had spent hours leaning out of the window swearing at them? I left the dog flat after a year. I became vulnerable (for life, as I now realize) to all sudden noises.' Andrew got married and moved to the country, but, due to the noise of the traffic going past his house, was back in North London after 18 months, only to discover he had bought a house under the flight path to Heathrow.

---

of the noise in ancient Rome or on the streets of medieval Europe to understand the problems it presented. But the type of noise was different to that so common in the modern world – Thompson called it 'the organic sounds created by humans and animals at work and at play.' Dr J H Girdner itemized these sounds in *The Plague of City Noises* (1896): 'horse-drawn vehicles, peddlers, musicians, animals and bells.' Actually, not very different from the 'ten great noises' listed in the Buddhist scriptures.

It was the spread of industrialization that changed the kind of noises which came to dominate people's lives. In an article in the *Saturday Review of Literature*, published in America in 1925, quoted by Thompson (2004), the author talked of very different noises: 'The air belongs to the steady burr of the motor, to the regular clank of the elevated, and to the chitter of the steel drill. Underneath is the rhythmic roll of the clattering of the subway; above, the drone of the airplane. The recurrent explosions of the internal combustion engine, and the rhythmic jar of bodies in rapid motion determine the tempo of the sound world in which we have to live.'

When New Yorkers were surveyed in 1929 about the noises which bothered them, the ten most annoying noises were all related to 'machine age inventions'. The human street sounds that had troubled people down through the ages had, by 1930, been replaced by mechanical noises. The roar of 'the roaring twenties' was very different from what had gone before.

Fast-forward a century to the present day. The 'machine age' noises are still dominant: the motor car, the aeroplane, the train and the factory. But our modern age has brought its own distinctive 'machine' noises: stereo-systems, air-conditioning, central heating, fridges, washing-machines, spin-dryers, mobiles phones, musak and iPods.

Attitudes shaped by the consumer society

The number of people now disturbed by noise runs into millions in the UK alone. (We look in detail at how prevalent noise pollution has become across the world in the next chapter). But there are also fascinating signs, most obvious in the richer countries of the world where the consumer society has become embedded, that a growing number of people not only accept noise but see it as something positive because it is associated with the consumer goods they value. It is not noise which disturbs them, but silence.

Fear of silence

It seems that attitudes towards noise are being shaped and changed by the consumer society. Many of the gadgets we acquire as consumers produce a noise: fridges, washing machines, central heating, vacuum cleaners, dishwashers, sound systems, televisions, radios, iPods, computers and mobile phones. At the most obvious level, this means that we can be growing up among a constant melee of mechanical noise. This lessens our awareness of background noise – particularly if we are from a home where the television, radio or music system is on much of the time and where family members are constantly attached to their iPods or linked into their computers. It also means that many people do not know life without noise; if it was not there, a void would open up in their lives. They would notice the silence. They have become oblivious to the noise.

Michael Bull (2000) explores many of these issues in *Sounding out the City*, subtitled 'the personal stereos and the management of everyday life', which looks at the way so many of us are constantly (and literally) attached to our iPod. One of the people Bull interviewed for his book talked about his iPod like this: 'It's a little like another person. But you can relate to it. You get something from it. It shares the same things as you do. You relate to it as if it is another person. Though you can't speak to it. The silence is freaky for me. That is kind of scary. It's almost like a void if you like.'

Another interviewee told Bull: 'I don't like silence. I hate it at night. I suppose it's night and you're on your own. I just don't like being alone. I just have to have someone with me or, if not with me, some type of noise. That's why I have the music on.'

Given the importance these people place on noise and their hatred of silence, to take the noise out of their world, or even to reduce it, would be disorientating. The personal stereo is not being used by these people to cut out undesirable noises – from traffic, aircraft, barking dogs, and so on. It is being used as a substitute for silence. Many of these children of the technological age are using technology not to fight against the noise it brings but to create their own noise. To escape the world, they choose noise, not silence. Many have become addicted to noise.

Defining our identity

It can go even deeper than this, though. The noise is coming from gadgets that we like, things that bring pleasure and value to our lives. Fewer and fewer of us any longer identify with a church, an ideology, a political party, a trade union or even our neighbourhood or extended family. We define ourselves by what we have. If many of these possessions are gadgets that make noise, then that noise, far from being disturbing, is associated with things that give us pleasure, increase our convenience and help define our identity. Thus noise becomes something positive, something that has good associations, something which is an integral part of ourselves. It does not of course mean that we have not all still got our pet hate irritating noises – the scraping of the nail file, the high-pitched whirr of the fan – but it does suggest a quite new attitude to mechanical noise has emerged. An attitude shaped by the consumer society.

Oliver James (2007) wrote in *Affluenza*: 'The great majority of people in English-speaking nations now define their lives through earnings, possessions, appearances and celebrity.'

Martin Pawley (1973) wrote in *The Private Future*: 'Consumer goods today determine social realities; they are the only reliable guide to income, lifestyle and aspirations. The marketing formula A, B, C1, C2, D and E is every bit as definitive as the Hindi caste system for the purposes of any consumer society.' This was written years before the consumer society became as dominant as it is today.

We have accepted and even welcomed noise as part of our embrace of the consumer society.

The loudness of modern noise

But we have not just embraced the *constant* noise from consumerism, many of us have also taken on board and indeed learnt to love the *loudness* of the noise. The noise in modern clubs, cinemas, restaurants and even on our home stereo-systems is of a decibel level unimaginable even 40 years ago. This is not a specifically youth problem, it applies across the age spectrum. Barry Blesser and Linda-Ruth Salter (2008) argue in 'The unexamined rewards for excessive loudness' that 'when a culture accepts loudness as being a legitimate right in recreational sound venues, that acceptance tends to legitimise all forms of noise pollution'. They go on: 'As a culture with advancing sonic tools and amplification, there are increasing opportunities to be immersed in destructively loud sound fields. We believe that acceptance of loudness in entertainment then carries over to a tolerance of disruptive noise from airplanes, jackhammers, powered garden equipment, and so on. Loudness becomes the cultural norm.'

If this argument is correct, it has profound implications for tackling noise. Will decision-makers feel under the same pressure to deal with noise if loudness has become the cultural norm for at least a percentage of the population? Indeed, how many decision-makers themselves will fall into that category? And where will that leave the millions who will still be disturbed by noise, far less the 10 per cent of people who are particularly noise-sensitive?

What we are beginning to see are two worlds colliding: those people who embrace loud and constant noise, who see no real problem with it; and those who are increasingly disturbed and, in some cases, utterly distressed by the noise around them. It means people will have markedly different attitudes to their neighbours' stereo-system, to living under a noisy flight path, to background music in a shop, to the constant stream of loud announcements pumped out on London's underground system.

A new attitude towards public space

There is another factor at play. In the richer countries, a new attitude towards public space and the public realm has emerged. New technology, designed typically for individual use, has meant that, for most of us, our lives have become centred round our own homes and our own families in a way that was not the case with previous generations. The television has replaced the trips to 'the pictures', the washing machine has seen off the laundry, the mobile has almost made the public phone box an anachronism. Of course, it is not sensible to exaggerate this. People still do go to the cinema and many high streets still have a launderette. But the trend is unmistakable and relentless. More and more activities take place within the home.

The result has been an historic retreat from the public realm. When most of us do venture out, we travel by car. We pass through, rather than use, public space. The result is we no longer recognize that we have any responsibility for the public realm. We regard it as the job of others to look after it: the police to keep it safe, the local authorities to maintain it, the state to manage it. Many people, indeed, have come to regard the public realm as alien territory. This lack of responsibility for, or even understanding of, the public realm can also mean that people do not see the need to modify their own behaviour when using it.

Again, we do not want to exaggerate this. Most of us spend time in the public realm but we are not *dependent* on it in the way that all previous generations were and that most people in poorer countries still are. We do not *need* to interact with other people in public spaces in a manner that was once unavoidable. The consumer society has ensured that we can live much of our lives behind the closed doors of our individual homes.

Noise in public spaces

The noise implications of this are huge and are already being worked out all around us. If we enjoy our 'noises' at home and at the same time feel little need to modify our behaviour in public spaces, it is only a natural desire and a logical step to recreate these 'noises' outside the home. The ghettoblaster in the street is the kid's sound system made public. The iPod on the train is no more than the chance to hear favourite songs when travelling – iPod man is fashioning the public realm around his private world.

The iPod is the sophisticated grandchild of the early, tinny transistor radio. The old transistor enabled us to bring our music with us – on the bus, to the park, to the beach. But the personal stereo goes much further. It enables us to create our own little world. When travelling, working or playing we can see the real world, but we are separate from it. We are in a public place but we are not communicating with it. Through our music on our personal stereo we are in our own privatized world.

One of Michael Bull's interviewees in *Sounding out the City* (2000) put it like this: 'I don't necessarily feel I'm there. Especially if I'm listening to radio. I feel I'm there, where the radio is … he's talking to me and only me and no one else around me is listening to that. So I feel like, I know I'm really on the train, but I am not really … I like the fact that there is someone still there.'

Bull argues that people retreat into this privatized, personal stereo world for a number of reasons. It can be out fear of public space, of mixing in an anonymous society. It can also be a tool of control, a way a person can impose their own world on a world that frightens them, or bores them, a world they cannot cope with or one that they have come to hate or despise. Asking someone to switch off, or even turn down, their music can therefore become tantamount to killing off their private world and forcing them to return to the mundane, and possibly frightening, outside world.

While doing our research we came across a strange little book called *The Perfect Thing*, by Steven Levy (2006). Levy, the chief technology writer on *Newsweek*, has written a paean of praise to the iPod, which he terms 'the defining object of the 21st century'. He calls it 'a near-universal object of desire'. To the smitten Levy, the iPod can do no wrong. He recalls how his spirits lifted as he 'bonded' with his iPod, which he argues is one of the most beautiful objects ever created.

Levy enthuses that the iPod, 'a totally cool product', not only gives people the chance to escape but to fashion an identity and to feel in control – control of their own world, control of their own playlist: 'A really good playlist can even generate an aphrodisiac effect'. He does acknowledge that 'it's not surprising that a new wave of finger-wagging editorialists has lambasted the iPod for isolating its users from human discourse, just as they did with the Walkman' but dismisses its critics as 'outsiders getting frustrated at the party they haven't been invited to' and as those who 'fit into a long tradition of neo-Luddite discomfort about the way people tweak their environments – and mess with their minds – to alter their mental and emotional state'. He seems to celebrate the fact that 'the iPod is only the most recent, and most compelling, advance in a movement of portable cocooning that's been going on for decades'.

Even if few people would endorse Levy's childlike admiration of it, the iPod is the perfect illustration of the changing attitude towards noise: as something that kills silence, which provides the opportunity for us to immerse ourselves in our own music, our own noise, played at the volume of our own choosing.

Attitudes could change again

This new situation could change. As is explained in the health chapter (Chapter 3), the level of noise that many people are now exposing themselves to over lengthy periods, particularly through music, is almost certain to damage their hearing and lead to premature deafness. Within a decade or two, the iPod in the ear could be replaced by the hearing aid. That could change attitudes. To hasten a change of attitude, probably the most immediate challenge is to find effective ways of weaning people off their addiction to loud music. It will not be easy, even if the political will were to be there. The personal rewards of loud music are immediate; the costs are subtle and delayed over years. Blesser and Salter (2008) argue we will only wean people off it if we first understand why they are addicted to loud music – the sense of power it can give, the arousal it produces, the escapism it allows – and then find less damaging alternatives that produce equivalent rewards. This is probably correct but it is long-term. Changing the culture of noise may require more immediate action.

The role of business

At this point, it would be useful to pause to consider a related argument: the view that it is business interests, rather than consumer attitudes, that are the real driving force behind the tolerance of noise in our society.

Professor Stuart Sim (2007), in his fascinating book *Manifesto for Silence*, argues that: 'Noise is in fact a key part of the business ethic that drives our culture, a means of capturing and holding our attention. The assumption in bars, for example, is that loud music increases alcohol consumption by drowning out talk; so as the night goes on the sound level goes up too, until by the evening's end you can hardly hear those standing next to you, even if they are shouting in your ear. Shopping malls are awash with music – some of it relatively bland and placid, some strident; so are airports.'

Sim expands his theme: 'Noise is used extensively as a marketing tool; as a way of stimulating consumption. Put crudely, noise sells, and the corporate world is very aware of this and concerned to exploit it to the full ... I will argue that such marketing techniques work to homogenise behaviour and restrict individualism; thus to resist them is to make a political statement. The areas of silence in our society are systematically being colonised by big business ... Noise in bars is unashamedly aimed at the younger generation because of their purchasing power, which corporations will always chase.'

Sim is arguing that noise, and particularly music, is used by corporations to influence and control. At one level this is certainly correct. But it would be a mistake to argue, and I am not sure Sim does, that business corporations are imposing loud music and other noise on an unwilling population. Our embrace of noise is part of our willing embrace of a consumer lifestyle. We may be influenced by corporations but we are not slaves to their music.

The implications for the poorer world

We need to consider whether these new attitudes towards noise that are emerging in richer countries are also to be found in industrializing countries as they strive to buy into the consumer society.

We must, of course, be careful not to look at the situation in the poorer world from our perspective; to, as it were, hear the street sounds of Cairo or Karachi through Western ears. The point is sometimes made by some noise officials from poorer societies that the very high noise levels found in their countries have not resulted in the deluge of complaints that would have come from people in the richer world exposed to similar levels. These officials argue that the people in their countries have been born into the noise, have adapted to it and simply regard much of it as a part of daily life. But, though there may be some truth in what they say, it would be a big mistake to imagine that just because the shanty town dwellers across the globe have not rioted over high noise levels that they find them acceptable. They do not regularly riot over a lack of sewerage facilities, filthy garbage heaps, drug dealers or communal violence either. They know they have little choice but to get on with life as best they can; to prioritize their problems. These officials' assertions may in part be to do with justifying their own inaction as the community voices that do filter through the global media from communities in the poorer world suggest that noise is a very real problem for many, many of its inhabitants.

Dr Yeshwant Oke, a medical consultant and anti-noise campaigner in Mumbai, put it like this: 'People and patients are silently suffering as they feel helpless. People feel agitated and angry, impotent to some extent. Indians are very docile. They would rather suffer than have enmity with the neighbours. But lately patience is wearing thin, and more and more people are complaining to get relief' (*Things Asian*, 2009). The head of the legal team at Beijing's Municipal

Environmental Protection Bureau, said: 'People's discontent about increasing noise harassment tops other complaints about the environment they live in' (China Daily, 2005). A survey in Vietnam found that more than a fifth of residents in both Hanoi and Ho Chi Minh City are highly annoyed by the typical daily noise levels in the cities (Phan et al, 2010).

The reasons for the high noise levels and their impact on people are not hard to identify. They come from cities that have developed rapidly, where homes, buildings, industrial premises, offices and shanty towns have sprung up beside each other in a pretty unplanned and unregulated way. Population numbers and traffic levels have soared. Airports have expanded. It all means people are subjected to very high levels of noise.

So far, for most of the citizens, few of the noises in poorer countries are associated with pleasure in the way that is increasingly common in richer countries. This will change with the influx of consumer goods. One crucial difference, though, will remain. For the foreseeable future, most people in poorer countries are likely to use and share public space in a way that is no longer the norm in most of the rich world. They will continue to have invest- ment in communal spaces. This may lead to stronger demands from the popu- lace for effective measures to be put in place to curb noise pollution. Certainly the driving force behind China's noise strategy – one of the few industrializing countries to have one in place – is a fear that its rapid embrace of the consumer society may lead to public disorder unless noise mitigation measures are put in place. It would be ironic if, at a time when in industrialized countries our love of consumerism has led to a more widespread acceptance of the noise it brings and lessened the pressure on governments to deal with it, the advent of the consumer society in poorer countries acted as the spur to more effective policies to tackle noise. Only time will tell.

Measuring noise

Noise is measured by its loudness (decibels) and its frequency (hertz). It is when we put the two together that we can get an idea of how disturbing a particular noise may be. Just to confuse matters, frequency does not mean how often a noise happens; it about how high or low the pitch of the noise is. A squeaky toy has a high-pitch. The bass of a sound system has a very low one.

How loud must noise be to become a problem?

- An increase of 10dB represents a doubling in perceived noise levels.
- The average person can pick up a 3dB change in noise levels, although some people can detect a 1dB change in noise.
- When daytime noise averages out at 50dB people start to get moderately annoyed.

TABLE 1.1 Sound levels and human response

Common Sounds	Noise Level (dB)	Effect
Boom Cars	145	Beyond threshold of pain (125 dB)
Jet Engines (Near)	140	
Shotgun Firing	130	
Jet Takeoff (100–200 ft)	130	
Rock Concerts (Varies)	110–140	
Oxygen Torch	121	
Symphony Orchestra	110	
Discotheque/Boom Box	120	Threshold of sensation (120 dB)
Thunderclap (Near)	120	
Stereos (Over 100 watts)	110–125	
Power Saw (Chain Saw)	110	Regular exposure of more than 1 min.
Pneumatic Drill/Jackhammer	110	risks permanent hearing loss (over
Snowmobile	105	100 dB)
Jet Flyover (1000 Feet)	103	
Electric Furnace Area	100	No more than 15 min. unprotected
Garbage Truck-Cement Mixer	100	exposure recommended (90–100 dB)
Farm Tractor	98	
Newspaper Press	97	
Subway, Motorcycle (25 ft)	90	Very annoying 85 – level at which
Lawnmower, Food Blender	85–90	hearing damage (8 hrs.) begins
Recreational Vehicles, TV	70–90	
Diesel Truck (40 mph, 30 ft)	84	
Washing Machine	78	
Dishwasher	75	
Average City Traffic Noise	80	Annoying, interferes with conversation,
Garbage Disposal	80	constant exposure may cause damage
Vacuum Cleaner, Hair Dryer	70	Intrusive, interferes with telephone use
Inside a Car (Loud Engine)		
Garbage Disposals	50–60	
Normal Conversation	50–65	Comfortable (under 60 dB)
Quiet Office	50–60	
Refrigerator Humming	40	
Living Room. Bedroom		
Whisper	30	Very Quiet
Broadcasting Studio	20	Just Audible
Rustling Leaves	10	Threshold of normal hearing (1000–
Normal Breathing	0	1000 Hz)

Source: Talbott and Thompson (1995)

- When it averages out at 55dB people start to get seriously annoyed.
- At night people start to get annoyed when the noise averages out at 30dB.
- The occasional loud noise can make us jump but rarely bothers us long-term. What really gets to people is frequent noise.

How loud does it need to be to make us deaf?

- A one-off noise above 150dB would probably produce instant hearing damage.
- A one-off noise of 130dB would produce a 'threshold of pain', without necessarily causing hearing damage unless the exposure continued for some time.
- The gradual loss of hearing from continuous exposure to high noise levels is a greater problem than one-off noises.
- Exposure to noise of 90dB or above for a relatively short time will produce temporary loss of hearing.
- If exposure to high noise is frequent, the speed at which normal hearing returns decreases and the threshold of hearing gradually becomes higher and reaches the point where it does not return to the normal level.

A look at frequency (Hz):

The frequency, or pitch, of noise is often neglected. Yet it has a real impact on whether or not we find a noise disturbing. So what is frequency?

- The frequency (or pitch) of noise is measured in hertz (Hz).
- The range of human hearing extends from around 20–20,000Hz – but a few people can hear lower frequencies.
- It is rare, though, that a sound occurs just at one frequency. Usually sound consists of many simultaneously occurring frequencies.
- Really low frequency noise is known as infrasound.

So why does it matter? Picture this scene. It is 2am. The dance floor is throbbing, packed with people gyrating to the latest sounds, the heaving mass of bodies picked out by the flickering flashes of the strobe lighting darting across the club. The music is good, but it is more than the music the clubbers are enjoying. It is the sensation of the sound and the strobes that are filling their whole body. This combination of the bass blaring out of the sound systems and the visual strobing is producing a physical effect. However, the sound system is not dependent upon the visuals to have this effect. The body would respond anyway to the low-frequency noise in the bass of the sound systems. The military have been aware for years that regular exposure to low frequency noise and infrasound (the lowest of all frequencies) can destabilise the human body.

It is these physical symptoms, allied to the noise disturbance, that tend to mean noises containing high amounts of low-frequency can be much more stressful than standard noises. This is thought to be the reason why most people find aircraft noise or the constant thudding of wind turbines worse than noise from traffic. Low-frequency noise is also present in many of our modern gadgets, such as the fridge, the washing machine, air conditioning or

TABLE 1.2 Physical symptoms of exposure to noise at very low frequencies

Symptoms	Frequency (Hz)
General feeling of discomfort	4–9
Influence on speech	13–20
Lump in throat	12–16
Chest pains	5–7
Abdominal pains	4–10
Urge to urinate	10–18
Influence on breathing movement	4–8

Source: Rasmussen (1982)

the bass of the sound system. The rise and rise of low-frequency noise is part of the reason for the growing number of noise complaints in society.

The hum

Most, though not all, acousticians, accept that 'the hum' is related to low-frequency noise. People who are affected by the hum often call themselves 'low-frequency noise sufferers'. They say that the noise in their ears is like the sound of thunder or the constant drone of a distant aircraft or the idling of a diesel engine. It is different from tinnitus, the ringing in the ears people get after exposure to loud noise. Tinnitus can become permanent. The hum usually goes away and it is generally site-specific. A number of studies have now taken place across the world into the hum. Nothing conclusive has been found but most agree that the cause is related to very low-frequencies, possibly emitted from gas pipelines, microwave levels, sonar defence systems or badly installed electrical equipment. There is a lot of debate regarding whether wind turbines can be a source of the hum.

The hum is very selective, approximately 5 per cent of the population 'hear' the noise at some stage in their lives, almost all are aged 50 or over, and 70 per cent of these are women. The hum is not constant in intensity and the physical effects which accompany it also vary in both type and intensity.

Apart from these physical symptoms, the hum sufferer can feel very isolated mentally as she may be the only person in the household to hear the hum. Other members of the house may well accuse her of making it up. Local authority officers can be unsympathetic. Often their equipment is not sophisticated enough to trace the very low-frequency sounds associated with the hum. Rarely is the source of the hum obvious, although in some cases it can be traced and the problem can be rectified. At other times, the only solution is for the sufferer to move permanently from her home or the area where she experiences the hum. The hum then nearly always disappears, though some sufferers argue that the experience has left them with very sensitive hearing for life. Given the huge predicted growth in technology in

---

BOX 1.3 The intensity of the hum

This scale was derived by the German Hum site (www.igzab.de)

0 = no hum audible

1 = moderate. The hum is constantly audible, but only as a quiet, soft background noise. Sleeping is not affected.

2 = disruptive. The hum is apparent even above other noises, becoming annoying and irritating. Any of the following may also be experienced: a rumbling noise, pressure on the ears, inability to concentrate, sleep disruptions or difficulty falling asleep. If the affected person is attempting to work in a quiet situation, the hum makes it difficult to think.

3 = very disruptive. Volume and/or vibrations at a higher level. Affected person feels a compulsion to seek the outdoors to escape the noise, and may become aggressive. If sleeping, then the periods of being unable to sleep exceed the periods of sleep. The affected person is therefore fatigued during the day.

4 = physical (bodily) symptoms. The noise is so insistent that thinking is prevented. The affected person is left with only the wish that the noise would stop. Symptoms such as the following may be experienced: dizziness, a feeling of pressure in the chest, perspiration, sleeplessness, uncontrolled twitching of the eyes, muscular vibrations or cramps, uncontrolled muscular twitches, a stiff neck, tension headache, irregular pulse, muscle and joint pain. The associated tension and excitation results in exhaustion. Vibrations are experienced at an intense level and perhaps in combination with a rumbling.

5 = hardly bearable. The hum is overpowering and survival is the only remaining thought. The affected person retreats into a fetal position in reaction to the onslaught of sensory perception. The symptoms described for level 4 may be combined with the feeling of the body being subjected to electrical current.

---

all countries, the hum is likely to become more widespread across the world. It is a dismal prospect.

The controversy over noise measurements

One might have thought that the task of measuring noise would be simple and uncontroversial. Far from it. It *is* easy to stand with a noise meter in your hand next to a busy road or beside your washing machine and record the decibel level. It shows you the noise levels you are experiencing. But it may underestimate the low-frequency. Most noise measurements are taken using what is known as 'A' weighting. That means that the measurements are 'weighted' so that the noise levels recorded are those heard by the human ear. But 'A' weighting doesn't work too well for low-frequency noise. The World Health Organization (WHO) suggests that, if the difference between 'A' weighted and 'C' weighted results is more than 10dB, the use of 'C' weighting should be considered when taking the results (Berglund et al, 2000). However many

---

BOX 1.4   A small sample of press cuttings collected from UK newspapers over the past 25 years about the hum

The Independent, March 1992

The search is on for the source of a low frequency hum that is ruining the lives of thousands of people in Britain. 'Hummers', the name given to people who hear a low, droning sound have been recognised at last as having a legitimate problem. A ten year fight to persuade the utilities and government departments that they are not imagining the hum has paid off. The Department of the Environment is funding a two year study in which scientists will try to find the source of the hum for 25 sufferers. The department acknowledges that some 500 new cases are reported each year.

Sunday Telegraph, May 2001

Unidentified low frequency humming continues to be a problem around the country. A throbbing or whirring sound known as the Largs hum has plagued coastal towns in Strathclyde for more than 20 years causing discomfort, nausea and nosebleeds. 'You are lucky if you can get an hour's sleep at night,' said Georgie Hyslop, a former Royal Air Force radar operative, who has suffered from the hum every day for a year. 'It gives you headaches, your ears pop, you feel your nose bursting and your chest crushing in.'

The Herald, March 2001

An Aberdeenshire couple has become the latest victims of the mysterious phenomenon known as the low frequency hum. It is a nuisance so bad that at times they have been forced to sleep in their car and take refuge in hotels. The hum at Whitehills, near Banff, a continuous whirr accompanied by high pressure in the head, is the second example of the phenomenon in Scotland, after the so called Largs Hum in Ayrshire which has baffled scientists for 20 years.

Birmingham Evening Post, July 1993

A distraught Birmingham husband today told how his wife killed herself because of a noise in her ears. The body of Mrs Hewlett was found in a bath in her hotel room yesterday. It is thought she had died of a massive drugs overdose. Mr Hewlett added 'The noises were particularly bad at night when there were no distractions. It was a constant buzzing in her ears. I came home on Monday and she'd packed a suitcase and left a note to me saying, I'm sorry, but I can't take it any more.'

---

officials are reluctant to use 'C' weighting. It means that the noise we actually hear from sounds that have a big low-frequency content may not be reflected in the measurements taken. We go into more detail about this when discussing aircraft noise in the transport chapter.

The other controversy surrounds the practice of averaging out noise over a given period, very often a day. There are a number of methods of doing this but the one which is probably the most widely used is known as LAeq (results are given as xdBLAeq). The concept of averaging out noise might work in the case of a busy road where traffic levels are pretty constant. But it does not accurately reflect the actual noise we hear when the noise is loud but less constant, such as aircraft flying overhead. Again, we say more about this in the transport chapter.

References

Berglund, B., Lindvall, T., Schwela, D. and Goh, K. (2000) *Guidelines for Community Noise*, World Health Organization, Geneva

Blesser, B. and Salter, L. (2008) 'The unexamined rewards for excessive loudness', paper given to the 9th International Congress on Noise as a Public Health Issue, Connecticut

Bull, M. (2000) *Sounding out the City*, Berg, New York

China Daily (2005) 'Beijing residents shout loud over noise pollution', 3 March

Girdner, J. (1896), 'The Plague of City Noises', *North American Review*, 163, pp296–303

Guski, R. (1999) 'Personal and social variables as co-determinants of noise annoyance', *Noise and Health Journal*, vol 1, no 3, pp45 – 56

James, O. (2007) *Affluenza*, Vermilion, London

Levy, S. (2006) *The Perfect Thing*, Ebury Press, London

Menon, B. (2004) 'What do you hear?', www.buzzle.com

Pawley, M. (1973) *The Private Future*, Thames & Hudson, London

Phan, H. Y. T., Yano, T., Phan, H. A. T., Nishimura, T., Sato, T. and Hashimoto, Y. (2010) 'Community responses to road traffic noise in Hanoi and Ho Chi Minh City', *Applied Acoustics*, vol 7, no 2, pp107–114

Rasmussen, G. (1982) 'Human body vibration exposure and its measurement', *Technical Review*, vol 1, p5

Sim, S. (2007) *Manifesto for Silence*, Edinburgh University Press, Edinburgh

Talbott, E. and Thompson, S. J. (1995) *Health Effects from Environmental Noise Exposure*, Lewis Publishers, New York

Things Asian (2009) 'Fighting noise in India's maximum city', www.thingsasian.com, 10 February

Thompson, E. (2004) *The Soundscape of Modernity*, MIT Press, Cambridge, MA

Washington Post (1994) 'Coping With the Noise of Summer: Regulators Struggle to Dull Season's Roar', 3 August 1994, *HighBeam Research*, 26 February 2011 http://www.highbeam.com

CHAPTER 2

Noise: Widespread and Worldwide

Across the world more people are disturbed by noise
on a daily basis than by any other pollutant on Earth.

It is a surprising fact. Noise regularly tops the list of complaints in Rio de Janeiro. Despite its poverty, crime and shanty towns, it is noise which can account for more than 60 per cent of *all* public complaints in the Brazilian city (Schafer, 1998). And Rio is not untypical. Noise is a problem that is widespread and worldwide. From the elegant boulevards of Paris to the crowded streets of Calcutta, from the open freeways of the US to the country lanes of rural England, from Heathrow to Hong Kong, noise is a problem.

In Europe, 450 million people, that is 65 per cent of the total population, are exposed daily to noise levels that the World Health Organization (WHO) regards as unacceptable (Berglund et al, 2000). In Paris, 59 per cent of people say noise is the biggest nuisance in their lives, more than double the numbers who complain about air pollution (Stanners, 1995). Even in a country such as Norway, where noise is treated reasonably seriously, nearly 30 per cent of the people live with noise levels above the WHO standard (Norway Climate and Pollution Agency, 2010). In New York, noise has regularly been the number one complaint to the city's 311 helpline number. In Australia, nearly 40 per cent of people are exposed to high levels of traffic noise (National Noise Transport Commission, 2001).

Despite the fact that, in richer countries, more people than ever before are embracing noise as they buy into the consumer society (see Chapter 1), it remains a huge problem for millions of their fellow citizens. There are fewer detailed statistics from the poorer and recently industrialized countries but all the evidence shows the situation to be even worse. 'Karachi – degraded by noise pollution' headlines the *Economic Review*. 'Most Koreans in cities suffer from noise pollution', says *AsiaPulse News*. 'Noise pollution is a killer in Cairo', writes the *Geographical*.

This chapter will attempt to assess the extent of the noise problem from a worldwide perspective, sampling noise in some of the more developed nations as well as the poorer ones. It will also present hypotheses as to why governments and policy-makers have been reluctant to tackle the noise issue.

Noise in the UK

Noise has become a huge problem in the UK with millions saying they have been disturbed by it. Half a million people move from their homes each year because of noise (MORI, 2006) and local authorities report that it regularly tops the list of complaints they receive. The 2001 *National Noise Attitude Survey* found that 12 million people are disturbed by traffic noise, 11 million by neighbour noise and more than 3.5 million by noise from aircraft (Building Research Establishment, 2001). What the otherwise first-rate survey did not fully capture is the *totality* of noise in modern Britain. For ease of reporting, the survey broke down noise into different sectors – aircraft, traffic, neighbourhood, and so on – but that meant it did not get across just how noisy day-to-day life actually can be. These days, as we outlined in Chapter 1, our houses are packed with noisy machines. Home now means the hum of the fridge, the whirr of the dishwasher and the pulsating bass of the stereo system. We shop to the sound of music playing. We eat out with the Arctic Monkeys, the Rolling Stones or the voice of Frank Sinatra reverberating around the restaurant. A quiet pint is virtually a thing of the past. Noise has become all-pervasive.

Decades of getting noisier

In recent decades, noise levels have increased significantly. A few figures give an indication of what has been happening:

- Noise complaints have risen fivefold over the past 20 years (*Sunday Times*, 2006).
- According to the Chartered Institute of Environmental Health (2007) noise complaints to councils had increased fivefold over the previous 20 years.
- The number of quiet areas in England has fallen by a fifth in the past 30 years (CPRE, 2006).

This big increase in noise should not really surprise us. There are more vehicles on our roads than at any time in our history. Aircraft noise is no longer confined to areas close to airports. We have access to more sound-producing consumer goods than ever before.

Les Blomberg, the executive director of the Noise Pollution Clearinghouse in the US, put it like this: 'In the past three decades, we have built noisier and noisier devices that are not subject to any regulations. Think about it. The car alarm is a 1970s invention, as is the leaf blower. The stereo sound systems we have in our cars are much louder than the sound systems the Beatles used for their concerts in the 1960s. All they had back then were 300-amp speakers' (in Chepesiuk, 2005).

Poor and vulnerable people are most exposed

Although noise can and does impact on all sectors of society, it tends to be the most vulnerable communities who are most affected. A MORI survey (2003) revealed that almost 20 per cent of people with a household income of less than £17,500 regularly hear noise from neighbours, including 93 per cent of social housing tenants. In contrast only 12 per cent of people with an income of more than £30,000 could hear their neighbours.

In poorer communities, more people are frequently crowded into smaller apartments, thus subjecting the inhabitants to increased noise within these apartments. Back in 1964, Deutsch, an American psychologist, hypothesized that children reared in noisier environments would become less attentive to acoustic cues, and, this in turn could explain their lower reading scores in school. Both Deutsch (1964) and Cohen et al (1973) found evidence for this hypothesis when they discovered a relationship between noise and reading deficits. Children reared in noisy environments and then placed in noisy classrooms may not treat the lessons presented by the teacher as being more important than the noise from overhead planes, nearby traffic, or classmates' chatter. This would very likely be as true in the UK as in the US.

Traffic noise is also more of a problem for poorer communities. A study found a fifth of council tenants in the London Borough of Greenwich rated traffic noise as big a problem as crime, with those living on main roads the most concerned (Stewart, 1998). Traffic noise, certainly in urban areas, has almost become only a main road problem (since many 'residential' roads have been traffic-calmed: cutting traffic volumes, speed and, usually, noise). This has a particular impact on poorer households who live in disproportionately large numbers on the main roads.

Excessive noise runs like a loud thread through many of the UK's most broken communities.

Noise in Europe

In many parts of Europe, recommended noise levels are exceeded every single day of the year. WHO, the one global body that takes noise seriously, has found that people start to get moderately annoyed by noise when it averages out throughout the day at 50dB and seriously annoyed when it averages out at 55dB (Berglund et al, 2000). Millions of people in Europe live with noise above these limits. Any gains from the manufacture of quieter cars, lorries, planes and trains over the past few decades have been off-set by the growth in travel, particularly by aircraft and motor vehicles. Add to that, the explosion in the number of consumer goods across much of Europe and the continent has become deluged by noise.

A national survey examining the perception and attitudes towards noise in France found that 68 per cent of the respondents heard traffic noise in their homes, 17 per cent heard aircraft, 8 per cent rail and 56 per cent heard neigh-bourhood noise (Lambert and Philipps-Bertin, 2005). Of those, 30 per cent were annoyed, and 13 per cent highly annoyed, by traffic noise; 6.6 per cent annoyed by the aircraft noise, with almost 3 per cent highly annoyed; just over 2 per cent were annoyed by rail noise, with 0.8 per cent highly annoyed. Because the study focused on transport noise, data on the percentage of people annoyed by neighbourhood noise was not available. The study also revealed that people had become more annoyed by all types of transport noise over the past 20 years.

The figures are lower than the Building Research Establishment survey carried out in the UK. This may reflect somewhat different definitions used in the two studies. However the overall picture is similar. Perhaps the most notice-able difference is in the numbers who hear aircraft noise. This is maybe a reflec-tion of the very high number of people overflown by planes using Heathrow.

Research carried out for the European Commission found that in Germany 17 per cent of citizens were seriously affected by traffic noise (RPA 2010). Another German study (Hoffman et al, 2003) found that 'noise pollution in environments is unevenly distributed', with people of lower socio-economic status suffering more than others because they are 'more likely to live in busy to extremely busy main roads and through roads.'

A report published in 2007 by Moscow's Environmental Health Service, cited by Chloe Arnold (2007), found that noise levels in Moscow had reached critical levels, with 70 per cent of Muscovites living with 'unacceptable' noise levels.

We could go on citing study after study – for example, the fact that a European Environment Agency (2009) report found that Bratislava has the highest transport noise levels of any city in Europe, followed closely by Warsaw and Paris – but it would simply serve to re-emphasize what is a very clear picture: Europe is a continent where noise is ubiquitous. It troubles, disturbs and disrupts the lives and well-being of men and women from the warm shores of the Mediterranean to the icy blasts of the Baltic. Although there has probably been more progress in tackling noise in the countries of Northern Europe than elsewhere in the continent, it cannot hide the fact that Europe has not come anywhere close to conquering the noise epidemic it is experiencing.

Little action

Unlike air pollution, the European Union (EU) has set no noise reduction targets for individual countries to meet. Nor has any comprehensive assess-ment of the human and economic costs of noise been carried out. There is evidence that the governments of Europe are under pressure from business interests to go easy on noise. The aviation industry has effectively neutered the European Noise Directive on airports. The EU is not able to set Europe-wide noise standards – noise limits can only be applied on an airport-by-airport basis. This effectively keeps things much as they are since no airport is willing to impose tough limits in case it loses business to its rivals. Equally, the tyre industry fought for years to delay the introduction of tougher standards to reduce tyre noise. Perhaps most seriously, reports have emerged from the WHO that it has been under strong pressure from multinational companies, particularly those based in the US, to stop doing work on noise.

It is not surprising that business is exerting pressure. Any attempt to bring down noise to acceptable levels would have major consequences for both the aviation and motor industries. To meet the WHO standards, night flights at most airports would need to be banned and the number of cars on many of Europe's roads would have to fall significantly (unless, with the introduction of electric or hybrid vehicles, cars and lorries were to become noticeably quieter). The industry argues that this proves the WHO guidelines are unrealistic.

The EU's attempt to deal with noise has been leaden-footed and bureaucratic rather than crisp and effective. It has mandated member states to draw up noise maps to identify noisy areas and then produce noise action plans to deal with the worst spots. But the noise maps are pretty pointless as most people know where the problem areas are. They hear them! And the noise action plans are proving to be little more than toothless bits of paper. If any country was serious about tackling noise, it would be better doing so from outside the EU or at least opting out of the noise directives.

The potential of new technology

We look at technology in more detail in the transport chapter. It is worth saying, however, that new technology has the potential to play a significant role in cutting noise levels. To achieve this requires action by both governments and the private sector. Governments are not good at micromanagement. Attempts to micromanage tend to end up in a bureaucratic jungle, reminiscent of the worst aspects of the EU. Governments need to confine their role to setting the overall regulatory framework and incentivizing the private sector to come up with the quieter goods. There is evidence from the demand for quieter household appliances, such as fridges and washing machines, that there is a market for less noisy products.

A question, however, which runs through this chapter, and indeed through this book, is whether the soaring demand for products, particularly for cars and air travel, will outstrip the developments in quieter technology. If that proves to be the case, then governments will be faced with much tougher decisions in order to tackle noise effectively. They would need to look to measures that limit the growth in flying, car use and possibly shipping. In the richer world, they might need to cut current levels of use. We return to this theme again at the end of the chapter and make a more considered assessment of it at the end of the transport chapter (Chapter 6).

Noise in the US

The US has a history of activism against noise going back nearly 100 years. And, today, it has more anti-noise pressure groups than anywhere else on Earth and almost certainly the most rules and regulations covering noise. Yet, despite the undoubted successes of the noise activists, it continues to be a very noisy place. This is perhaps hardly surprising. Noise and the American way of life tend to go together like Fannie Mae and Freddie Mac once did. This is the mother of all gadget-based societies. The place where car-based living is the norm, where air-con abounds and where planes are used like buses. The American Dream is not a quiet one.

Back in the 18th century, America's founding fathers had something to say about noise. They understood that noise intrudes on thinking and writing when they asked that mud be packed upon the cobblestone street in front of Independence Hall in Philadelphia so that the noise of the carts and horses passing by would be less intrusive on the men who were inside the hall drafting the Constitution. Yet, despite this early recognition in the nation's history of the intrusiveness of noise and the many American authors and poets that have written over the years of the importance of quiet in our lives, the US in the next two centuries continued to grow noisier and, from the end of the 19th century to the early 20th century, noise grew in leaps and bounds as the result of the Industrial Revolution.

Noise proliferated as Americans became more dependent on noise-producing and noise-related technology. Annette Zaner (1991) provided a list of sources of noise: transportation, industrial, home appliances, emergency signals. She wisely acknowledged that her list would probably be outdated shortly after the publication of her chapter and she was correct. She did not write of the noise associated with mobile phones, boom cars, the rumbler horn used by police departments and other 21st century gadgets.

Writers such as James Kunstler (2005) and Vernon Coleman (2008) argue that the American lifestyle has been built on plentiful supplies of cheap oil. Kunstler notes that cheap oil created America's car-based culture: the interstate highways, the urban motorways, the sprawling suburbs, the office parks, strip malls, chain stores and fry-pits. Cheap oil and an increased standard of living for many Americans in the latter part of the 20th century allowed aircraft travel to become the norm. Coleman similarly noted that the American suburban lifestyle depended largely upon cheap oil. Thus, the vast highway system of the US and its cheap air travel added immeasurably to the increase in noise.

In the early 1970s, the US federal government became more environmentally conscious, passing both the Clean Air Act and the Noise Control Act. This followed an outcry from its citizens who asked for cleaner air and a quieter environment. The Noise Control Act of 1972 gave Americans the right to a quiet environment and delegated the responsibilities of enforcement of this act to the Office of Noise Abatement and Control in the Environmental Protection Agency. The passage of the Noise Control Act placed the US at the forefront of curbing noise which it recognized then as a health hazard. The Office of Noise Abatement and Control (ONAC) was especially noteworthy for its publications that educated people to the dangers of noise and informed them of ways to lessen the sounds around them.

ONAC also produced educational materials for schools to teach students about the hazards of noise. It worked with states and cities, helping them monitor and limit noises in their local communities. ONAC, while it did not have the authority to regulate aircraft or railroad noise, produced pamphlets highlighting the dangers of transportation. It was also moving in the direction of regulating noise emissions of products. Some of the materials released by ONAC can be viewed on the Noise Pollution Clearinghouse's website, www.npc.org.

Sadly, in 1982, Ronald Reagan, who believed noise pollution should be handled by the states rather than the federal government, cut the funds to ONAC and Congress supported him in his efforts to strip ONAC of its ability to lessen noise pollution. Noise control exists in a very limited fashion in the US Environmental Protection Agency (US EPA) today. Recently, EPA set up a noise section on its website, providing some information on noise pollution in the US. When Reagan cut the money to ONAC, he effectively terminated funds to states that depended on them to maintain their noise control efforts (Bronzaft, 1998).

New York City, however, had passed its own Noise Control Code in 1972 and has been involved in trying to limit the noises of a city that has had a worldwide reputation as being extremely loud. While it is true that New York City's subway system is known to be noisy – as are the crowded streets of Times Square – New Yorkers, like citizens in the quietest towns of the country, expect less noise when they close the doors to their apartments and homes. They may be willing to deal with the noisy street traffic, crowds and subways, as they traverse the city but they are less tolerant of noisy intrusions into their homes. However, despite the existence of a noise code and an office in the Department of Environmental Protection dealing with noise, the past 30 years has witnessed a growth in noise in New York as evidenced by the fact that noise leads the number of calls to the 311 hotline. Thus, in 2007, a revised Noise Code was passed to try to better cope with the noise of the city. It is still too early to speak of the overall effectiveness of the revised Noise Code but the section on construction noise has been singled out as limiting noise from construction sites. A copy of the updated Noise Code can be seen on the New York City's Department of Environmental Protection website, www.dep.org.

The US, as a whole, has also experienced a growth in noise in the past 30 years but, within the last ten years, there has been increased action on the part of cities and states to pass legislation to lessen the noise of motorcycles, boom cars and other local entities that disturb communities. This action has been in response to the outcry from citizens for laws to lessen the din around them as well as the activities of some vocal anti-noise groups that have been formed during the past 15 years (such as Noise Pollution Clearinghouse, NoiseOff, Lower the Boom, NoBoomers). However, transportation noise issues and consumer product noise emissions are handled at the federal level and that is why anti-noise groups have been campaigning to refund the Office of Noise Abatement and Control. Congresswoman Nita Lowey introduced legislation in 1997 to reactivate this office but was unable to garner the number of votes in Congress needed to get the funding. She has reintroduced this legislation several times but she has been unable to get it passed. The presidents following Reagan have shown no interest in asking Congress to refund the office.

Several groups (such as Aviation Watch, Our Airspace, New Jersey Citizens for the Abatement of Aircraft Noise) have been formed to try to deal with aviation noise and have even brought lawsuits to reduce air travel noise. So far they have been largely unsuccessful. The airline industry points to the quiet aircraft they are now flying but the increase in air traffic as well as the inappropriate sound levels set by the Federal Aviation Administration to assess noise impacts have largely negated the impact of quieter planes. For now, Americans have to rely on local legislation to limit noise in their communities and continue to urge their Congress people to deal with noise on a federal level.

Dr William H. Stewart, former Surgeon General of the US, in a keynote address to a 1969 Conference on Noise as a Public Health Hazard stated the following: 'Must we wait until we prove every link in the chain of causation? I stand with (Surgeon General) Burney's statement of ten years ago. In protecting health, absolute proof comes late. To wait for it, is to invite disaster or to prolong suffering unnecessarily' (US EPA, 1978). Russell E. Train, the former administrator of the US EPA, in 1976, discussing aviation noise stated: 'We really know what needs to be done. We have simply lacked the will to do it. Let's get on with the job' (US EPA, 1976).

The founding fathers of the US knew that noise intrudes on thinking and discussion; two former American Surgeon Generals understood the health impacts of noise; and the former administrator of the US EPA believed in 1976 that the knowledge to limit aviation noise existed but the will to do something to lessen it was lacking. Even President Obama understood that noise intrudes on learning when he noted in a speech to the joint houses of Congress in 2009 that a South Carolina student who was in the audience had her classes intruded upon by a train barrelling past the school five times a day. However, the fact that the current US Congress does not understand that noise is hazardous to both mental and physical health might explain why, to paraphrase former administrator Train, it lacks the will to do something about noise pollution. Unfortunately, the American people have not pressed the federal government to abate noise.

However, the US may be forced to become more environmentally conscious in the next few years. Coleman (2008) writes in *Oil Apocalypse*: 'The sort of suburban lifestyle many people live today will become impossible. The suburban lifestyle has been described as the greatest misallocation of resources in the history of the world. Only the very rich will be able to afford to heat large homes or to own and run a car. Most people who work for a living will have to live within walking or cycling distance of their place of employment. There will be no more imported television sets, PlayStation games or out-of-season foods from the other side of the world.' If these predictions are correct, the US will be forced to downscale, to think local, to drive and fly less and to get rid of many of its household gadgets. It will become a more environmentally concerned country. It will also be a much quieter one.

Noise in Australia

The Australians are wrestling with much the same problems as Europe. We noted earlier that around 40 per cent of Australians are exposed to high levels of traffic noise (National Noise Transport Commission, 2001). In Sydney there are more than 100,000 noise complaints a year, most of which relate to noisy neighbours. The noise situation has become worse in recent decades as people are living more closely together – noise complaints in Melbourne doubled in 2000 after higher density housing was permitted – but even in thinly populated Tasmania, about half the environmental complaints relate to noise (Nova Science in the News, 2001).

In Australia there is no single government authority with overall responsibility for noise. The national government is responsible for aircraft noise and standards for new motor vehicles. An environmental protection agency regulates noise in each state. The indications now are that the states are starting to legislate in response to a noise climate that has deteriorated badly over the past few decades. There is more about this in the chapter on noise law (Chapter 9).

Why the lack of effective action?

What is so striking is that, despite this litany of problems, no country in the rich world has come up with a strategy to tackle noise effectively. We have identified some reasons for this: the pressure on governments from business interests to introduce only 'light touch' legislation; a belief that improved technology will solve the problems without governments having to do much; and, in Europe, the EU's tendency to react in a bureaucratic rather than an effective manner.

It is too simplistic, though, to put all the blame on big business, Brussels bureaucrats and an unwarranted faith in new technology. We need to throw into the mix what we identified in the previous chapter: the impact the consumer society has had on people's attitudes towards noise. Noise, even loud noise, is tolerated because a growing number of citizens regard it, at worst, as an unavoidable by-product of their lifestyle and, at best, something positive, something that has good associations for them, something to be embraced. They do not see noise as a problem, cannot understand those who do and do not feel that governments should give it a priority, except in exceptional circumstances. It is this attitude, shared by many in power, which may be the biggest barrier to getting effective policies in place.

There is another important reason, too, for the failure of modern governments to tackle noise: a lack of conviction that certain types of behaviour, including behaviour causing noise disturbance, are wrong and that the perpetrators need to be dealt with. Over the last few decades the clear line between responsible behaviour and irresponsible behaviour has been blurred. Everything has become too relative. As far as noise is concerned, it means noise-makers are often not held to account for their behaviour. This attitude is more prevalent in some countries than others but it has been a factor in the reluctance to tackle noise.

In hock to the consumer society

As an illustration of these points, we use the 13 years Labour were in power in the UK (1997–2010) as a case study. New Labour was the government that championed the consumer society more than any other in UK history; indeed, it was the government whose finances depended upon consumer spending (made possible by easy credit). It had little time for the peace and quiet so many yearned for. It tended to see those who complained about the noise created by modern consumer goods – cars, planes, sound systems, and so on – as 'elitist'; people who were putting their own selfish interests before the right of 'hard-working British families' to acquire the latest gadget or go on a cheap flight abroad.

Inevitably these are generalities and certainly do not apply to every individual New Labour politician or supporter. However, having made and stressed that caveat, I think it is fair to say that New Labour, seemingly so keen to represent the political face of material man and material woman above all else, refused to take noise seriously. In fact, it downgraded noise. Noise was excluded from the list of areas that local authorities were required to prioritize. It featured in none of the Labour government's much-vaunted policy targets. Under Labour, noise was simply left out of key policy announcements. Its blueprint for better neighbourhoods was entitled *Greener, Safer, Cleaner*. Quieter? Missing. Forgotten (Department for Communities and Local Government, 2006). Its guidelines for the controversial 'eco-towns' excluded any mention of noise. Its Decent Homes programme, intended to improve social housing, failed to include the need for adequate sound insulation between properties as a key criteria. In 13 years of government it frequently promised, but never delivered, a noise strategy.

For all its talk about 'rights' and 'responsibilities' New Labour came dangerously close to losing many of its moral bearings. It bowed down before the altar of consumerism. It also failed to ensure there were clear standards in the UK as to what was acceptable behaviour. It failed to change, or sometimes even challenge, the culture where everything had become relative. Many of its individual politicians wanted to and tried to change things but New Labour left largely intact a non-judgemental culture, which was particularly widespread in local government and the voluntary sector, the very sectors that often had the key responsibility for tackling noise. This meant that all too often noise-makers faced no meaningful sanctions. Their irresponsible behaviour was allowed to continue by local authority officers or housing association officials so that 'they could work through their problems' or was excused on the grounds of 'lifestyle differences.'

To reverse this sort of thinking in these sectors is a huge task. In many ways the equal opportunities and 'rights' legislation of the past 30 years has made things worse. This is not to argue that legislation to promote the interests of disabled people, and other groups who were discriminated against was not required. But the legislation has had the unintended effect of embedding in the culture of too much of the voluntary and public sector an oppressive 'non-judgemental' attitude.

Susan Neiman, in her book, *Moral Clarity: A Guide for Grown-Up Idealists*, argues that these attitudes have become the norm on the left in politics. She says that in all sorts of policy areas, much of the left has lost its moral bearings (Neiman, 2008). She maintains it has become deeply afraid of notions of good and evil, dignity and nobility; all given second place to untrammelled consumer choice.

Neiman's assessment of the left has caused controversy, but it is difficult not to recognize some of what she says in New Labour, whose attitudes made things very bleak for the millions of noise sufferers in the UK, particularly those that were poor and vulnerable – the very people who tend to be most exposed to noise and have the least chance to do anything about it. Indeed, to sort out their noise problem, many of these people are dependent on an army of professionals and bureaucrats – housing officials, local authority officers, social workers, community workers – many of whom have bought into the 'rights' culture and have little desire to seriously clamp down on the noise-maker. Labour failed to tackle this. It is terribly ironic that Labour politicians, who were so ready to brand anti-noise campaigners as 'elitist', actually let down the most vulnerable people in society through their inaction on noise. New Labour, in its blind determination to allow people to buy into the consumer dream, ended up discriminating against the poorest and most vulnerable people in society.

A new attitude required

In this book we make practical recommendations for tackling noise. But they will be irrelevant if the basic attitude of those in power fails to change. New values are required: people less in awe of the consumer society, more willing to regulate big business where necessary (but also to release its potential to provide some of the solutions). Above all, the new attitude needs to be guided by a moral compass. There has to be a move away from the current emphasis on 'rights' – where people are not forced to face up to the consequences of their own behaviour – and towards the notion of 'responsibility'. Not just the responsibility people have to modify their own behaviour but also the responsibility the state and others in authority have towards different groups in society. Until there is this change in basic attitudes, detailed policies to tackle noise will achieve little.

Noise in the industrializing world

We prefer this term, 'the industrializing world' to 'the poorer world'. It conveys the idea of countries at different stages of development. It more accurately describes what is happening on the ground. It is certainly more helpful when assessing the noise policies of the different countries.

Countries with newly industrialized economies such as South Korea, Taiwan or Hong Kong have developed comprehensive noise policies. Fast-industrializing nations, such as China and India, are putting in place policies to cope with the impact of the process of industrialization. But many other countries, particularly in Africa, have few noise policies in place.

We will be looking at a number of these countries in turn as several of them are developing policies that can stand as templates for many other places. But first it is worth painting a picture of noise levels across much of the industrializing world. It really requires a visit to a mega-city in the industrializing world to appreciate the extent of the noise. In India's four major cities, for example, noise levels regularly average out at more than 82dB – that is almost 30dB above the level at which the WHO says people start to get seriously disturbed (Berglund et al, 2000).

The big problems have been caused by the rapid, largely unregulated development and industrialization in the urban areas which has take place over the last few decades (Mehdi, 1999).

Noise levels can be very high indeed. During rush hours in Karachi, Pakistan, the noise levels can exceed 140dB, louder than a jet landing at Heathrow. It is estimated that road traffic accounts for at least 65 per cent of the noise. But, in certain places, industrial noise is also very high – for example, the average noise levels at the main wharf of Karachi Port range between 90dB and 110dB on any given day (Berglund et al, 2000).

In Bangkok, the capital of Thailand and home to more than 10 million people and 5.5 million vehicles, a fifth of the population is suffering from hearing loss, the main problems coming from street noise, traffic, industrial and leisure noise (Berglund et al, 2000).

Bangladesh is much the same: 'Noise pollution ... has reached almost intolerable limits in recent times posing a serious threat to the nation's health ... [according to the survey], 98% of respondents felt that traffic control should be improved and industrial activities banned in urban areas ... 91% of the people identified the car horns as the main cause of noise pollution ... the pernicious pollution will only come under control when the authority implement the laws strictly' (*The Independent*, 2003). The article from the *South Asia Voice* (2002) gives a taster of what noise levels can be like in a mega-city in the poorer world (see Box 2.1).

BOX 2.1 Managing environmental noise in India

This article was sent to us by a resident of New Delhi who has been suffering from noise-related ailments for many years, and wished our readers to become more aware of the dangers of long-term exposure to unwanted industrial and urban noise.

Any traveller in India sensitive to noise will probably attest to the difficulties in finding quiet accommodation that is also conveniently located and affordable. If it is not the incessant howling and barking of stray dogs, it might be the television set in the next room that will be blasting loud music or intense melodramatic dialogues well into the wee hours of the night.

Businesses think nothing of employing noisy gadgets and machines well past sunset, and with most cities and towns lacking adequate zoning laws that might provide meaningful separation of commercial or industrial areas from residential neighbourhoods, hazards from unwanted noise are almost unavoidable for most of the citizenry. Even when zoning guidelines exist, implementation is spotty and marred by rampant corruption and administrative indifference.

Particularly menacing is the noise pollution that emanates from construction activities that continue throughout the day and well into the night. In Delhi, due to the banning of truck traffic during the day, much unloading of construction equipment and related raw materials takes place throughout the night, and since all kinds of wholesale markets are located adjacent to residential colonies, there is no escape from the crashes and thuds that accompany the manual unloading of bricks, timber, steel and other building materials that are necessary at construction sites. And non-insulated generators, which have become very common, can be particularly annoying and especially unsettling at night.

To make matters worse, ordinary citizens (particularly in Punjab and the Northern Plains) compound the problem with their penchant for raucous wedding celebrations complete with marching bands that weave through city streets blasting away pop tunes all through the night. The practice of bursting firecrackers on festivals and other holidays is also common as is the tendency to amplify all manner of religious celebrations at odd hours of the night.

Although the trend towards the loudspeaker 'jagran' began with some Sikh communities during the Khalistan years, Hindu, Jain and Muslim communities have now adopted this tortuous custom with a vengeance. In doing so, they have all revealed an appalling lack of concern of the right of the general population to a good night's sleep. Whereas the Muezzin in the mosque will use the loudspeaker only for a limited time to signify the start of prayers, all-night sessions are not at all unusual in periodic Hindu or Jain religious gatherings. In some Punjab Gurudwaras, the use of loudspeakers is a daily occurrence, and in some towns, miked Sangeet sessions can start at 3am.

Recent Supreme Court rulings have acknowledged the gravity of the problem, but noise prevention statutes do not yet offer provisions for hefty fines or other serious punishment, even for chronic and repeated offenders.

Although a number of Public Interest Litigations (PILs) have been filed by concerned citizens and lawyers, there has not been enough attention and support from the mainstream media, educators, community health providers and other influential public figures. Politicians have not been particularly helpful, preferring to pander to obscurantist religious forces or cater to selfish commercial or private interests. Print and television media especially need to do more in raising awareness concerning the growing menace of noise pollution and the general insensitivity to this growing health hazard.

As India's towns and cities become more densely packed, the problem of unwanted noise is likely to increase both during the day and at night. While recent pronouncements by the Supreme Court are an important victory for noise-control activists, it is but a very small step forward. Much more needs to be done if India's laws and implementation are to match what has been achieved in the EU and Australia in recent years.

Africa has gathered fewer noise statistics than Asia but the situation that emerges is similar. Here is an account of the situation in Ethiopia: 'Noise pollution is the least addressed issue in Ethiopia and in Africa in general. It does not only affect humans but also animals and nature.

Because the competition between churches and mosques is also so rife, the loudspeakers come in handy to win the battle. In big cities, especially in Addis, the condition is worse. Having a house next to a church or a mosque is a nightmare. Government officials rarely intervene to quell such rampant and ugly competitions. Though there has been a law (starting from 1957) that addresses noise pollution, it has never been implemented properly.

In addition to churches and mosques, vehicles are other noise polluters. A short trip to Addis and to other regional cities will help one understand my frustration. Unnecessary honking, for example, mostly by men to get young girls' attention or to annoy someone who accidentally blocks one's way, remains one of the most unpleasant noises. It is almost impossible to have a peaceful, undisturbed day walking in the streets. Urban planning, which is one of Ethiopia's weaknesses, also contributes significantly to noise pollution. One should not be surprised to see industrial buildings (small or big) next to hotels, residential areas, and schools. Slums, results of poor urban planning, are bonus sources of noise pollution' (*Free Voice*, 2009).

And from Egypt: 'Excessive noise levels in Cairo are increasing stress-related illnesses and hearing impairments among the Egyptian capital's 15 million residents ... noise levels in Cairo regularly reach an average of 90 decibels during the day and seldom drop below 70 decibels' (*The Geographical*, 2008).

It is little different in South America. In Argentina's capital Buenos Aires noise pollution has been increasing year on year. Noise levels on several city centre avenues exceed 100dB (Berglund et al, 2000). Research into noise levels in the sprawling Brazilian city of Sao Paulo found noise complaints are becoming more frequent: 'An important local newspaper has recently been publishing letters of complaint about noise problems very frequently. However, no answer from the authorities has been given to these letters' (Moura-de-Sousa and Alves Cardoso, 2002). The research goes on to explain why the noise has become worse: 'In Brazil, the investment in the road system, as a stimulus for the new national motor vehicle industry in the 1950s, resulted in an enormous increase in the number of vehicles in circulation throughout the cities. The city of Sao Paulo, which is the centre of the most influential metropolitan area of the country, has now a vehicle fleet of more than 5 million units. Atmospheric and noise pollution related to vehicle traffic is thus some of the most serious environmental problems faced by the city in these days' (Moura-de-Sousa and Alves Cardoso, 2002).

Our list could go on but the point is made: noise is at epidemic levels.

A question of social justice

There is an obvious question of social justice in what is happening. The high noise levels in many poor areas are caused, at least in part, by the activities of much wealthier people. Poor people have no cars to drive on the roaring new motorways that cut an ugly swathe through their fragile communities. The congestion on the city streets is not of their making. The flash new airports are not for them. They are the victims of other people's lifestyles.

Never were the words of Les Blomberg, executive director of the Noise Pollution Clearing House, more appropriate: 'Second hand noise is increasingly used to describe noise that is experienced by people who did not produce it. Like second hand smoke, it's put into the environment without people's consent and then has effects on them that they don't have any control over' (in Chepesiuk, 2005).

Action being taken

There are currently few effective, properly enforced rules and regulations in place to tackle noise in most of the industrializing and newly industrialized countries. But there are some notable exceptions and it is to these we now turn.

South Korea

South Korea is a successful newly industrialized economy. As it industrialized, so noise complaints rose. Now 90 per cent of environmental disputes are about noise and vibration. It has become a very noisy place. *Asia Pulse News*

(2002) reported that the majority of metropolitan residents in South Korea are suffering from serious noise pollution. It found that 63 per cent of Seoul residents said noise levels were 'very serious'. In the smaller cities it was 49 per cent. And 88 per cent of metropolitan residents expected noise levels to get worse. Cars, trains and planes were selected as the main culprits of noise pollution in the major cities.

South Korea has developed noise policies similar to those in Europe and the ones adopted by its closer neighbours, Taiwan and Japan. It has regulations covering all types of noise. There is a considerable amount of research being done into the development of quieter machines and vehicles. The aim is for a step-by-step reduction in noise from cars, lorries and aircraft as well as from factories and construction sites. Progress is being made. But the advances could be undermined by the sheer growth in the volume of vehicles on the roads and planes in the sky. The number of cars produced rose from 50,000 in 1986 to more than 4 million today (some of these, of course, were for export). A new international airport is being planned for the southern part of the country. We will return to this point later in the chapter when we will assess it in more detail, but this growth in car and air travel in newly industrializing countries threatens to seriously undermine efforts to cut noise.

India

India has almost been synonymous with noise but things are changing. Professor M. L. Munjal, chairman of India's National Committee on Noise Pollution Control, argues that there was a sea-change in 1991 when India, under its new finance minister, Dr Manmohan Singh, now the prime minister, embraced globalization and market reforms. For decades, India had a large number of noise laws in place but they were only enforced in a patchy way. Usually they simply got lost in the country's bureaucratic systems. Professor Munjal argues that competition began to sweep away that rigid bureaucracy that had acted as a barrier to effective action. He also maintains that exposure to the global market forced India to manufacture goods that would meet the much tighter noise requirements in places such as Europe, the US and Japan.

Certainly there is a new desire to deal with noise in India, particularly the ubiquitous noise on the street. Freed from the shackles of a previously stifling bureaucracy, there is a new effectiveness in tacking noise from loudspeakers, portable generators, firecrackers, public address systems and the incessant 'honking' of the vehicles.

The National Committee on Noise Pollution Control is framing simple rules in a language that is comprehensible to the sometimes poorly educated person on the street. The committee argues that everybody has to understand the rules in order to get compliance. It is, however, using market mechanisms wherever possible. For example, it tends to favour simple labelling, using colours, to give consumers the choice rather than direct regulation.

But India still has a long way to go. According to Sumaira Abdulali, who runs the campaign group the Awaaz Foundation, the citizens of Mumbai are forced to endure constant noise three times as loud as recommended by the WHO. Despite the campaign achieving a notable success in 2009 in persuading the authorities to crackdown on 'honking' drivers, Abdulali fears that urban planners in Mumbai are forcing its 14 million residents to accept extreme noise as part of life.

India is facing the same problem as other developing economies. Will the growth in gadgets available through the globalized market – cars, flights, washing machines, stereo-systems, and so on – scupper the country's noise-curbing efforts that have become more effective in recent years since its more market-based approach began to sweep away the old bureaucracy?

Hong Kong

The models for controlling noise in fast-developing economies – and, indeed, in much of the poorer world – may be China and Hong Kong.

We turn to Hong Kong first. Noise is a big problem. More than a million people are affected by traffic noise alone (EPD, 2006). That is nothing unusual for a mega-city, but where Hong Kong is different is in its response to the problem. It has put a strategy in place that is among the most comprehensive in the world. The strategy recognizes that 'poor planning in the past and cramped development have resulted in such thorny problems as highways running just outside people's living rooms' (EPD, 2006).

Hong Kong has prioritized noise since 1986 when its Environmental Protection Department (EPD) was established. The EPD has based its strategy to tackle road noise, the main problem, on four principles: the use of the planning process to cut the impact of traffic; legislation to cut noise from individual vehicles; the introduction of measures to reduce noise from existing roads; and a programme of public engagement and education.

Hong Kong recognizes that reducing noise from new or widened roads is easier than cutting it on existing roads since more use can be made of the planning process. When the authorities plan new roads, they must ensure that the noise experienced by people in the vicinity is kept within acceptable limits. Noise reduction measures are required to be incorporated at the design stage. These include adjusting the alignment of the road where practicable, looking at the possibility of alternative land-use arrangements, the use of low-noise materials for surfacing, the erection of noise barriers and the creation of a buffer zone between residential properties and the new road. More than 30km of barriers and screens have been erected along new roads since 1990, benefitting 120,000 people.

Reducing noise on existing roads has proved more difficult but some progress has been made. The EPD has calculated that 70dB (averaged over an hour) is exceeded on 655 roads. It estimates that barriers or low-noise surfaces could be used on about 100 of these roads to cut noise. Low noise materials are now standard for resurfacing all high-speed roads. A programme of retro-fitting barriers is also underway but the costs are high and progress is fairly limited. Hong Kong has also spent millions of pounds insulating thousands of classrooms, benefitting more than half a million pupils.

In 1996, Hong Kong introduced the Noise Control (Motor Vehicles) Regulation, which sets standards that all new vehicles must meet. In 2002, it tightened these standards further to bring them into line with international standards. (They do not, however, apply to existing vehicles.)

Hong Kong's public engagement and education programme merits a mention. There is a big concern in many industrializing countries that the public, while often disturbed by noise, does not always appreciate the full extent of the harm it can do to them. Hong Kong is using a creative 3D noise modelling tool that can provide information about noise and its impacts in an easily understandable form and to allow the public to feed their ideas for noise reduction and mitigation to the authorities.

However, for all the thought and resources which have gone into cutting traffic noise, the authorities admit they are far from conquering the problem. More than 1.1 million people are still exposed to traffic noise levels in excess of 70dB (averaged out over one hour); with 2.5 million exposed to 60dB or higher. The EPD puts this down to 'a combination of factors including the scarcity of habitable land, a significant increase in population and housing needs in the past 20 years, and a huge transportation demand to support economic growth and social activities' (EPD, 2006).

The EPD estimates that by 2016, if no further action were to be taken, increased traffic levels 'could lead to a 50% increase in the population exposed to excessive traffic noise as compared with the situation in 1997' (EPD, 2006). Hong Kong, therefore, has further plans for resurfacing more roads, installing additional noise barriers, bringing in tougher regulations for vehicles, exploring a night-time noise standard and further enhancing public engage-ment and partnership.

But the authorities do not try to hide the fact that the torrent of traffic flooding the streets threatens to overwhelm their efforts to cut noise. Hong Kong is spending millions just to stand still. It has seen traffic growth as the inevitable consequence of growing prosperity. Ironically, that prosperity may actually be threatened by costs of taming the traffic. We return to these prob-lems at the end of the chapter.

Aircraft noise

Hong Kong also has strategies to tackle noise from other sources. The problem of aircraft noise was dramatically reduced when the airport was moved off-shore from Kai Tak to Chek Lap Kok in 1998. Kai Tak was in the midst of a densely populated area where at least 380,000 people were affected by the noise. Now it is claimed to be down to little more than a few hundred. Nevertheless there are strict regulations in place. Aircraft are expected to use a Continuous Descent Approach when landing and adhere to speed restrictions. Preferential use of the runway that impacts less on residents is required.

Construction and other noise problems

Construction noise was a major problem when the EPD was set up in 1986. Pile-drivers operated 12 hours a day in urban areas, affecting one in 12 people. The EPD brought in a noise control ordinance which limited piling to 3–5 hours a day in built-up areas and required quieter equipment to be used. However, the EPD admits, construction noise remains a problem and it is looking at ways to deal with it, particularly of encouraging greater compliance among builders.

Hong Kong has also put in place comprehensive regulations to tackle neighbour and neighbourhood noise. They cover noise from animals, birds, musical instruments, loudspeakers, games, trades, businesses and loud-speakers. There are particular provisions to deal with noise at night.

It will have become clear that Hong Kong's strategies to tackle noise are well ahead of those of most other countries in the industrializing world and, indeed, put many richer countries to shame. Only China matches the breadth of its strategy. It is to China we now turn.

China

China has developed one of the most comprehensive strategies to tackle noise in the world. It has been built on the pioneering work of Professor Maa Dah-You. A physics graduate from Peking University in 1936, he identified noise as a key issue as far back as the late 1950s. It is largely due to his work that China recognized noise as an environmental problem as early as the 1960s.

In recent years the driver for tackling noise has been the phenomenal growth China has been experiencing. The authorities have recognized that such a rate of growth would be untenable if the noise impacts of it were not dealt with. The strategy has produced some real results. For example, there is the remarkable fact that, despite a huge increase in the number of vehicles on its streets, the average noise from traffic in Beijing is down from 77dB(A) in 1976 to 69dB(A) in 2004.

The strategy, devised by the central government over the past 20 years, has been a top-down one. It contains rules and regulation, as well as target levels, for everything from traffic and aircraft to loudspeakers and air-conditioning units. It is based around the concept of zoning. Each zone, or area, is desig-nated for a particular type of activity. That then determines the permissible noise levels in the neighbourhood. There is a rule, for example, that no civil aircraft may fly over the urban areas of cities unless they are landing or taking off. There is also a requirement on local authorities to work out plans for mitigating noise from trains when they pass through urban residential, cultural and education districts. There are strict limits on the levels of noise industrial units and factories may emit. And there is a lot of legislation surrounding roads and traffic, most notably the building of new roads. Residential dwellings, for example, must not be built within 50–100m of a new road. Noise barriers, quiet road surfaces and canal and channel-like roads are required in noise sensitive areas. To deal with noise on existing roads, there is a programme to improve the quality of the road surfaces and to reduce the residential density alongside these roads by moving the population. Mufflers and horns of motor vehicles driven within urban areas must meet strict noise laws. China is also taking measures to deal with the vehicles themselves. It is forbidden to manufacture, sell or import automobiles that emit noise beyond the limits set. The car industry is undertaking major research into quieter vehicles. The Chinese see land-use planning as key to managing noise levels.

In 2003, China was rated first in the world by the World Trade Organization (WTO) for the improvements it had made to noise from household appliances. The Chinese regard quieter gadgets in the home as a priority both because of the density of the population and of the particular sensitivity which Asian people appear to have to low-frequency noise (see Box 2.2). China is also making big efforts to ensure that people are aware of the impact of noise so that there will be consumer pressure on the authorities to act.

China of course still has noise problems. Professor Jing Tian, director of acoustics at the Chinese Academy of Sciences, told the international Inter-Noise Conference in Istanbul in 2007 that China was facing three major concerns: noise from traffic on existing roads; complaints from people around current airports (and this is likely to get much worse); and the growing menace of low frequency noise. There is also a concern that China's enforcement of its impressive array of legislation is not as rigorous as it should be. But China has shown what can be done when a fast-developing country takes noise seriously. Along with Hong Kong and Korea, it may well provide a model that countries in the industrializing world could adapt to meet their own needs.

BOX 2.2 Sensitivity to low-frequency noise

There is evidence emerging from China that Asian people may be more sensitive to low-frequency noise than Europeans. Professor Dongxing Mao from Tongi University and others argue that Asian people have a different canal infracture and a different language perception. Studies carried out have found that the 'A' weighting used to measure noise did not correlate with residents' responses to the noise (Xie et al, 2007). Mao is therefore working on developing a metric more suitable for Asian people.

Positive signs from the industrializing world

There are positive signs, then, from industrializing countries that action is being taken to tackle noise. But it is still only in a small minority of countries. A paper from Schwela, Finegold and Stewart (2007) identified some steps that could be of benefit to those industrializing countries currently doing very little to tackle noise.

1. The importance of an overall strategy.
    Ideally the strategy would include improved land-use planning and investment in public transport as well as specific measures to tackle noise.

2. The importance of implementation and enforcement.
    Quite a few developing countries have theoretical policies in place, but the implementation and enforcement of them is poor. This is partly the result of a lack of political will and partly because of the cost. It is probably unrealistic to expect a rapid improvement in implementation and enforcement, so a step-by-step approach would be more realistic.

3. The importance of low-cost solutions
    It is going to be difficult to persuade developing countries to give priority to noise and put in place an effective strategy if they believe it is going to cost a lot of money. Therefore, low-cost solutions are important. That should rule out any idea of adopting the EU's practice of noise mapping. It is quite unnecessary since most people know where the noisiest areas are. The cost-benefit advantages of tackling noise also need to be highlighted – for example, money spent on noise reduction could have real savings in health costs.

4. The importance of active citizens' groups
    Governments are most likely to respond effectively to an issue when they feel under pressure from citizens' groups and campaign organizations. There are protests in the industrializing world about noise but concerted pressure is missing. This is in part due to a lack of understanding on the part of the population as a whole about the serious impact noise can have, particularly on people's health. But when people are annoyed and stressed out by noise they do not need to fully understand the impact it is having on them to protest! It is likely that protests will grow as development brings an increase in noise. It will be important that citizens groups from industrializing countries link up with their counterparts in the more industrialized world.

Need to curb growth?

The question which remains unresolved, however, is whether all the costly efforts to tackle noise in industrializing countries will be overwhelmed by the huge growth in the number of cars on the road and planes in the air. Or will new technology come to the rescue?

Individual aircraft have become a lot quieter during the past 30 years but there is no similar step-change on the horizon over the coming decades. In both the industrializing and more industrialized countries there seems little prospect of keeping aircraft noise in check without slowing the rate of growth in industrializing countries and reversing it in more developed economies. However, as we explain in the chapter on transport (Chapter 6), we need to make the distinction between long-haul and short-haul flights. Aircraft noise only really presents a noise problem when they approach or leave an airport. If the number of short-haul flights could be curbed, long-haul flights would become more manageable.

What about traffic? At its present rate of growth, it threatens to undermine any efforts being made to tackle noise in industrializing countries. Unless the noise of vehicles can be cut considerably at source, the cost of dealing with traffic noise will become prohibitive. If there was a rapid and universal move away from petrol vehicles to ones powered by electricity or hydrogen, then the noise picture might be transformed. Without it, there will be little choice but to curb car use.

Concluding remarks

It remains the case that, in most countries of the world, noise is given a low priority. But we can draw lessons about the most effective way to tackle noise from the experiences of different countries.

First, and above all, there needs to be the political will to take action. We noted, for example, the progress made in places such as China and Hong Kong once their governments became convinced of the need to tackle noise. Equally, we saw what happens when there is no motivation to deal with noise in the case study on New Labour's performance while in government in the UK: it is excluded from key policy areas and, indeed, is regarded as an unavoidable consequence of consumerism.

Second, the evidence suggests that for a country to get to grips with noise, a national strategy is required. Progress in the US more or less came to a halt when Reagan handed responsibility for tackling noise to the individual states. By contrast, the nationally driven approach of China, Hong Kong and some of the Northern European countries has been fruitful. Unless noise reduction is an integral part of policy at a national level, it will lose out. That is not to say that local action is not important – some of the American states have shown what can be done – but it is clear that it is countries with national strategies that have made the greatest progress in tackling noise.

Third, we need to distinguish between the importance of a national strategy and the state micromanaging noise policy. The latter can lead to bureaucracy, stalemate and sterility. There is a real danger, for example, that the EU's detailed requirements for noise mapping and noise action plans are turning into little more than expensive and time-consuming paper exercises that bring little real improvement to the noise climate. By contrast, India's experience is interesting and instructive. It was only when it sought solutions through market mechanisms rather than locally and centrally controlled bureaucracy that it began to make progress. That is not to argue that business cannot be a problem! The delaying tactics of the tyre industry stalled moves towards quieter tyres in the EU for many years. But it would be a mistake to see business as just part of the problem. The evidence suggests it is also part of the solution. Governments should confine themselves to setting a tough regulatory framework and then, wherever practicable, incentivize business to deliver the solutions.

Fourthly, we found that official action is often prompted by citizens' campaigns. A good example of this was the outcry from citizens in the US about the state of their environment which prompted the US government to pass the Clean Air and Noise Control Acts in the 1970s. We noted that there would be more pressure on governments if campaign groups were able to coordinate their activities across national boundaries. In particular, it is important that citizens groups from industrializing countries link up with their counterparts in the industrialized world. In Chapter 4 we explore the reasons why there is no worldwide 'anti-noise' movement to match the vibrant green movement against climate change. Such a movement would exert real pressure on governments to take action against noise.

Finally, we considered whether the huge, predicted growth in travel, particularly by plane and car, could be off-set by the introduction of quieter technology. Our tentative conclusion was that this was unlikely to be so in the case of planes but, with motor vehicles, it may be possible with the introduction of quieter vehicles powered by electricity and hydrogen. This relationship between travel, movement and economic growth is something which will be explored more fully in following chapters.

References

Arnold, C. (2007) 'Russia: Moscow's noise pollution reaches dangerous levels', Radio Free Europe, accessed 19 September, www.rferl.org/content/article/1078719.html

AsiaPulse News (2002) 'Most Koreans in cities suffer from noise pollution', Asia Pulse Pty Ltd., *HighBeam Research*, accessed 26 February 2011, www.highbeam.com

Berglund, B., Lindvall, T., Schwela, D. and Goh, K. (2000) *Guidelines for Community Noise*, World Health Organization, Geneva

Bronzaft, A. (1998) 'A voice to end the government's silence on noise', *Hearing Rehabilitation Quarterly*, vol 23, pp6–12, 29

Building Research Establishment (2001) *The UK National Noise Attitude Survey*, Building Research Establishment, London

Chartered Institute of Environmental Health (2007), 'Noise complaints increase five-fold', 21 April, www.cieh.org/ehn/ehn3.aspx?id=4226&terms=noise+complaints

Chepesiuk, R. (2005) 'Decibel hell: The effects of living in a noisy world', *Environmental Health Perspectives*, vol 113, no 1, pp34–41

Cohen, S., Glass, D. and Singer, J. (1973) 'Apartment noise, auditory discrimination and reading ability in children', *Journal of Experimental Social Psychology*, vol 7, pp407–422

Coleman, V. (2008) *Oil Apocalypse*, Blue Books, London

CPRE (Campaign to Protect Rural England) (2006) *Saving Tranquil Spaces*, Campaign to Protect Rural England, London

Department for Communities and Local Government (2006) *Greener, Safer, Cleaner*, Department for Communities and Local Government, London

Deutsch, C. (1964) 'Auditory discrimination and learning: Social factors', *The Merrill-Palmer Quarterly of Behaviour and Development*, vol 10, pp277–296

EPD (Environmental Protection Department) (2006) *An Overview on Noise Pollution*, Environmental Protection Department, Hong Kong

European Environment Agency (2009) *Transport at a Crossroads*, European Environment Agency, Denmark

Free Voice (2009) *Noise Pollution*, accessed 21 September, http://etyopian.wordpress.com/2009/09/21/noise-pollution/

Hoffman, B., Robra, B. and Swart, E. (2003) 'Social inequality and noise pollution in the living environment', German Federal Health Survey, Germany

Independent (2003) 19 August, Bangladesh, 'Law to curb noise pollution soon', *HighBeam Research*, accessed 26 February 2011, www.highbeam.com

Kunstler, J. (2005) *The Long Emergency*, Atlantic Books, London

Lambert, J. and Philipps-Bertin, C. (2005) 'Perception and attitudes to transportation noise in France: A national survey', CBEN, Cambridge, MA

Mehdi, M. (1999) 'Karachi – Degraded by noise pollution', *Economic Review*, Economic and Industrial Publications, *HighBeam Research*, accessed 26 February 2011, www.highbeam.com

MORI Poll (2006) commissioned by Environmental Protection UK

MORI Survey (2003) *Neighbour Noise*, Department for Environment, Food and Rural Affairs, London

Moura-de-Sousa. C. and Alves Cardoso, M. (2002) 'Urban noise in the City of Sao Paulo, Brazil: An important problem of public health', *Noise and Health*, vol 4, pp57–63

National Noise Transport Commission (2001) *Australia's Vehicle Noise Limits Too Loud*, National Noise Transport Commission, Australia

Nieman, S. (2008) *Moral Clarity: A Guide for Grown-Up Idealists*, Harcourt, Florida

Norway Climate and Pollution Agency (2010) *State of the Environment*, Climate and Pollution Agency, Norway

Nova Science in the News (2001) *Quiet Please! Fighting Noise Pollution*, Australian Academy of Science, Australia

RPA (2010) *Final Report on Task 3, Impact Assessment and Proposal of Action Plan*, for DG Environment, European Commission, May

Schafer, R. (1998) *The Book of Noise*, Arcana Editions, Ontario

Schwela, D., Finegold, L. and Stewart, J. (2007) *A Strategic Approach on Environmental Noise Management in Developing Countries*, Inter-Noise, Istanbul, Turkey

South Asia Voice (2002) 'Decibel assault – Noise pollution in Indian cities', 2 February

Stanners, D. (1995) *Europe's Environment, The Dobris Assessment*, European Environment Agency, Denmark

Stewart, J. (1998) *Poor Show*, Alarm UK and GASP, London

Sunday Times (2006) 'Barking dogs, drum'n bass – noise from next door can drive you mad. So what can you do about it?' 6 August

The Geographical (2008) 'Noise pollution a killer in Cairo', Circle Publishing Ltd, April, *HighBeam Research*, accessed 26 February 2011, www.highbeam.com

US EPA (Environmental Protection Agency) (1976) *Aviation Noise: Let's Get on With the Job*, US Environmental Protection Agency, Washington, DC

US EPA (1978) *Noise: A Health Problem*, US Environmental Protection Agency, Office of Noise Abatement and Control, Washington, DC

Xie, B., Zhong, X., Rao, D. and Ling, Z. (2007) 'Head-related transfer function database and its analyses', *Science in China Series: Physics, Mechanics and Astronomy*, vol 50, no 3, pp267–280

Zaner, A. (1991) 'Definition and sources of noise', in T. H. Fay (ed) *Noise and Health*, New York Academy of Medicine, New York

CHAPTER 3

Hear Me Now!
Noise Can Harm Your Health!

ARLINE L. BRONZAFT

*Noise is not just an annoyance or an inconvenience
that must be tolerated; it is a health hazard.*

Introduction

Many people define health as an absence of observable symptoms but health is more properly defined by the World Health Organization (WHO) as a complete state of well-being. Good health also implies a decent quality of life. Individuals who are intruded upon by noise from overhead planes, the neighbour's barking dog or the passing of loud boom cars are often not able to carry on with their everyday activities such as talking on the telephone, watching television, listening to their radios or conversing with others in their home. Even sleep can be disrupted. In essence, intrusive noise diminishes the quality of life for these people. In the long run, the continuous noise and the concomitant diminished quality of life can bring about actual physiological and psychological symptoms. In other words, noise is a health hazard.

Defining noise

We too often hear that noise is in the ear of the beholder or one person's music is another's noise. It would then follow that noise is subjective and it would differ from sound, which is a measurable physical phenomenon. As noted in Chapter 1, sound can be measured and it is generally described as having two physical properties: speed or the frequency of its vibrating waves and intensity or the sound pressure level of each vibration. When sound travels to the ear, the frequency is interpreted as pitch and the intensity is interpreted as loudness, recognizing that higher pitched sounds are deemed to be louder.

47

It is the outer ear that picks up the sound that travels to the hair cells of the inner ear and then on to the temporal lobe of the brain along the eighth cranial nerve. The frontal lobe of the brain gives meaning to the different sounds but it also contributes to the emotional significance of these sounds – it is this part of the brain that determines whether a particular sound is pleasant or unpleasant, wanted or unwanted. Noises are those sounds that are judged to be intrusive, bothersome, uncontrollable and unpredictable.

If noise is judged on an individual basis, can we assess the presence of noise in an objective way? Yes, when we realize that certain sounds would be deemed intrusive and annoying by people of reasonable sensitivities. While there are people who may be more annoyed by certain sounds and others less annoyed by these same sounds, if most of the population of reasonable people would be bothered by a particular set of sounds, then we would deem these sounds to be noises. Overhead aircraft noise affects large numbers of people as does the traffic of passing cars. Most people would be bothered by basketball playing in the apartment above and similarly most people would find it difficult to fall asleep living above a noisy bar playing loud music. Sound becomes noise when a person of reasonable sensitivities is bothered by the sound and this noise can adversely affect that person's mental and physical health. That sound need not be loud to be annoying, for example, a dripping tap or a partner's snoring.

Noise control agencies tend to measure loudness of sounds on the A scale of the decibel meter but such measurements ignore the influence of the low frequency sounds that can be disturbing. The bass of the music from the bar below can disturb the individual living above as can the low hum of a neighbour's air conditioner. To measure the impact of these sounds requires employing the C scale of the decibel meter. New York City's 2007 Revised Noise Code permits measurement on the C scale for commercial music.

Noise does more than annoy – it is hazardous to our mental well-being

Borsky (1969, 1980) early on wrote about the common response to noise – annoyance. In his earlier paper, he noted, that both in the UK and the US, less than a quarter of the population exposed to noise complained about it. Borsky believed that the degree of the annoyance, the seriousness of the noise intrusion, compared to other problems, and the likelihood that a complaint would abate the noise were factors that accounted for the low number complaining. In his later paper, Borsky found too few complained about being annoyed, and even those who were especially annoyed and did complain still believed there was little chance of successfully lessening the noise. Kryter (1985) concurred with Borsky in that many more people are annoyed by noise than is reported by surveys because many believe that their complaints will fall on 'deaf ears'. According to Chepesiuk (2005), about 65 per cent of the European population is exposed to ambient sounds exceeding 55dB(A) and about 17 per cent are exposed to sounds above 65dB(A). If these percentages are accurate, then a large number of people are very likely annoyed by noise. As we saw in Chapter 2, a considerable number of people are indeed disturbed by noise.

By 1990 there was a definite growth of community groups opposing noise intrusions especially those from airports (Ruben, 1991). Zaner's (1991) review of survey data indicated that motor vehicles and aircraft were the major sources of noise complaints. Bronzaft et al (1998) and Cohen et al (2008) reported that residents living near airports are annoyed by both the aircraft noise and the traffic noise of the vehicles traveling to and from the airport. That aviation noise is a major annoyance for citizens living near airports is evidenced by the lawsuits filed in the US against the Federal Aviation Administration's (FAA) Airspace Redesign, which has brought increased noise over the homes of people living near airports in New York, Pennsylvania, Connecticut, Delaware and New Jersey (www.ourairspace.org). Similarly, the opposition to Heathrow's expansion has been founded on the fear of residents that this expansion will result in increased noise to their communities.

Berglund and Lindvall (1995) in a review of surveys on noise concluded that annoyance was the most prevalent response to noise intrusions. Later studies (Bronzaft et al, 2000; Bronzaft and van Ryzin, 2004, 2006, 2007) found that New Yorkers, as well as citizens across the US, identified annoyance as the number one response to a list of stated noises. In New York City, the 311 complaint line reports that noise is its number one complaint (Gootman, 2010).

However, simply to say that noise annoys people is to underestimate the effect it has on our mental well-being. As the chair of the noise committee of GrowNYC, a mayoral-appointed committee, I have been the recipient of phone calls and emails from New Yorkers with noise problems asking for help when neither landlords nor city agencies were able to assist them. When these people call, the anguish and distress in their voices indicate that noise is more than an annoyance. As a psychologist, I spend the first few minutes of the call simply listening and this response tends to calm the callers to the point where they can speak of their noise problems. Then I try to help them with their problems. My having served on GrowNYC, formerly the Council on the Environment, for many years, having been named by four mayors, has given me first-hand experience of how stressful and disturbing noise disruptions can be. Annoyance leads to feelings of anger, helplessness and agitation in these callers and my personal experiences with these callers were supported in a study in which respondents to a questionnaire were asked to identify their feelings when bothered by noise (Bronzaft et al, 2000).

When the FAA in the US holds hearings on proposed airport expansions, it is very evident that the reactions of the communities go beyond annoyance; their anger and distress are readily expressed. Similarly, UK citizens opposing Heathrow's expansion have displayed their unhappiness through a wide range of emotional responses. Citizens, when they complain about noise at community meetings regarding loud sounds from discos, bars, new construction and neighbours frequently do so with anger, frustration and distress in their voices. Unfortunately, too often complaints about noise go unheeded, as the studies above note. It is then complainants develop a feeling of learned helplessness in which they believe that nothing can be done to alleviate the noise problem and this, in turn, increases the distress of the individual.

To avoid the added stress that comes with learned helplessness, citizens have joined groups that have been set up to lessen noise in their environments through educating public officials about the deleterious effects of noise. Additionally such groups provide the opportunity for individuals to learn that others are similarly inflicted by noise. This knowledge does not alleviate much of the unhappiness brought about by the noise but brings some comfort by informing people they are not alone. People who complain about noise to authorities are often told that they are overly sensitive to noise and should learn to live with it. This is especially true when complainants live in large cities or near airports. Following are some noise group websites: www.noiseoff.org, www.lowertheboom.org, www.noboomers.org, www.ukna.org.uk, www.nonoise.org, www.quiet.org.

We must also realize that when individuals are not able to ameliorate their noise problems, especially when the source of the noise is someone in the community (for example, an upstairs neighbour who plays her piano loudly five hours a day, neighbourhood children who play in front of one's window), then arguments may arise between the complainant and the noisemaker. Such arguments can become shouting matches or result in fist fights and even shootings. Early psychological laboratory studies in the 1970s found that noise could lead to aggression but, more to the point, today's media in both the UK and the US have reported serious disputes over noise. In the US, the website www.noboomers.org carries newspaper stories on such disputes including the story of a Cleveland firefighter who, angered over the 4 July 2007 noise from his next door neighbour's home, shot three of the people in that neighbour's house. As is true in many of these neighbour arguments, the firefighter had complained to the neighbour many times about keeping the noise down but to no avail. That someone could murder because of noise reflects the amount of distress noise can bring about.

It should be noted that individuals who are less emotionally stable may be even more disturbed by noise. The noise throws these individuals into heightened states of anxiety. I have responded to noise complaints from residents in New York City and elsewhere for many years and have identified some callers for whom the noise exacerbated an already existing state of anxiety. However, this does not mean that the caller's noise complaint was not a legitimate one.

Loud sounds, noise and hearing loss

Before discussing the impacts of emotional reactions to noise on overall physical health, I would like to examine the most obvious adverse and measurable
health effect of exposure to loud sounds and excessive noise – hearing loss.
Even when listening to loud sounds that are desirable, such as music at a rock
concert or disco, exposure to this loud music can still be damaging to the ear.
When leaving a loud concert, the attendee may feel some ringing in the ear
but if this ringing alerts the individual to avoid further exposures then there
will probably be no damage to the inner ear's hair cells. However, a very loud
intense sound close to the ear can lead to an immediate loss of some hearing. It
has been claimed that former US President Ronald Reagan lost some hearing
when a loud gunshot went off near his ear when he was filming a movie. More
frequently, it is the continuous exposure to loud sounds or loud music that
leads to a gradual loss of hearing over time.

Many people suffer from gradual loss of hearing, largely due to exposure
to loud sounds over time. It has been said that former President Bill Clinton's
loss of some of his hearing was the result of exposure to the loud sounds of his
'baby boom' generation, his saxophone playing and his frequent trips on loud
helicopters. Our increasingly noisy urban society has resulted in an increase
in the numbers of older people who have poorer hearing, according to the
research of Bat Chava and Schur (2000). After taking hearing measurements
of large samples of people over the age of 60 in New York City over a 19-year
period, they found a higher percentage of these individuals did poorly on the
hearing test administered with each passing year.

What is especially alarming is the growing numbers of younger people
who are losing some of their hearing. Lipscomb (1972) found significant loss
of high frequency hearing amongst college freshmen. Cozad et al (1974) found
an increase in numbers of students between the ages of 6 and 18 suffering
from hearing loss and Niskar et al (2001) reported that about 12.5 per cent of
American children between the ages of 6 and 19 suffered from noise-related
hearing loss. In the UK, according to a BBC News programme (2003), youngsters attending clubs with loud music were experiencing ringing in the ears
and some loss of hearing. It would be safe to assume that the increase in exposure to loud sounds by our youngsters, for example, discos, concerts, boom
cars and video arcade games, accounts for this increase in hearing loss.

Brian J. Fligor (2010), a researcher examining the causes of hearing loss,
especially in the younger population, writes about the link between recreational noise and hearing loss. He looked at the data of the 'Listen Up! Project' at
the Oregon Museum of Science and Industry and found that young adult men
and women engage in noisy recreational activities that he believes significantly
correlates to the hearing loss among some of the participants who completed
questionnaires and had their hearing tested at this Oregon exhibit. Amongst
an older group (aged 20–45), compared to the younger group (aged 11–19),

a larger percentage of men than women had some hearing loss, partially explained by the fact that more men in this age group rode a motorcycle or snowmobile. While most of the participants did not have hearing loss, the dangers of loud recreational activities were clear. Similarly, the researchers affiliated with the Ear Science Institute Australia (ESIA) and the University of Western Australia's Ear Science Center (www.earscience.org.au), who took sound measurements at music venues in and around the Perth metropolitan area in 2005, warned young people that attendance at these loud venues put them at risk of permanent hearing damage. Furthermore, their study found that, although young people believed that sound levels of these venues were very high, they were reluctant to wear hearing protection. Dr Marcus Atlas, director of ESIA, believes that this attitude very likely contributes to the findings that younger people both in Australia and abroad are wearing hearing aids earlier in life.

Then there are the people, who when they experience some hearing loss, deny they have a problem. Rather, they feel more comfortable compensating for their loss by playing the television or CD player louder. They often accuse people of speaking too softly and then ask them to repeat themselves. At other times, they simply accept missing some of the conversation because they are too embarrassed to speak up. While hearing aids can improve hearing ability, many people do not like wearing them. Hearing aids are not yet as acceptable as eyeglasses.

Another hearing problem which has received more attention lately is tinnitus, a constant ringing in one's head, that is the result of frequent exposure to loud sounds. Some believe tinnitus is due to the damage of the hair cells of the ear but they also note the relationship between the hearing system and two other parts of the brain – the amygdala, which is associated with anxiety, and the hippocampus, which is associated with memory. Baguley (2010) explores more fully the causes of tinnitus and examines possible therapies to correct the problem. Singer Pete Townshend of The Who, a 1970s band known for loud performances, suffers from both hearing loss and tinnitus. Townshend notes that his hearing has been irreversibly damaged from using extremely loud studio headphones. He uses his weblog to warn iPod users that they may face hearing loss if they continue to pump up the volume on their devices as he once did.

Beyond hearing loss – other bodily impacts

The direct impact of loud sounds on the ears is hearing loss but sounds can indirectly affect other parts of the body. They need not be loud – a dripping tap or the constant hum of a neighbour's air conditioner. Intrusive, unwanted sounds that disturb our ongoing activities are called noise and the body responds with a stress reaction. This stress triggers off bodily responses:

increases in blood pressure, increased heart rate, contraction of muscles, and so on. If these intrusive sounds or noises continue, for example, overhead aircraft, a neighbour's loud music, passing boom cars, then the resultant sustained stress can bring about changes in the bodily systems affected: high blood pressure, hardening of the arteries, indigestion and insomnia.

Studies conducted in industrial settings, where workers are exposed to loud intrusive sounds, have demonstrated relationships between cardiovascular disorders and exposure to noise (Tomei et al, 1995; Melamed et al, 2001) but today there is increasing evidence that noise adversely impacts on individuals who are exposed to it at home, with the strongest evidence for cardiovascular and circulatory disorders (Jarup et al, 2008; Babisch, 2006; Ising and Kruppa, 2004; Passchier-Vermeer and Passchier, 2000). Niemann et al (2006) undertook a study in eight European countries in which they examined noise-induced annoyance and morbidity and concluded that one's health is at risk from exposure to noise-induced annoyance. They urged governments to reduce noise in residential areas.

While the subjects for studies cited above are generally exposed to transportation noise, for example, traffic and aircraft, the findings of these studies can be generalized to specific cases where individuals are similarly exposed to continuous noises. Although, one might argue that, in the larger picture, noise may account for a small percentage of cardiovascular and circulatory disorders, the fact that these disorders are growing significantly in our society only underscores the importance of lessening the impact of any contributing factor that may bring about the onset of these disorders. It should also be added that noise may possibly exacerbate existing cardiac ailments. Hospitals traditionally have been aware of maintaining quiet in the hospital setting but lately intensive care units have introduced noisy monitoring equipment. The medical staff in these units have become concerned about exposure of patients to these noises, not to mention how many commented on how relieved they are when they leave the units. On the other hand, hospitals have recognized that shared televisions may disturb patients who are resting and have been switching over to personal television sets. Similarly, nursing stations are being placed in areas that are less intrusive.

The impact on children's health

Of special concern is the impact of noise on the health of children. Goines (2008) warns that the noise of neonatal intensive care units (NICUs) puts neonates at risk of hearing loss. She adds that the noise of staff activities also triggers off undesirable physiological responses that include fluctuations in blood pressure and heart rate. In her article, she warns parents about reducing noise exposure when these young infants are brought home from the hospital. Evans et al (1993) Belojevic et al (2008), Babisch (2006) and van Kampen et al

(2006) have found that living in noisy environments exposes children to conditions that may elevate their blood pressure levels but these findings require additional confirmation. However, warnings may still be appropriate.

It should be pointed out that the US Environmental Protection Agency (US EPA) in its 1978 *Noise: A Health Problem* brochure cautioned about the potential harm of exposing the foetus to noise and further expressed concern that the stress on the mother who was exposed to a noisy environment might impact the developing foetus. Their statements were based on studies that indicated lower birth rates and lower levels of certain hormones among women exposed to noisy environments. While future studies in this area were not conducted to confirm earlier findings, one should note the statement that ended this section of the brochure: 'In the case of noise, it is not known how much is required to have an effect. Whatever the effect, the risk of even a slight increase in birth defects is considerably disturbing.'

Noise: A state of well-being

With the WHO definition of health as a complete state of well-being, one need not experience the symptoms of disease to feel 'less than healthy'. It should be sufficient to state that, when noise intrudes on an individual's activities, a person's quality of life is diminished. Bronzaft et al (1998) found that many residents living with overhead aircraft noise reported that the noise from these planes prevented them from opening their windows, talking on the telephone, talking with others in their homes, sleeping and listening to radio or television. These residents also perceived themselves to be in poorer health when compared to a comparable group not exposed to the aircraft noise. Additionally, an individual's perception of poor health has been considered a valid indicator of actual health status. Clearly, noise intrudes on well-being, even if the individual has not yet evidenced actual symptoms of a disorder.

The US in the 1970s produced materials that recognized noise as a health hazard, long before many of today's studies, largely conducted in Europe, confirmed the deleterious effects of noise. Dr William H. Stewart, the former Surgeon General stated the following in a 1969 Conference on Noise as a Public Health Hazard: 'Must we wait until we prove every link in the chain of causation ... To wait for it is to invite disaster or to prolong suffering unnecessarily' (US EPA, 1978). Frequently the attitude toward noise is compared with the one toward smoking 50 years ago when governments did not believe there was sufficient evidence to curtail smoking. While waiting for confirmation of the smoking/health link, many people died and many more developed chronic illnesses. I wonder if Dr Stewart was not reflecting on the relationship between smoking and ill health when he made his statement in 1969.

When noise disrupts sleep, our health is harmed

It has long been recognized that a good night's sleep is essential for good health. Sleep brings us requisite rest and allows the body to restore itself from the day's activities. Thus, the noise intrusions that prevent people from getting their needed sleep can be viewed as hazardous to good health. A significant number of residents in two studies, in which I was one of the researchers, complained about noise intruding on sleep (Bronzaft et al, 1998; Cohen et al, 2008). Studies by Okinawa Prefectual Government (1999), Passchier-Vermeer and Passchier (2000) and Griefahn (2007) similarly reported that night-time noise disturbances increased awakenings. Of special concern is the disruption of sleep among children (Ohrstrom et al, 2006). Jarup et al (2008) found that individuals living near airports had higher blood pressure. The authors believed that the exposure to the noisy aircraft was a factor in raising the pressure.

A 2009 WHO report entitled *Night Noise Guidelines for Europe* reviewed the available studies examining the impact of night noise on health and concluded that there was 'sufficient evidence that night noise exposure causes self-reported sleep disturbances, increase in medical use, increase in body movements and (environmental) insomnia'. The report also found evidence to suggest a stronger link between night noise exposure and cardiovascular effects than daytime exposure, echoing the findings of Jarup et al (2008). However, this report found limited evidence supporting impacts of disturbed sleep on performance levels the next day, accidents or fatigue. While the evidence might be limited in these areas, there is still the possibility that lack of sleep may make one less attentive to cues of danger in their environment and less able to perform their jobs proficiently. The WHO report singled out children, older people and those in ill health to be more vulnerable to sleep disruptions. Again, it should be pointed out that more than 30 years ago, the 1978 EPA brochure *Noise: A Health Problem* contained a statement in keeping with results of more recent studies: 'When sleep is disturbed by noise, work efficiency and health might suffer.'

Noise disrupts children's development: Cognition, language and learning

As a member of America's premier honour society Phi Beta Kappa, an organization that recognizes the highest achieving students in college who have demonstrated excellent grades and have taken many credits in the liberal arts, I have been long interested in the factors that contribute to academic success. This led to my research on the lives of Phi Beta Kappa members after they graduated college as well as exploring what their childhoods were like. The resulting book *Top of the Class* (Bronzaft, 1996) found that these academic high-achievers did well professionally and personally after graduating from college. Their parents inculcated a love of reading and learning in these achievers early on in life, which contributed to their success in school and afterwards. However, my interest in noise led me to inquire in telephone conversations with many of the older subjects regarding the sound level in their homes. They reported that their homes provided them with the requisite quiet needed for reading, studying and thinking. Televisions and stereos were not blasting loudly in the background when they read and did their homework and parents did not chide them with loud voices. Apparently, the quieter homes in which these high academic achievers lived helped them do well in school.

This should not have surprised me because I already had published two studies on the effects of noise on children's learning when their school was adjacent to noisy elevated train tracks in Manhattan, New York (Bronzaft and McCarthy, 1975; Bronzaft, 1981). In PS98, children whose classrooms were adjacent to the rail tracks heard the trains passing by every four and a half minutes. When we examined the reading scores of these children in the second, fourth, and sixth grades for three years and compared the reading scores to those of children who attended classes on the quiet side of the building, we found that by the sixth grade, the children exposed to transit noise were about 11 months behind children on the quiet side. Children reported they could not hear the teachers when the trains passed and, in fact, teachers stopped teaching for about 11 per cent of the time. Additionally, teachers sometimes shouted above the din. The results of this study influenced the Transit Authority to place rubber resilient pads on the tracks to lessen the noise and the Board of Education to install acoustic ceilings in the affected classes. The 1981 study found that the abatement techniques lessened the noise by 6–8dB but, more importantly, this was sufficient enough to enable the students on the track side to read at the same level as the children on the quiet side. As a result of this study, the Transit Authority decided to install rubber resilient pads on their elevated tracks, understanding that other schools were similarly located and that people, including children, lived in homes alongside the elevated structure.

The results of these two studies indicating that noise affects reading scores were confirmed by later research. Green et al (1982) examined the reading ability of children attending schools near New York's major airports and compared their reading ability to children not exposed to aircraft noise and found the reading ability of children near airports to be poorer. Lukas et al (1981) also found that children attending schools near Los Angeles freeways had lower reading scores. More recently, Haines et al (2001) found in their London study that aircraft noise impaired reading comprehension as did Stansfield et al (2005) who examined the impact of aircraft noise on children attending schools in the UK, Spain and The Netherlands. The Federal Interagency Committee (FICAN, 2000) examined 20 studies and concluded that aircraft noise intrudes on children's learning. These studies have resulted in the FAA issuing a contract in 2010 to examine the impact of aircraft noise on children's learning. Even children in day-care centres can be affected by nearby noise as Hambrick-Dixon (1986) found when she looked at the poorer psychomotor performance of children who attended day-care centres near New York's elevated trains.

Noise in the home and the neighbourhood also impacts on children's development. Wachs and Gruen (1982) found that children living in noisy homes were slower in cognitive and language development and Lercher et al (2003) reported that chronic neighbourhood noise can result in poorer intentional and incidental memory in school-aged children. Noise impacts could be especially detrimental to children who already have some hearing loss or who have learning and language disabilities.

Despite strong research findings on the deleterious effects of noise on children's development and learning, not enough has been done to lessen the children's exposure to noise in the home, community and classroom. The US House Education and Labor Committee passed legislation in 2009 that would reduce children's exposure to noise in schools but the bill has not yet been passed by Congress. President Obama, in a speech to the joint houses of Congress in February 2009, bemoaned the exposure of a student, attending this Congressional session, to train noises that pass her South Carolina school six times a day. It would be wonderful if President Obama used his office to encourage passage of the legislation that would reduce noise in schools. His actions would further support the classroom acoustical standards set by the American National Standard Institute in 2002 (www.nonoise.org). While it is fine for researchers to call for additional studies, there is apparently sufficient evidence linking noise to children's learning deficits.

Lacking federal legislation requiring schools to keep the noise levels down from within and without the school, cities and states in the US can pass their own legislation. Information on how classrooms can be quietened, as well as information on the importance of quieter classrooms, can be accessed by cities in the US and abroad by going to the Noise Pollution Clearinghouse website (www.nonoise.org). Educational and environmental departments in cities and towns can educate parents, teachers and children on the need to lessen noise in the children's lives. In New York City, the Department of Environmental Protection has developed its own educational programme and sends out representatives to New York schools with information on noise pollution and what to do to reduce noise levels (www.nycdep.org). The Toronto, Canada, Public Health department has published a document entitled *Noise and Children: Reducing the Level of Noise in Your Home* (www.city.toronto.on.ca/health).

Concluding thoughts

My goal in writing this chapter was not only to educate readers to the hazards of noise pollution but to arouse them to action to lessen the din in their environments. I hope that I have succeeded in alerting readers to the fact that noise is not just an annoyance or an inconvenience that must be tolerated. Too often, you hear people say that noise is part of living in a city or in a shared housing situation. While it is true that cities and shared dwelling spaces result in an increase in surrounding sounds, the amount of noise emitted can be curtailed. Residents in apartment buildings do not have to slam their doors nor hit the loud button on their television sets. Youngsters do not have to boom their music as their cars travel through neighbourhoods. In addition, noise-making is not just limited to urban centers. Motorcross raceways are being planned for relatively quiet communities and even a serene, small town neighbourhood can be disrupted by an extremely noisy neighbour. One cannot really escape the 'noisy intruder'.

While it is true that governments can pass legislation to abate noise and manufacturers can produce quieter products, we must remember that many noises are the result of people not caring about their neighbours. We all should question whether we have added to the noises in our environments and, if so, correct the situation and reduce our own noise-making. We should also question whether we are responsible for the behaviour of others in our family, for example, children, and then make an effort to teach them to keep their sounds down. Remember, children learn from adults and adults have to set examples for them. Beyond our own families, we can reach out to others with whom we are in contact to educate them about trying to 'keep the sound down'. By advocating a quieter environment, I am not suggesting that louder sounds cannot accompany joyous events such as parades and parties, provided they do not intrude on others who are not participating.

A quieter environment is also rewarding in and of itself. It can be a time of reflection and relaxation and these in turn contribute to good health. I would like to borrow from the common expression 'stop and smell the roses' to 'quiet down and enjoy the silence'.

References

Babisch, W. (2006) 'Transportation noise and cardiovascular risk: Updated review and synthesis of epidemiological studies indicate that the evidence has increased', *Noise & Health*, vol 8, pp1–29

Baguley, D. M. (2010), 'Tinnitus and hyperacusis', in M. Chasin (ed) *The Consumer Handbook on Hearing Loss and Noise*, Auricle Ink Publishers, Sedona, AZ

Bat-Chava, Y. and Schur, K. (2000) 'Longitudinal trends in hearing loss: Nineteen years of public screenings', Annual Meeting of American Public Health Association, November, Boston

BBC News (2003) 'Clubbers risk premature deafness', 8 May

Belojevic, G., Jakovljevic, B., Stojanov, V. and Paunovic, K. (2008) *Environmental International*, vol 34, pp226–231

Berglund, B. and Lindvall, T. (1995) *Community Noise*, Center for Sensory Research, Stockholm

Borsky, P. N. (1969), 'Effects of noise on community behavior', in W. D. Ward and J. E. Fricke (eds) *Proceedings of the Conference on Noise as a Public Health Hazard*, American Speech and Hearing Association, Washington, DC

Borsky, P. N. (1980), 'Review of community response to noise', in J. Tobias, G. Jansen and W. D. Ward (eds) *Proceedings of the Third International Congress on Noise as a Public Health Hazard*, American Speech-Language-Hearing Society, Rockville, Maryland

Bronzaft, A. L. (1996) *Top of the Class*, Ablex, Greenwich, CT

Bronzaft, A. L. (1981) 'The effect of a noise abatement program on reading ability', *Journal of Environmental Psychology*, vol 1, pp215–222

Bronzaft, A. L. and McCarthy, D. (1975) 'The effect of elevated train noise on reading ability', *Environment and Behaviour*, vol 7, pp517–528

Bronzaft, A. L. and van Ryzin, G. (2004, 2006,2007) 'Neighborhood noise and its consequences', www.etownpanel.com/results.htm

Bronzaft, A. L., Ahern, K.D., McGinn, R., O'Connor, J. and Savino, B. (1998) 'Aircraft noise: A potential health hazard', *Environment and Behaviour*, vol 30, pp101–113

Bronzaft, A. L., Deignan, E., Bat-Chava, Y. and Nadler, N. B. (2000) 'Intrusive community noises yield more complaints', *Noise Rehabilitation Quarterly*, vol 25, pp16–22

Chepesiuk, R. (2005) 'Decibel hell', *Environmental Health Perspectives*, January, A35–A41

Cohen, B. S., Bronzaft, A. L., Heikkinen, M., Goodman, J. and Nadas, A. (2008) 'Airport-related pollution and noise', *Journal of Occupational and Environmental Health*, vol 5,pp119–129

Cozad, R. L., Martson, L. and Joseph, D. (1974) 'Some implications regarding high frequency loss in school-age children', *Journal of School Health*, vol 44, pp92–96

Evans, G. W. and Lepore, S. J. (1993) 'Non-auditory effects on children: A critical review, *Children's Environments*, vol 10, pp42–72.

FICAN (Federal Interagency Committee on Aviation Noise) (2000) 'FICAN position on research into effects of aircraft noise on classroom learning', Federal Interagency Committee on Aviation Noise, Washington, DC

Fligor, B. J. (2010), 'Recreational noise', in M. Chasin (ed) *The Consumer Handbook on Hearing Loss and Noise*, Auricle Ink Publishers, Sedona, AZ

Goines, L. (2008) 'The importance of quiet in the home: Teaching noise awareness to parents before the neonate is discharged from the NICU', *Neonatal Network*, vol 27, pp171–176

Gootman, E. (2010) 'Thank You for Calling 311', *The New York Times*, 16 May, MB1, MB 8

Green, K. B., Pasternak, B. S. and Shore, R. E. (1982) 'Effects of aircraft noise on reading ability of school-age children', *Archives of Environmental Health*, vol 37, pp24–31

Griefahn, B. (2007), 'Noise and sleep', in D. Prasher and L. Luxon (eds) *Noise and its Effects*, John Wiley & Sons Ltd, New York

Haines, M. M., Stansfield, S. A., Soames Job, R. F., Berglund, B. and Head, J. (2001) 'A follow-up study of effects of chronic aircraft noise exposure on child stress responses and cognition', *International Journal of Epidemiology*, vol 30, pp839–845

Hambrick-Dixon, P. J. (1986) 'Effects of experimentally imposed noise on task performance of black children attending day care centers near elevated subway trains', *Developmental Psychology*, vol 22, pp259–264

Ising, H. and Kruppa, B. (2004) 'Health effects caused by noise: Evidence in the literature from the past 25 years', *Noise and Health*, vol 6, pp5–13

Jarup, L., Babisch, W. and Houthuijs, D. (2008), 'Hypertension and exposure to noise near airports: The HYENA study', *Environmental Health Perspectives*, vol 116, pp329–333

Kryter, K. D. (1985) *The Effects of Noise on Man*, second edition, Academic Press, Orlando

Lercher, P., Evans, G. W. and Meis, M. (2003) 'Ambient noise and cognitive processes among primary schoolchildren', *Environment and Behaviour*, vol 35, pp725–735

Lipscomb, D. M. (1972) 'The increase in prevalence of high frequency impairment among college students', *Audiology*, vol 11, pp231–234

Lukas, J. S., DuPree, R. B. and Swing, J. W. (1981) *Effects of Noise on Academic Achievement and Classroom Behavior*, Office of Noise Control, Department of Health Service, Berkeley, CA

Melamed, S., Fried, Y. and Froom, P. (2001) 'The interactive effect of chronic exposure to noise and job complexity on changes in blood pressure and job satisfaction: A longitudinal study of industrial employees', *Journal of Occupational Health Psychology*, vol 6, pp182–195

Niemann, H., Bonnefoy, X., Braubach, M., Hecht, K., Maschke, D., Rodrigues, C. and Robbel, N. (2006) 'Noise induced annoyance and morbidity results from pan-European LARES study', *Noise and Health*, vol 8, pp63–79

Niskar, A. S., Kieszak, S. M., Holmes, A., Esteban, E., Rubin, C. and Brody, D. J. (2001) 'Estimated prevalence of noise induced hearing threshold shifts among children 6 to 19 years of age: The third national health and nutrition examination survey, 1988–1994', *Pediatrics*, vol 108, pp40–43

Ohrstrom, E., Hadzibajra, E., Holmes, M. and Svensson, H. (2006) 'Effects of road traffic on sleep: Studies on children and adults', *Journal of Environmental Psychology*, vol 16, pp116–126

Okinawa Prefectual Government. (1999) 'A report on the aircraft noise as a public health problem in Okinawa', Okinawa Prefectural Government, Department of Culture and Environmental Affairs, Japan

Passchier-Vermeer, W. and Passchier, W. F. (2000) 'Noise exposure and public health', *Environmental Health Perspectives*, vol 108, pp123–131

Ruben, B. (1991) 'On deaf ears', *Environmental Action*, March/April, pp16–19

Stansfield, S. A., Berglund, B., Clark, C., Lopez-Barrio, I., Fischer, P., Ohrstrom, E., Haines, M., Hygge, S., van Kamp, I. and Berry, B. F. (2005) 'Aircraft and road traffic noise and children's cognition and health: A cross-national study', *The Lancet*, vol 365, pp1942–1949

Tomei, F., Tomao, E., Papaleo, B., Baccolo, T. P., Cirio, A. M. and Alfi, P. (1995) 'Epidemiological and clinical study of subjects occupationally exposed to noise', *International Journal of Angiology*, vol 4, pp117–121

US EPA (Environmental Protection Agency) (1978) *Noise: A Health Problem*, US Environmental Protection Agency, Office of Noise Abatement and Control, Washington, DC

van Kampen, E., Van Kamp, I., Fischer, P., Davies, H., Houthuijs, K., Stellato, R., Clark, C. and Stansfield, S. (2006) 'Noise exposure and children's blood pressure and heart rate: The RANCH Project', *Occupational Environmental Medicine*, vol 63, pp632–639

Wachs, T. and Gruen, G. (1982) *Early Experience and Human Development*, Plenum, New York

WHO (World Health Organization) (2009) *Night Noise Guidelines for Europe*, World Health Organization, Copenhagen

Zaner, A. (1991) 'Definition and sources of noise', in T. H. Fay (ed) *Noise and Health*, New York Academy of Medicine, New York

CHAPTER 4

Noise: The Neglected Green Issue of Our Age?

The threat to the planet's sound systems is silently passing the world by.

The green movement has so far shown little interest in noise. Its principal concern has been climate change. Understandably so. The consequences of runaway climate change do not bear thinking about. This chapter makes the case for noise as a green issue. It draws a parallel between the way in which climate change is threatening to alter the planet's ecosystems and 'man-made' or human noise is threatening the planet's natural sound systems.

These natural systems, which have evolved over the centuries, are fragile and complex. The sounds of the oceans, the forests, the deserts and the prairies send important signals to marine and wildlife. When human noise distorts or destroys these sounds, the very survival of the species that depend on them can be threatened. Although there is some evidence of adaptation to new, noisy situations – such as urban birds singing more loudly – there are also signs that human noise has become so intrusive that it is threatening to destroy the delicate balance of nature's sound systems on which so many species depend.

As a general rule, the noise impact on marine and wildlife depends on the extent to which noise disrupts a functioning ecosystem or a natural sound system. Noise has the greatest effect on the marine and wildlife that rely most heavily on auditory signals for survival. Increases in background noise levels can interfere with or mask communication signals that animals, birds and mammals use in their daily lives: in courtship, to warn of danger (often critical to survival) or to stake out territory.

It is in the oceans and forests that the natural sound systems are being most dramatically distorted. The natural sounds of the ocean are magnificent in their range, beautiful in their delivery and stunningly varied. But these sounds are in danger of being overwhelmed by human noises and vibrations such as never before in recorded history. It is estimated that underwater noise has doubled each decade during the past 50 years (McDonald et al, 2006). Scientists and conservationists are increasingly concerned that noise pollution poses a significant threat to whales, dolphins and other marine wildlife.

The sounds of the jungle rival those of the ocean. They are at once beautiful and frightening, awesome and awe-inspiring. But they are under threat. As the jungle is chopped down or invaded, its natural noise rhythms are disappearing. Dr Bernie Krause, the eminent American acoustician who has recorded nature's sounds for the past 40 years, estimates that in that time nearly a third of the ecosystems he has captured have become aurally 'extinct' because of habitat loss or the presence of noise-making machines (in Hull, 2007).

Noise in the ocean

We turn to look at the ocean in more detail. From the shore, it may seem quiet. But beneath the waves is a world of sound. Whales sing. Earthquakes roar. And over the past 100 years, humans have increasingly intruded with their noise machines. The exact impact of this sea of sound on the mammals and fish, while significant, is still difficult to define with pinpoint accuracy. Scientists feel they have only scratched the surface due in part to the difficulties inherent in ocean research. Michael Jasny, senior policy analyst at the American-based Natural Resources Defense Council (NRDC) and one of the world's leading experts on oceans, put it like this when interviewed in the *Boston Globe*: 'In general, this stuff is hard to study. All of these impacts on marine mammals and fish, they are occurring at sea, and their bodies often are not recovered' (Lazar, 2006). The Scientific Committee on International Whaling Report found there was 'compelling evidence' that entire populations of marine mammals are potentially threatened by increasingly intense underwater noise from human activities (Scientific Committee of the International Whaling Commission, 2005). And the Marine Mammal Commission Report (2007) found 'human activities are increasing the level of sound in the oceans causing widespread concern about the effect on marine mammals and marine ecosystems'.

Whales and dolphins rely on sound

It is whales and dolphins that can be particularly badly affected by noise. Cetaceans, the family to which they belong, live in a world dominated by sound. In the dark sea waters where they live, they rely on their acute and highly specialized hearing for communication and navigation. It is their primary sense. Adding alien and often very powerful sounds to this environment is like adding a blinding and confusing light to our world. It totally disorientates. Although different forms of cetaceans make different sounds and sing different songs, they all rely on sound to communicate and, ultimately, to survive. Sight is limited for marine mammals because of the way water absorbs light. Smell is also limited. Sound is all-important for them.

Perhaps the best-known sound of the sea is the song of the humpback whale. It communicates using a pattern of regular and predictable sounds that are reminiscent of human singing. Since male humpback whales sing only during the mating season, it is assumed that the purpose of the songs is to attract a mate. Whether the songs are a competitive behaviour between males seeking the same mate, a means of staking out their territory or a 'flirting' behaviour from a male to a female is not known, but what is beyond doubt is that the ability to sing songs is vital for whales. Interestingly, whales that occupy the same geographical area (which can be as large as entire ocean basins) tend to sing similar songs, with only slight variations. Whales from other regions sing entirely different songs.

It is believed that, because whales and some other mammals communicate over such large distances, their chain of communication is particularly vulnerable to human noises. This is not just because such a lengthy chain can be broken in many more places, but also because the low-frequency content in the noise from ships, seismic equipment and other mechanical noises humans have introduced travels much further through the ocean than higher-frequency sounds. A particular problem arises if mammals are communicating at the same low-frequencies as the 'man-made' noises. It totally disorientates them. It is estimated that low frequency noise has increased by 3dB per decade in the period 1950–1998 (McDonald et al, 2006).

Acidification of the oceans

These problems are compounded by the phenomenon of ocean acidification which climate scientists attribute to high concentrations of carbon dioxide (CO_2) in the atmosphere. The Intergovernmental Panel on Climate Change (IPCC) forecasts that this could lead to a drop of 0.3 in the pH (a sensitive function of its alkalinity and total inorganic carbon concentration) of ocean surface waters by the middle of the century (IPCC, 2007). It could be as much as 0.5 units by the end of the century (Caldeira and Wickett, 2003). Although this acidification has many damaging effects on marine life, it has a particular significance where underwater noise is concerned in that it weakens the concentration of noise-absorbing chemicals in seawater. As a result of this, low frequency noise can now travel uninterruptedly for ever greater distances through the sea. Tatiana Ilyina, an oceanographer at the University of Hawaii, found in her research that sound absorption will drop by up to 70 per cent by the end of this century (Ilyina et al, 2009).

Impact of sonar testing

Sonar testing is having an impact on mammals and fish. One obvious effect is that it drives them away, which can be harmful when they are forced to leave feeding or mating areas. Scientists have found that in areas off the coast of Russia, where oil companies do sonic surveys, endangered gray whales cannot search for food in their normal habitat. Writing in *Current Science Magazine*, the science writer Chris Jozefowicz argues that sonic sound may also drive deep-diving whales too quickly into shallow water: 'A few years ago, researchers investigated whales that had washed up on the coast of the Canary Islands after sonar testing had been carried out in the area. The researchers found signs of gas embolisms in the whales. They had bubbles in their tissues, most likely because they had risen into the low-pressure water at the surface too quickly. Gas embolisms can make internal organs rupture and bleed, and those injuries can disorient an animal' (Josefowicz, 2006). Jasny said of the incident, 'This physical evidence has led scientists to understand that the sonar is injuring the whales in addition to causing them to strand' (in Josefowicz, 2006).

In its paper, 'Current noise pollution issues', the Antarctic and Southern Ocean Coalition (ASOC) argues that 'mounting evidence indicates that high-intensity anthropogenic sound from sonar and airguns leads to strandings, injury and mortality of beaked whales and other cetacean species' (ASOC, 2006). ASOC goes on to itemize some of the strandings that have taken place:

> *A multi-species stranding of 33 short-finned pilot whales, a minke whale and two dwarf sperm whales in North Carolina, United States, in January 2005. A mass stranding of Cuvier's beaked whales occurred on the Spanish coast of Almeria in January 2006. A further mass stranding in which at least 145 long-finned pilot whales perished occurred in Tasmania, Australia on 25th–27th October 2005. In a further compelling case, a non-stranding event in Hawaii, in July 2004 involving 150–200 melon-headed whales. Each of these events was linked to the use of military sonar.* (ASOC, 2006)

The navy under fire

The US navy has drawn particular fire over its low-frequency active sonar system. The navy argues it is essential for detecting super-quiet enemy submarines developed for the post Cold War seascape. The author Leora Broydo says it works 'by generating blasts of sounds upwards of 230 decibels (a jet engine is about 120 decibels at source) from massive transmitters that ships drag through the water; technicians then interpret the echoes. The navy wants to use this technology in 80% of the world's oceans' (Broydo, undated).

The big problem is that some marine mammals use the same or similar low-frequency sounds as the navy emits to communicate, feed and navigate. Chris Clarke writing in *Earth Island Journal* says, 'Bottlenose dolphins can distinguish between a cube and a sphere of similar size just by listening to their echoes' (Clarke, 2000).

The US navy has admitted that its sonar systems can have an impact on mammals. Its own research showed that the vocalizations of fin and blue whales decreased, gray whales deviated from their migration paths and about a third of humpback whales stopped singing. But the navy argues that the effect is temporary. However, the number of mass strandings linked to sonar noise suggests the impacts may be more serious. Jasny argues that 'the lesson to be taken is to be precautionary. There are too many uncertainties and risks to deploy a [sonar] system of such wide geographic reach' (Jasny, 2010).

Impact of airguns

Jasny (2010) has also outlined the severe impact on marine wildlife of the airguns used by the oil and gas companies. He writes: 'It's important to remember that environmental impacts don't start with drilling. Before companies drill for oil and gas, they explore for oil and gas, and it's not a pretty scene. Industry scopes the seafloor using long arrays of airguns that send extremely intense blasts of noise into the water column, about once every ten seconds, for weeks or months at a time. The impacts that this continual booming has on the marine environment – on species as varied as whales and cod – are profound.' Jasny says that some marine biologists argue that airgun surveys are 'the most intrusive form of man-made undersea noise'.

Impact of ships

However, it is ships that are responsible for the majority of the human-induced noise in the oceans. The noisiest ships are the huge vessels which carry oil, food and manufactured goods between ports all over the world. It is the propellers that are the cause of most of the noise from ships. As the blades turn, they create thousands of tiny bubbles, a process known as 'cavitation'. It is the sound of these bubbles bursting that causes the noise. Ship engines are a distant secondary contributor.

The Chamber of Shipping of America, a trade association, estimates that there are 100,000 large commercial vessels criss-crossing the world's oceans. This is expected to double or even treble by 2030. It is the cumulative effect of the noise from all these ships that scientists believe poses a greater threat to mammals than the intermittent blasts from sonar or the impact of drilling and dredging.

Campaigners are calling for improved ship design as a critical first step to reducing the noise caused by cavitation. It would also be in the interest of the maritime industry itself to cut cavitation noise since it reduces fuel efficiency: the higher the cavitation, the higher the fuel costs. The industry argues that retrofitting existing ships would be both costly and impracticable as far as the large vessels are concerned, but is supportive of improved design standards being mandatory for all new ships.

Some campaigners are also advocating that the speed of the ships be cut and that they be routed away from particularly important marine areas. Jackie Dragon, head of the marine sanctuaries campaign section of the US pressure group Vessel Watch, told the *Oakland Tribune*: 'The magic number is 10 knots.

If ships were travelling slower, they'd be cleaner, they'd be quieter and they would be safer' (Bohan, 2009).

But Dragon acknowledges the issue is a non-starter with the shipping industry. Kathy Metcalf, the director of maritime affairs for the Chamber of Shipping of America, argues that slowing down ships from cruising speeds of 25 knots would lead to more ships on the ocean because it would delay arrival times for key products and it would add many more hours to the voyages, piling on the costs.

The industry also opposes widespread rerouting of ships. But rerouting already happens on a limited scale. The International Maritime Organization (IMO), a specialized agency of the United Nations (UN), which acts as a global forum for the adoption of uniform rules and standards for the shipping industry, does designate places that are felt to be at particular risk from the impact of international shipping as Maritime Protection Areas (MPAs). The need for 'ship quieting' is now being taken seriously by the IMO, which has set up a Marine Environment Protection Committee to focus attention on the problem of ship noise. Its specialist Correspondence Group reported on 23 July 2010, recommending four areas of research: propulsion, hull design, on-board machinery and operations – the last covering such matters as speed, load variations, hydrography and routing (IMO, 2010). Article 194(1) of the UN Convention on the Law of the Sea sets out a general duty to protect marine biodiversity and prevent, reduce and control pollution 'from any source', which it is reasonable to assume includes noise pollution.

However, there is no real evidence that, of themselves, these measures will be sufficient to significantly reduce the tumult of noises that reverberates across the oceans, what Christopher W. Clark, the bioacoustics expert from Cornell University, calls, 'an acoustics traffic jam'.(Clark, 1999) It is the *number* of ships criss-crossing the oceans that is the fundamental problem. It is a problem for noise but also for climate change. Shipping is now the fastest-growing contributor to carbon dioxide emissions. Ships, perhaps even more than planes, have become the work-horse of the globalized economy with 95 per cent of the world's trade tonnage carried by ships. It would require fundamental policies to alter the situation. We explore this in more detail at the end of the chapter.

The impact on fish

Little research has been undertaken with regard to the impact of human noise on fish although it is clear that like all creatures they are affected by stress, which can make them vulnerable to disease, among other things. A US report (Natural Resources Defense Council, 2005) found that noise from oil and gas exploitation has been linked to lower catch rates of halibut, cod and other species. It also found that some species of fish suffer severe injury to their inner ears from noise that can seriously compromise their ability to survive. Sound is particularly important to fish as they rely on acoustic information to hunt, navigate, reproduce and avoid predators especially when their vision is impaired by the clouding of water by plankton and microorganisms. Human noise can cause fish to alter their migration patterns and avoid habitual feeding areas and spawning grounds. The intensive and increasingly noisy use of our seas, estuaries and rivers by commercial shipping, offshore wind farms and such activities as dredging, construction and mineral exploration is affecting the behaviour and physiology of fish. This is happening at a time when fish populations are under pressure from a variety of other sources including climate change and overfishing.

Action to cut noise

The authorities are starting to understand that measures need to be taken to tackle the noise pollution of the oceans. Spain implemented a moratorium on military activities in the waters around the Canary Islands in response to the beaked whale mortalities. A number of other countries have put guidelines in place for the protection of cetaceans from the potential impacts of military and seismic activities. These include the UK, the US, Brazil, Canada, Russia and New Zealand. We are, however, just at the earliest stage of protecting the ocean from 'man-made' noise.

Animals talk … and sing

We are all familiar with the phrase 'dumb animals'. It comes from the days when we assumed that animals could not talk to each other. We now know differently. Dr Bernie Krause, the musician turned acoustician, coined a word for this: biophony. It is what the world sounds like in the absence of humans. It is quite remarkable. Krause has found that animals divide up the acoustic spectrum so they do not interfere with one another's voices. It is like a musical score for an orchestra, with each instrument in its place. No two species are using the same frequency. Krause told *Wired Magazine* (Thompson, 2008): 'That's part of how they co-exist so well.' When they issue mating calls or warning cries, they are not masked by the noises of other animals.

This is best illustrated in the rainforest. John Wilkinson, writing for the BBC, takes up the story: 'It is dusk in a Central American rainforest. The sun drops below the hidden horizon and there is a brief silence as the calls of many birds and diurnal insects (those active during the day) fade away. In the nearby creek, a male toad makes his first tentative call of the evening, rather like the trilling of a mobile phone. He is soon joined by tens of others of his kind and the contrasting calls of several treefrogs from the leaves overhead. To a human listener, the multitude of different sounds to be heard under the rainforest canopy represents a bewildering variety of squeaks, chirrups and whistles' (Wilkinson, 2004).

When human noise – what Krause calls 'anthropony' – intrudes on this natural symphony, the information flow of the animal world is disturbed. It

---

BOX 4.1 Bernie Krause

Bernie Krause listens to nature for a living. He began his ground-breaking work in bioacoustics in the 1960s. He was a successful young musician. He and his music partner, the late Paul Beaver, had introduced the Moog synthesizer to pop music and had contributed to hundreds of albums and soundtracks. In 1968, he was having lunch with Van Dyke Parks of the Beach Boys. Parks suggested that he 'do an album on ecology'.

Krause told *Conservation Magazine* (Stover, 2009): 'The instant I switched on my recorder in the forest, my life changed. I was so intrigued by what I heard that I made a decision that this was what I wanted to do for the rest of my life.' Back in his studio, Krause examined the recordings of the forest: 'It was clear to him that what he had heard was a sequence of sounds so carefully partitioned that they read like a musical score. Different species vocalise at specific frequencies or times so they can be heard above other animals – in the same way you can make out the individual sounds of trumpets, violins and clarinets as Beethoven's fifth builds to a crescendo' (Stover, 2009).

Krause sold his music business, obtained a PhD in bioacoustics and began his lifetime's work of recording natural environments across the world. Forty years on, his ten albums have grossed sales of more than $24 million. He has established his own company Wild Sanctuary. He gained national recognition across the US as the 'Pied Piper' whose audio wizardry lured 'Humphrey the Wayward Humpback Whale' from the Sacramento River delta back to the Pacific Ocean.

---

is increasingly happening: from cars, lorries, aircraft, logging and drilling. It does not take much to disrupt the delicate balance of a natural soundscape. California's Lincoln Meadows, for example, underwent only a tiny bit of logging but the acoustic landscape changed completely. Krause said: 'The area looks the same as ever but if you listen to it, the density and diversity of the sound has diminished' (Thompson, 2008).

The rainforests

It is not a surprise that people such as Bernie Krause and John Wilkinson were so moved by the rainforests. They are remarkable places. A single rainforest reserve in Peru is home to more species of birds than are found in the entire US. One pond in Brazil can contain a greater variety of fish than is found in all of Europe's rivers. The biodiversity of the tropical rainforest is so immense that less than 1 per cent of its millions of species have been studied by scientists. No wonder the sounds of the forest are so magical. Yet they are being drowned out by the progressive encroachment of our human culture: drilling, sawing, cars and aircraft. Indeed, the forests themselves are disappearing at an alarming rate. Rainforests once covered 14 per cent of the Earth's land surface; it is now down to 6 per cent and experts estimate the last remaining rainforests could be consumed within less than 40 years if the current state of development continues (Taylor, 2004). That would be a disaster for the planet. The rainforest has been described as the 'lungs of the planet' because it provides the essential service of continuously recycling carbon dioxide into oxygen. It makes the preservation of the rainforest vital if the world is to win its fight against climate change. Its soundscape is equally unique.

The impact of low-frequency noise

Low-frequency noises emitted from the likes of military sonar equipment, gas pipelines, low-flying aircraft and other sources can have a particularly devastating effect on types of wildlife that use a low-frequency range – sometimes not detectable by the human ear – to communicate.

Hans Slabbekoorn, an assistant professor of behavioral biology at Leiden University in the Netherlands, has found that it is animals and birds that depend on low-frequency calls to communicate and cannot switch to higher frequencies that are most under threat. He says that birds such as orioles, great reed warblers and house sparrows fit into this category and suspects that human noise has been a factor in the decline of house sparrows across Europe (Stover, 2009).

Krause has witnessed a similar phenomenon among spadefoot toads in the Mono Lake basin east of Yosemite National Park in America. He told *Conservation Magazine*:

> *Using its big front claws, the toad buries itself one metre below the desert floor and can survive there for up to six years. When rain finally comes, the toad emerges and joins others to sing in chorus, which makes it harder for predators such as owls and coyotes to get a lead on where the sound is coming from. The problem is that, during night-time periods when the toads do their singing, military jets often use the basin for training. Flying only 100 metres above the ground, the planes are so loud that the toads can't hear each other. Even after the planes leave, it takes 20 to 45 minutes for the toads to resume their synchronized chorus, and in the meantime they're vulnerable to predators.* (Stover, 2009)

Krause believes the noise is partly responsible for a precipitous decline in spadefoot populations, which he has studied since 1984.

Elephants are perhaps the best known of the animals which communicate at very low-frequencies. They largely use infrasound, the lowest of frequencies. They will stamp on the ground and send seismic waves that other elephants can pick up because the soles of their feet have passing corpuscles that act like ground-listening antennae or receptors. Using infrasound, elephants can communicate over distances of 40km. There is evidence to show that, when an elephant is shot in one area, elephant herds 30–40km away become distressed.

The animals escape the tsunami … thanks to their hearing

The way elephants use infrasound to communicate may have given them early warning of the Asian tsumani. The naturalist Gehan De Silva Wijeyeratne has speculated:

> *Did they perhaps have several hours of prior notice? We know that elephants communicate using infrasound. They pick up ground waves. One possibility is when the earthquake happened off Sumatra, some of those ground-waves were detected by them, giving them a forewarning. Another possibility is as a tsunami wave came in, there would have been some wave energy carried as seismic waves, some as infrasound, either ground-borne or airborne. Animals like elephants could have picked it up. And it's possible that they gradually moved away. This could be why there weren't many reports of animals fleeing in a hurry.* (De Silva Wijeyeratne 2008)

Widespread impact of noise

Although human noise can be *particularly* disorienting and damaging to creatures such as whales, dolphins and elephants it has an impact on all creatures and birds are no exception. Birds depend on songs and calls to define their territories, locate and attract potential mates, give warning of danger, draw attention to the presence of food, coordinate flock movements and maintain family contacts.

Bats also have their problems with human noise, especially 'gleaning' or 'listening' bats such as the greater mouse-eared bat, which finds its prey by listening for the small rustling sounds of insects and small mammals. These creatures are seriously disadvantaged by traffic noise which masks these sounds and they will starve if they do not move to a quieter area (Schaub et al, 2008).

Of course, for all creatures the extent of that impact depends on a number of variables, their age and sex, the season of the year, the life history of the species, the type of habitat where the animal lives (most desert creatures, for example, have very acute hearing) as well as the character and duration of the noise.

The most obvious impact is damage to hearing. As in the case of humans, deafness can set in as a result of prolonged exposure to noise or from a sudden burst of very loud noise. Even temporary deafness can put wildlife at risk. For example, the roar of a dune buggy can turn a kangaroo rat deaf for several days. In the meantime, the rat has no way to escape from its enemy, the sidewinder rattlesnake. A desert kangaroo rat can normally hear the snake at a distance of 75cm. This is enough time for the feisty rat to kick sand in the snake's eyes and escape. But the deafened rats have no warning to escape – and end up as an easy meal.

Noise can also cause stress which in turn can lead to physical illnesses and behavioural and psychological problems. Of course all animals live with a degree of stress – it is part of their natural world. This makes it difficult to quantify the exact proportion of the stress caused by human noises. What evidence there is suggests that it is at times when the noise is unnaturally and excessively loud that it disorientates. It can lead to what is commonly referred to as the 'fight or flight'. Flight takes place when wildlife becomes disturbed by, or stressed about, noise. They do not understand where it is coming from or what it means. Witness how dogs react to fireworks. When animals do take flight en masse from an area, it can have serious consequences: it can be left barren and increasingly devoid of natural life.

Wildlife can sometimes adapt to a noisy environment, particularly if they have been brought up in that environment. There is the wonderful, if somewhat disturbing, story of a male blackbird in Somerset in England who terrorized the neighbourhood. Dawn Stover (2009) takes up the story: 'For several months he started singing at around 5am each day, but this was no ordinary song. The bird imitated the sounds of ambulance sirens and car alarms at a jarringly lifelike volume. It even produced cell-phone ring tones that went unanswered for hours.' The Somerset terror is not unique. Hans Slabbekoorn in his research discovered numerous examples of blackbirds imitating the urban sounds around them. This ability of some wildlife to adapt explains the existence of animals and birds near high-noise places such airports and military installations. For animals that migrate into these areas, the noise exposure may be less important to them than other factors: they may, for example, feel safe in these places as they usually have few humans or other animals in them.

Loss of biodiversity and fragmentation

Notwithstanding the fact that some animals can adapt to noise, scientists are increasingly worried by the damage that humans are doing to the natural world through their impact on biodiversity and the ecological systems that support it. Human noise contributes to the fragmentation and degradation of these systems and, as we have noted in the case of urban birds, the masking of low frequency transmissions can eventually lead to the complete disappearance of some bird species from a local ecosystem. Examples of this dispersal and dislocation resulting from noise can be found in all areas of the animal kingdom from gleaning bats to amphibians and the Sonoran pronghorn antelopes of Arizona who have abandoned their habitat in order to escape the noise of low-flying jets (Krausman, 2003). Jesse Barber summed it up: 'Habitat destruction and fragmentation are the greatest threats to wildlife and the major causes of species extinction' (Barber et al, 2009).

It is important, though, to recognize that there are still many areas of the world where the animal kingdom is largely unaffected by human noises. But, equally, the unnatural sounds of the modern world are reaching new places all the time, increasingly upsetting the balance of the animal king-doms. Human-induced noise is threatening to change the natural world forever. The sound systems of many of its natural habitats are being threat-ened, possibly beyond repair.

Possible solutions

What can be done about it? The introduction of quieter equipment and the development of new technology are necessary, but the evidence suggests this may not be sufficient in itself. Sonar and seismic equipment, for example, can be so disturbing that tight restrictions would need to be placed on its use to have any significant effect. And the problem with shipping is not just the noise made by each individual vessel but the huge projected growth in their use. The ship has become integral to the globalized economy. This suggests it will be difficult to conquer the noise problems without moving to a more localized economy. Many climate change campaigners argue that a move to a different economic set-up – more localized, less dependent on international trade – is essential if carbon dioxide emissions are to be curbed. It may also be necessary if vital sound systems of the world are to be preserved.

It is interesting, though, that this threat to the planet's sound systems is silently passing the world by. Though there is concern among individuals and some campaigning groups, it has generated nothing to match the vibrant, worldwide movement urging action to stop runaway climate change. The lack of interest is almost certainly a by-product of the way that society has failed to tackle noise problems closer to home over the past decades. Noise has not been regarded as a major pollutant. It still is not seen as a key problem. But nature is telling us something different. How long will we remain deaf to its dying call?

Humans are losing out too

The destruction of natural soundscapes is not just damaging to wildlife; it is harming human beings as well. Krause (2004) argues that the sounds of nature are 'seminal to the health and well-being of most organisms … [They are] part and parcel of becoming reconnected to our natural roots'. He maintains that we have largely replaced natural sounds with music. He is not decrying music. As a classically trained musician he recognises that music can stir the emotions but he is saying that the sounds of nature are qualitatively different:

> There is no human music that achieves quite the same level of impact … natural sound is simple. It doesn't require an orchestra, or quartet, or rehearsals, a stage or expensive forum to perform, or a conductor, or an expensive ticket, or a recording studio, or the need for a fancy costume

*to attend a performance with social peers, or anything else but your ears
and some attentiveness. It's free! Just like the air we breathe. And best of
all, it really heals!* (Krause, 2004)

Krause argues that the biophony of nature's sounds – their natural symphony –
is what can restore our minds, bodies and spirits. It is what we have lost among
the noise, even among the music, of the modern world.

He cites the example of the Bayaka pygmies from the Central African
Republic (Krause, 2004). For centuries they lived a quasi-nomadic life in
Dzanga-Sangha rainforest. Today, they work in the cash economy, employed as
hunters, loggers and mill workers. Their contact with the modern world has
brought much ill-health, but on the occasions they are able to revisit the forest
'in a matter of weeks they are transformed back to an order of sanity and health'.
Krause spoke with Loius Sarno, an author and American expat who has lived
with the tribe since the mid-1980s, and who believes that a large part of the
healing can be put down to contact with the forest biophany which is the origin
of the tribe's music and spiritual roots. The Bayaka have learned to hear and
visualize this animal orchestration from the time they were first conscious.

Most of us are never going to have that experience but it does emphasize
the importance of getting away from the noise of the modern world from time
to time. Ian Skelly (2005) put it like this: 'We could all do with a pause. Our
world is saturated by unnecessary noise. On a recent trip around Britain I was
constantly reminded of lines by Wendell Berry, "Best of any song is bird song
in the quiet, but first you must have the quiet".'

BOX 4.2 Noise in US National Parks

The US is famous for its National Parks but in recent years these have been increasingly assailed by man-made noise ranging from snowmobiles to overflying air tours.
For obvious reasons, this can be damaging to resident wildlife but it can also destroy
the pleasure of human beings who visit these parks for refreshment and inspiration.
A survey by the National Park Service (NPS, 1994) found that as many people visit
national parks to experience 'natural quiet' as do those who are in search of visual
beauty. This has become an important issue in the US where complaints about noise
led to the establishment of the NPS Natural Sound Program that, among other things,
has researched the problem of overflying air tours. Complaints about these flights, and
in particular those over the Grand Canyon, gave rise to the National Parks Air Tour
Management Act 2000.

When Congress discussed this difficult problem it was provided with a paper
entitled: *The Eloquent Sounds of Silence* (Iyer, 1993) that contained the following
sentence: 'Silence is something more than just a pause, it is that enchanted place where
space is cleared and time is stayed and the horizon itself expands.'

In 2000 the then director of the NPS called on National Park managers to draft
noise action plans that would preserve or restore the natural soundscapes associated
with their parks. This was no easy task because such plans would almost certainly

have to deal with the demands of local politicians and reconcile the differing inter-ests of conservationists, hikers, manufacturers and businessmen. The Grand Canyon National Park illustrates this difficulty very well as numerous visitors have complained about noisy air tours and engine noise from motor rafts on the Colorado River. Tour operators responded by saying that motor rafts, helicopters and fixed wing aircraft are essential for visitors who are elderly, unfit, or short of time and who would be denied a memorable experience if these forms of transport were banned.

The Great Sand Dunes National Park of Colorado has been described by the NPS Natural Sounds Program as the most quiet National Park in the US but it is now at the centre of a major lawsuit and a growing national debate regarding the difficulty of balancing conflicting land uses and competing interests in federal lands. The dispute arose when the US Fish and Wildlife Service, which manages the neigh-bouring Baca National Wildlife Refuge, issued Lexam Explorations Inc with licences to drill two 4300m wells on the refuge. The NPS and two environmental groups joined forces to oppose this development and began by seeking an injunction to block the preliminary drilling. They were successful and US District Judge Walter Miller who issued an injunction restraining drilling until the Lexam case was tried said 'the plaintiffs have presented adequate evidence that the drilling of these wells is likely to cause irreparable injury not only to wildlife but also to the refuge's signifi-cant sense of place and quiet'.

Snowmobiles are at the heart of another high profile battle stemming from US District Judge Emmet Sullivan's landmark ruling in 2000 that the managers of Yellowstone Park must account for snowmobile noise in the park's winter plan. He wrote that the stewardship of park resources applies 'equally to the conservation of the park's natural soundscapes'. This precipitated an ongoing duel between himself and Judge Clarence Brimmer of Cheyenne Wyoming who struck down the snowmobile ban on the basis that it was imposed without adequate participation from the public and the States of Montana and Wyoming. Predictably, the International Snowmobile Manufacturers Association opposed the ban but its supporters included the Greater Yellowstone Coalition, Natural Resource Defense Council, the Sierra Club and the Wilderness Society and matters were further complicated by the fact that, while Judge Sullivan operates in Washington, DC, Judge Brimmer operates in Wyoming so their two courts lie within different districts of appeal.

The value of silence

The great religions of the world have stressed the importance for personal renewal of retreating into the natural world. Well-known examples are the silent mediation of Gautama Budda under the Bo Tree some time between 566 and 368 BC, the 40-day solitary fast of Jesus in the Sinai Desert and Muhammad's annual Ramadan retreat to Mount Hira near Mecca.

In her engaging work, *A Book of Silence*, Sara Maitland (2008) suggests that silence 'is the place, the focus, of the radical encounter with the divine'. C. S. Lewis, the Christian writer, argues that is the reason Satan hates silence. In *The Screwtape Letters*, (Lewis, first published 1942) the devil says:

Music and silence – how I detest them both! How thankful we should be that ever since Our Father entered Hell … no square inch of infernal space and no moment of infernal time has been surrendered to either of those abominable forces, but all has been occupied with Noise – Noise, the grand dynamism, the audible expression of all that is exultant, ruthless and virile – Noise which alone defends us from silly qualms, despairing scruples and impossible desires. We will make the whole universe a noise in the end. We have already made great strides in this direction as regards the Earth. The melodies of Heaven will be shouted down in the end.

Many of the secular philosophies and mediation theories place a similar stress on silence.

Maitland argues that the value of silence lies not just in the absence of noise. Silence, she says, has positive qualities of its own:

I began to sense that all our contemporary thinking about silence sees it as an absence or a lack of speech or sound – a totally negative condition. But I was not experiencing it like that. In the growth of my garden, in my appreciation of time and the natural world, in the way I was praying, in my new sense of well-being and simple joy – all of which grew clearer the more silent I was – I did not see lack or absence, but a positive presence. Silence may be outside, or beyond the limits of, descriptive or narrative language but that does not necessarily mean that silence is lacking anything … perhaps it is not an absence of sound but the presence of something which is not sound. (Maitland, 2008)

Maitland argues that the major physical forces of our planet are silent – gravity, light, tides, the whole cosmos spinning unseen and unheard. To have no opportunity to commune silently with these forces damages our well-being. When Maitland talks about silence she means the absence of human noise. She is talking, at least in part, about something very similar to Krause's biophany: being part of and listening to the sounds of nature.

The Quiet Garden Movement, based in the UK, discovered the restorative effect silence and peacefulness could have on prisoners. As a result it is in the process of establishing quiet gardens in a number of prisons. The first one was set up in Bedford Prison:

Funding was made available from the prison and a local garden centre provided advice and support from their main garden designer, who was glad for this to be an expression of his own faith. The small yard is now an attractive area with raised beds of shrubs and flowers, plants in patio pots and new seating. The Healthcare Care patients are able to develop their own skills and sense of responsibility by maintaining the area and keeping it clean. In a prison environment of harsh sounds, wire fences and brick walls, the garden provides a welcome breathing space which has demon-strably enhanced the well-being of patients. This improvement has been measurable as the numbers on constant watch have been reduced due to improved socialisation of patients. (Quiet Garden Movement, undated)

Living without silence

We noted in Chapter 1 that, as children of the 'gadget-generation', we are perhaps further removed in our daily lives from the natural sounds of the planet than any previous generation. Indeed it is the *absence* of mechanical sounds which disturbs many of us. We noted that many people use gadgets such as the iPod not primarily to block noise but as a substitute for silence. If Krause is right, this is a most unnatural state of affairs.

We do not want to exaggerate this. People still do enjoy and appreciate the sounds of nature. Most of us might value our iPods when they provide a soothing musical alternative to the harsh noise of a city street, but would not dream of wearing them when walking beside a babbling brook or trekking deep in ancient woodland. But it does remain true that, for many people, their gadgets leave little room for natural sounds or silence.

If humankind, with its multitude of mechanical noises, is threatening to destroy the natural sound systems of the world, that same dependence on technology is beginning to separate a growing section of humanity from any real interaction with the natural world.

References

ASOC (Antarctic and Southern Ocean Coalition) (2006) 'Current noise pollution issues', Antarctic and Southern Ocean Coalition, Washington, DC

Barber, J., Fristrup, K., Brown, C., Hardy, A., Angeloni, L. and Crooks, K. (2009) 'Conserving the wild life therein: Protecting park fauna from anthropogenic noise', *Park Science*, vol 26, no 3, pp31–37

Bohan, S. (2009) 'Large ships' propellers creating underwater din for whales, other marine animals', *Oakland Tribune*, 4 September

Broydo, L. (undated) '20,000 Decibels under the sea', www.earthnews.net/articles/2000decibels.htm

Caldeira, K. and Wickett, M. E. (2003) 'Anthropogenic carbon and ocean pH', *Nature*, vol 425, no 6956, pp365–365

Clark, C. (1999), *Natural Resources Defense Council Urges More Regulation of Super-tankers and Military Sonar*, www.nonoise.org/news/1999/jun27.htm#, 27 June

Clarke, C. (2000) 'Sound and Fury: US navy threatens whales to safeguard foreign interventions', *Earth Island Journal*, vol15, no 2, summer, www.earthislandprojects.org/eijournal/sum2000/eia_sum2000immp7.html

De Silva Wijeyeratne, G. (2008) 'Can animals predict disaster?', www.pbs.org/wnet/nature/episodes/can-animals-predict-disaster/eyewitness-accounts/gehan-de-silva-wijeyeratne/139

Hull, J. (2007) 'The noises of nature', *New York Times*, 18 Feb

Ilyina, T., Zeebe, R. and Brewer, P. (2009) 'Future oceans increasingly transparent to low-frequency sound owing to carbon dioxide emissions', published online: www.nature.com/ngeo/journal/v3/n1/full/ngeo719.html, 20 December

IMO (International Maritime Organization) (2010) 'Noise from commercial shipping and its adverse impacts on marine life', Maritime Environment Protection Committee, 61st session, agenda item 19, 23 July

International Whaling Commission Scientific Committee (2005) *Report of the Scientific Committee from its Annual Meeting*, International Whaling Committee

IPCC (Intergovernmental Panel on Climate Change) (2007) 'Fourth assessment report: Climate change', Intergovernmental Panel on Climate Change, Geneva, Switzerland

Iyer, P. (1993) 'The Eloquent Sound of Silence', *Time Magazine*, vol 141, no 4, 25 January, www.time.com/time/magazine/article/0,9171,977567,00.html

Jasny, M. (2010) 'Boom, baby, boom: Reviving the world's oceans', National Resources Defense Council, Washington, DC, 31 March

Josefowicz, C. (2006) 'Din in the depths: Is underwater noise harming sea-creatures – and driving whales onto beaches?', *Current Science*, a Weekly Reader publication, Weekly Reader Corporation, 7 April, *HighBeam Research*, accessed 26 February 2011, www.highbeam.com

Krause, B. (2004) 'The meaning of wild landscapes', www.greenmuseum.org

Krausman, P. (2003) 'Pronghorn use of areas with varying sound pressure levels', *Southwestern Naturalist*, vol 48, no 4, pp725–728

Lazar, K. (2006) 'Oceans of noise, a man-made undersea cacophony, threatens to drive marine mammals away', *Boston Globe*, 1 January, *HighBeam Research*, accessed 26 February 2011, www.highbeam.com

Lewis, C.S. (1942), *The Screwtape Letters*, Fontana Collins

Maitland, S. (2008) *A Book of Silence*, Granta Books, London

Marine Mammal Commission (2007) *Annual Report to Congress – Marine Mammal Commission*, Marine Mammal Commission

McDonald, M. A., Hildebrand, J. A. and Wiggins, S. M. (2006) 'Increases in deep ocean ambient noise in the Northeast Pacific west of San Nicolas Island, California', *Journal of the Acoustic Society of America*, vol 120, no 2, pp711–718

Natural Resources Defense Council (2005) *Sounding the Depths 2: The Rising Toll of Sonar, Shipping and Industrial Ocean Noise on Marine Life*, Natural Resources Defense Council, Washington, DC

NPS (National Park Service) (1994) *Report to Congress*, National Parks Service, Washington, DC

Quiet Garden Movement (undated) www.quietgarden.org/prisons.html

Schaub, A., Ostwald, J. and Siemers, B. M. (2008) 'Foraging bats avoid noise', *Journal of Experimental Biology*, vol 211, no 19, pp3174–3180

Skelly, I. (2005) 'Joy of silence', *Resurgence*, vol 228, www.resurgence.org/magazine/article697-joy-of-silence.html

Stover, D. (2009) 'Not so silent spring', *Conservation Magazine*, vol 10, no 1, www.conservationmagazine.org/2009/01/not-so-silent-spring

Taylor, L. (2004) *The Healing Power of Rainforest Herbs*, Square One Publishers, New York

Thompson, C. (2008) 'How man-made noise may be altering earth's ecology', *Wired Magazine*, 19 May, www.wired.com/science/planetearth/magazine/16-06/st_thompson

Wilkinson, J. (2004) 'The world around us: Why all the noise?' BBC and Open University, www.open2.net/sciencetechnologynature/worldaroundus/why_all_the_noise.html

CHAPTER 5

Noise in the Workplace

A majority of the world's workforce is still inadequately protected from noise in the workplace.

N oise in the workplace is a global problem. Worldwide, 16 per cent of hearing loss in adults is caused by occupational noise. This ranges from 7 per cent in some countries to 21 per cent in others (Nelson et al, 2006). Generally, it is a bigger problem in poorer countries than in richer ones but the advances that have been made in the richer world should not mask the fact that very real concerns remain there as well. In Europe, people are more exposed to noise in their workplace than to any other physical risk except for what the World Health Organization (WHO) terms 'painful positions' (Ezzati et al, 2004). In the USA 30 million Americans are daily experiencing workplace noise levels above the recommended safe level (Ezzati et al, 2004). Of these, one in four, about 7.5 million people, will develop a permanent hearing loss. In Germany as many as 5 million people, around 12.5 per cent of all those employed, are exposed to dangerous noise levels at work (Ezzati et al, 2004). It is almost a third in Australia (De Crespigny, 2009). The situation is similar in most of the industrialized countries. It is harder to get precise figures for countries in the poorer world but the WHO suggests it is much worse than in the richer countries and, indeed, getting even worse: 'The average noise levels in developing countries may be increasing because industrialization is not always accompanied by protection' (Concha-Barrientos et al, 2004).

This chapter looks at workplace noise in both industrialized and industrializing countries. Rather than give a scanty description of the position across a lot of countries, it concentrates on a few places to illustrate the overall situation, with a view to suggesting remedies. It has a dedicated short section on the construction industry. It ends with a longer section on the wind farm industry as wind turbine noise has emerged as a major source of contention.

Across the world

The WHO has found that exposure for more than eight hours a day to noise in excess of 85dB is potentially harmful. This level of noise is regularly exceeded in a number of industries. The WHO cites some examples (WHO, 2001):

- 'Air jets – widely used, for example, for cleaning, drying, power tools and steam values – can generate sound levels of 105dB.
- In the woodworking industry, the sound levels of saws can be as high as 106dB.
- Average sound levels in industries such as foundries, shipyards, breweries, weaving factories and paper and saw mills range between 92dB and 96dB. The recorded peak values were between 117dB and 136dB.
- Workers in a cigarette factory in Brazil involved in compressed air cleaning were exposed to sound levels equivalent to 92dB for 8 hours.

Richer countries

The WHO recognizes that, as far as noise from heavy industry is concerned, the situation in most of the richer countries has improved over the last few decades 'as more widespread appreciation of the hazard has led to protective measures' (Concha-Barrientos et al, 2004). But problems still remain. One of the most comprehensive studies into occupational noise was carried out by the European Agency for Safety and Health at Work (Schneider et al, 2005). It found that 'approximately a quarter to a third of the workforce is exposed at some stage (at least a quarter of the time) to high-level noise'. This ranges from 29 per cent in the 15 countries that had been European Union (EU) members for some years to 35 per cent in the new member states. The figures are high but the position is levelling out. There has only been a slight increase since 1990.

The study found that, for workers in the 'old' EU countries, the greatest exposure to noise comes from the construction industry followed by the manufacturing sector: 'In both sectors about 40% of workers are exposed to unacceptably high levels for at least half of their time at work' (Schneider et al, 2005). In the new member states 'the highest percentage of workers exposed to noise all or almost all of the time are in agriculture (40%) and mining (34%). A high percentage are also exposed to noise in manufacturing (19%).' The study points out that 'it has to be kept in mind that the proportion of workers working in these sectors is higher in the new member states'. It cites an example: 'The proportion of people employed in agriculture is higher (21% compared to 5%), but there are wide differences between countries.'

In each sector it was overwhelmingly blue-collar workers – skilled and unskilled people – who were exposed to the noise. This puts a slightly different slant on the average figure of around a third of all workers being exposed to excessively high levels of noise. In certain areas and among particular classes of workers, the numbers are considerably higher.

The report from the European Agency for Safety and Health at Work (Schneider et al, 2005) included a case study focusing on Poland. Between 1995 and 2003, exposure to all serious pollutants – noise, chemical substances, dust, vibrations and excessive physical exertion – fell. However, twice as many workers were still exposed to noise than to any other pollutant.

Legislation

In common with other places in the richer world, Europe has had legislation in place for some years to tackle noise in the workplace. In 1986, the EU adopted Directive 86/188/EEC, setting exposure limits for workers and outlining guidelines for employers to protect them. This was followed in 2003 by Directive 2003/10/EC, which set out a strategy to protect workers exposed to noise. The aim is to prevent exposure to noise levels which average out at 87dB or more. Directive 2003/10/EC also details information and training that should be given to workers regarding noise. It urges noise be eliminated at the source where possible.

The year before Directive 2003/10/EC came into force, a study was carried out in the UK in which a number of companies were surveyed about their noise practices (Hughson et al, 2002). It found that, on the whole, the larger companies had effective or partially effective noise protection programmes in place, while smaller companies lagged far behind. However, noise was not seen as a priority for the majority of companies, large or small. They tended to give a higher priority to physical or chemical hazards that had a more immediate impact on their employees. The study found that workers had a reasonably good awareness regarding the dangers of excessive noise. However, there is some doubt about how much use they are making of noise protective devices. The report from the European Agency for Safety and Health at Work (Schneider et al, 2005) cites a Dutch survey, carried out in 2002, which found that only 44 per cent of employees exposed to high levels of noise regularly used the noise-reduction equipment available to them.

The situation in most developed countries is not dissimilar to Europe. We have taken Australia as an example. A 2009 report found that 'between 28% and 32% of the Australian workforce are likely to work in an environment where they are exposed to non-trivial [above 85dB(A)] loud noise generated during the course of their work' (De Crespigny, 2009). However, the report found 'training on how to prevent hearing damage appears to be underprovided in workplaces: only 41% of exposed workers reported they had received training'. As in the UK, the Australian survey found that things were likely to be worse in small and medium-sized firms.

Australia has similar rules about regulating noise to those found in Europe. Australian regulations describe a hierarchy of risk management that employers should follow to prevent occupational hearing loss in their workplaces. As a general rule, employers should attempt to eliminate, control or reduce exposure to loud noise before resorting to providing workers with personal protective equipment. Workers should also be informed and consulted about the hazards of loud noise in their workplace and trained in the use of strategies or tools that reduce their exposure.

The new industries

Nowadays, noise is not only a problem in the traditional industries. It is also causing concerns for people working in some of the newer industries, such as call centres and music venues. A French survey into the hazards associated with call centres found them to be very noisy places – 27 per cent of operators are exposed to daily noise levels of more than 85dB. It also revealed telephone operators are likely to lack awareness of the seriousness of the problem (Trompette and Trompette, 2009).

In the music industry, it has long been known that many musicians develop hearing problems as a result of prolonged exposure to very loud noise levels. People who work in music venues and nightclubs are now facing similar problems

Progress

It is interesting that, despite the very real problems that remain, much more progress has been made in tackling noise in the workplace – certainly in richer countries – than in improving the noise climate for people in their homes. I would suggest that this has been down to collective action, particularly by the trade union movement. A noise-sufferer at home can feel isolated. In contrast, a noise problem in the workplace usually becomes a joint concern. It is seen as the responsibility of the employer to deal with it. If he does not, the trade union or other representatives of the workforce may well take it up. See Boxes 5.1 and 5.2 for a couple of examples from the UK.

BOX 5.1 Teenage work noise led to deafness

A member of the UK's general trade union, GMB, exposed to dangerous levels of workplace noise as a teenage apprentice became reliant on two hearing aids at the age of 48. Neil Dawson from Hull has received £5750 in damages after developing occupational deafness. The harm was caused by his first job as a 16-year-old apprentice for Richard Dunston Shipbuilders in Hessle, Yorkshire, where he trained to be a plater from 1977 to 1981. The yard was noisy but he was never given instruction or advice regarding the dangers it posed to his hearing. Richard Dunston Shipbuilders no longer exists so Thompsons, the personal injury law firm brought in by the GMB to represent Dawson, had to track down the firm's former insurers, who admitted liability and settled out of court. Dawson said: 'I was only 16 when I started working at the shipbuilders and I had no idea that the noise I worked in was damaging my ears. We were never provided with ear defenders and now at only 48 I have to wear two hearing aids.' Andy Worth from the GMB said: 'Many of our members have been negligently exposed to excessive levels of noise in the workplace by their employers. Sadly even with the knowledge of the long-term damage it can cause and the safety equipment available people are being exposed today. We won't let those who ignore health and safety laws or fail to provide the correct safety equipment to get away with it however long ago it happened.'

Source: Thompsons Solicitors (2010b)

BOX 5.2 Ferry workers warned about hearing risks

A ferry worker developed noise induced hearing loss after just eight years working on Stena Line ferries. Peter Hall, 49, a member of the National Union of Rail, Maritime and Transport Workers (RMT), had worked out of Holyhead for 18 years, but says he has had hearing difficulties for a decade. In a 2010 union-backed claim, he received a 'substantial' sum in damages for occupational deafness caused by his work on the vehicle decks of ferries. He now warns other RMT members who worked in the ferry industry to consider having their hearing tested as he believes many will have been affected by the working conditions. He worked on the car decks loading and unloading lorries crossing the Irish Sea. He was never provided with protection for his ears while working in an enclosed space among engine noise. Stena Line denied liability but Thompsons Solicitors, the law firm brought in by the RMT to represent Peter, secured a settlement out of court. Peter, who now works for RMT, said:

> *Even when I was diagnosed I put it down to getting older but when I started working for the union I realised my hearing was never protected while at Stena and decided to pursue compensation. I reckon that there are many former ferry industry workers who suffer from hearing loss but have not considered that it may have been caused by their work.*

RMT general secretary Bob Crow said: 'Hearing loss affects many of our members working in noisy environments and like Peter they often put it down to getting older. As Peter's case shows, members who have worked in a noisy environment and who have been diagnosed with hearing problems should get in touch.'

Source: Thompsons Solicitors (2010a)

Industrializing world

It is in the poorer, industrializing world where occupational noise is at its worst. Without proper regulations in place, and an often blatant disregard for those that do exist, many workers in the poorer world are left with little or no protection from excessive noise.

The majority of the world's workforce – 75 per cent of working people – are in the 'developing' world. This means that, whatever progress may have been made in richer countries, this majority of the world's workforce is inadequately protected from noise in the workplace. Look at these figures: 63 per cent of workplace accidents in Brazil are associated with noise (Dias and Cordeiro, 2008); more than 50 per cent of pulse processing workers in India have damaged hearing (Patel and Ingle, 2007); 23 per cent of miners who had worked in Zambian mines for more than 20 years became completely deaf (Nelson et al, 2006); employees who have worked at Karachi Airport in Pakistan for any length of time experience a considerable loss of hearing (Siddiqui and Siddiqui, 2008).

Not much research has been carried out into occupational noise in industrializing countries but what has been done all points in one direction: noise is a major occupational hazard in poorer countries. This very human story from Jordan illustrates the point:

> *Thirteen per cent of working children in the country are subjected to forced labour, with over 16 per cent earning a meagre JD 10–50 a month, according to a study released by the Ministry of Labour … The Worst Forms of Child Labour study … found that children in the country's informal labour market are exposed to health hazards on a daily basis, with many suffering from heavy coughs, shortness of breath and aching limbs and joints caused by long working hours and exposures to chemicals. Factors such as heavy vibrating machinery, noise pollution, poor lighting and exposure to chemicals stood out as some of the most commonly faced risks. Around 17.6 per cent of surveyed children complained of being affected by loud noise, while 6 per cent said they were exposed to chemicals. Around 10 per cent said they worked in poorly-lit environments. Programme Manager Nihaya Dabdub said poor awareness among working children and sub-standard conditions are the key challenges to address: "Most of these children are school dropouts aged 11 to 13 with no knowledge about the health risks they face in the workplace or the ability to differentiate between hazardous and non-hazardous conditions to their health."* (Dajani, 2007)

The situation in the industrializing world can partly be explained by the high numbers of people still working in mines, heavy industry and agriculture as well as the equally large number exposed to high levels of traffic noise in the course of their work, but much of it can be put down to a lack of any basic protection for workers and, in a lot of countries, little awareness among many of the workers of the damage noisy environments can cause.

A way forward

So what is the way forward? A lot is known about techniques to cut industrial noise at the source in mining, manufacture, construction and agriculture. We also know how to protect workers from the worst excesses of noise. The problem in the poorer countries lies in the race to industrialize … on the cheap. The pressure of the global market is forcing this race to the bottom. Quieter machinery, if it costs more, is not purchased. Protective devices are not installed. Workers very often are afraid to protest about the conditions for fear of losing the only job they can get. The main barrier to improvement is political rather than technical.

BOX 5.3 The construction industry

Noise-induced hearing impairment is the most prevalent irreversible occupational hazard, worldwide, in the construction industry. Noise levels on construction sites can range from 74–105dB(A) (Sinclair and Haflidson, 1995). Employees working on or around heavy equipment have a particularly high level of exposure to noise (Utley and Miller, 1985). Equipment found on construction sites is very noisy:

TABLE 5.1 Construction site equipment

Dozers, Dumpers range from	89–103dB
Front-end loaders	85–91dB
Excavators	86–90dB
Backhoes	79–89dB
Scrapers	84–102dB
Mobile cranes	97–102dB
Compressors	62–92dB
Pavers	100–102dB
Rollers (compactors)	79–93dB
Bar benders	94–96dB
Pneumatic breakers	94–111dB
Hydraulic breakers	90–100dB

Occupational exposure to high noise levels from such vehicles, tools and equipment places hundreds of thousands of construction workers at risk of developing hearing impairment and hypertension (NIOSH, 1990). A comprehensive study carried out in Kuwait paints a bleak picture: 'A total of 33 construction sites throughout the city of Kuwait were selected for monitoring noise. Their areas ranged from about 500 to 60,000 square metres. The overall mean equivalent noise level observed was 78.7dBA, ranging from 58.0 to 98.2. The maximum levels ranged from 70.3 to 112.4' (Hamoda, 2008). Although the situation is worst in fast-developing countries such as Kuwait, there remain problems in the richer world. A study of construction noise in Ontario, Canada reported average noise levels ranging from 93.1dB(A) to 107.7dB(A). Tools and equipment were found to be the major source of noise at construction sites (Sinclair and Haflidson, 1995).

Wind farms

Wind farms are controversial. They are supported by most environmentalists who see them as a key component of a renewable energy policy. A lot of governments agree. Many subsidize their development. But wind farms also face fierce opposition. Some energy experts argue their contribution to renewable energy will be erratic and relatively minor. Many local communities oppose them on aesthetic grounds. Some turbines are causing real noise problems.

These noise impacts have been downplayed, and sometimes denied, by governments, developers, the wind power industry and even some environmentalists. Garret Keizer (2010) writes in his book *The Unwanted Sound of Everything We Want*:

> *It has become increasingly clear that the noise effects of wind turbines have routinely been denied by ignorant or unscrupulous developers. In league with them are any number of disingenuous politicians hoping to avoid the hard work and political fall-out of a sustainable energy policy by certifying their pale-green credentials with a few visually imposing monuments. The irony is that the tone, methods, and motivation of their denials are uncannily similar to the denial of global warming itself.* (Keizer, 2010)

Have they become the noise-deniers? The common perception remains that noise is not a problem; that wind turbines are quiet. The noise impact is indeed quite complex but there can be no doubt that it has become a major concern, possibly the fastest growing industrial noise problem in the developed world.

Many people living in the vicinity of wind turbines are reporting severe problems.

> *Stressed and extremely anxious, as I am constantly disturbed by them when they are turning fast and facing towards me. We are having to live our lives around them due to the constant noise.*

> *Irritating noise from wind farm in easterly direction. You can almost feel it as well as hear it. It drives you mad over extended periods because of the nature of the noise, not the level per se.*

> *The strobing even when curtains are closed is hell. The noise is a pain. TV blocks it, night and day. Can't sit and read a book or write chapters.*

> *We will probably have to move. I can see no future for me here.*

> *I never suffered from any problems before the turbines. I am convinced that living in a continual state of anxiety over the past four and a half years since the noise nuisance started has contributed to my present problems.*

> *Our lives and home have been trashed and must be seen to be believed. We seem short tempered, unable to concentrate. Everything we have such as mattresses, duvets, cushions four inches thick, three rolls of sound deadening quilt, three sheets of corrugated asbestos, blankets, curtains, pillows, even floor carpet stacked against the walls to try and keep out the sound. Not the peace I volunteered to fight for.*

Wind turbine noise – particularly disturbing

These quotes are from the UK (Stewart, 2006) but people are telling similar stories all over the world. And the research backs them up. A Swedish study found that 40 per cent of people became very annoyed when the noise from wind turbines averaged out at 40dB or more, much lower than the level at which the World Health Organization (WHO) would have expected people to become so disturbed. Turbines, in other words, are causing particularly difficult noise problems (Pederson and Persson Waye, 2002). This was illustrated in a related Swedish study that showed that people tended to become more annoyed more quickly by noise from wind turbines than by noise from other industrial sources or from traffic noise (Pederson and Persson Waye, 2005).

A recent study into the Mars Hill Wind Farm in Maine, US, found that 100 per cent of those interviewed said that they had considered moving away since the 28 turbines were erected within 1040m of their homes (Nissenbaum, 2009). And 73 per cent said the only reason they had not done so was because they could not afford to. They felt trapped by the turbines: 'No options – can't leave, and can't live here.' In an admittedly small survey, 93 per cent of people complained of sleep disturbance, 53 per cent of increased headaches with 100 per cent saying the quality of their life had been affected.

What is causing the problem? Pedersen put it like this:

> *The informants' descriptions of their feelings when exposed to wind turbine noise, as well as shadows and the rotating movement of the rotar blades, were in our analysis interpreted as an intrusion into private domain. For some informants, the intrusion went further into the most private domain, into themselves, creating a feeling of violation that was expressed as anger, uneasiness, and tiredness.* (Pederson and Persson Waye, 2002)

It appears that the dancing shadows and the rotating blades can significantly add to the annoyance and stress caused by noise from the turbines. Stewart concluded that the particularly disturbing nature of wind turbine noise could be explained by 'a cocktail of effects – the noise, low-frequency, rotating blades, the shadows and the strobing – leading to ill-health out of proportion to the noise turbines make' (Stewart, 2006).

It may, though, go even deeper than this. Some people talk of 'feeling' the noise in addition to, or even instead of, hearing it. This idea of feeling noise is controversial and complex and is rejected by a number of acousticians. But there are medical experts who are beginning to believe that the dramatic impact that wind farms have on some people's health cannot be explained by sheer annoyance. They argue that the low-frequency content of wind turbine noise (even if it is not heard), along with the 'flicker', can destabilize the human body.

The UK-based GP Dr Amanda Harry, who has done surveys into noise disturbance from turbines, argues:

The low frequencies contribute to the overall audible noise but also produce a seismic characteristic which is one of the common complaints from people when they say not only can they hear the noise but they can also feel it. This happens because the various parts of the body have a specific natural frequency or a resonance frequency. The human body is a strongly damped system. Therefore, when a part of it is excited at its natural frequency, it will resonate over a range of frequencies instead of at a single frequency. (Stewart, 2006)

This is the same argument made by Dr Nina Pierpont. The core of her recent publication (Pierpont, 2009) is a scientific report presenting original, primary research regarding people living near large industrial wind turbines erected since 2004 in the US. In the research Dr Pierpont, who practices medicine in Upper New York State, found that people were more than simply annoyed by the noise. She reports that many of them experienced 'sleep disturbance and deprivation, headache, tinnitus (ringing in ears), ear pressure, dizziness, vertigo (spinning dizziness), nausea, visual blurring, tachycardia (fast heart rate), irritability, problems with concentration and memory, and panic episodes associated with sensations of movement or quivering inside the body that arise while awake or asleep'. In some cases the symptoms became so severe that people were forced to move home away from the turbines.

Pierpont has coined the term 'wind turbine syndrome' to explain what is happening to people. The name reflects the fact that when the people moved away from the turbines, even temporarily, the symptoms disappeared. Dr Pierpont is thus at pains to point out that wind turbine syndrome is not the same as vibroacoustic disease (VAD). VAD is a chronic, progressive, cumulative, systemic disease brought on by exposure to high-intensity/low-frequency sound and infrasound. Essentially, the disease is caused by a thickening of the blood cells, which can impede normal blood flow. Professor Mariana Alves-Pereira, the leading authority on the disease and based at Lisbon University, has found that DJs, rock musicians or people working with powerful car audio equipment are at risk of developing VAD (Alves-Pereira and Branco, 1999). She also argues that people living close to wind farms are at risk. But its progressive nature makes its different from wind turbine syndrome, which disappears when sufferers move away from the turbines.

Dr Harry is scathing about the refusal of most acousticians to even acknowledge there may be some merit in the arguments the doctors are making: 'On searching the current literature I can find no papers written showing that turbines are harmless, only statements from acousticians giving their personal thoughts. I feel that these comments are made outside their area of expertise and should be ignored until proper, epidemiological studies are carried out by independent medical researchers.' Certainly over the years the military has been aware of the way the human body can be destabilized by a combination of persistent low-frequency noise, infrasound and visual strobing (Stewart, 2006).

Wind turbine noise – getting worse?

There is no reason to believe, despite the claims of the wind power industry, that noise from wind turbines is decreasing. The evidence suggests that both the industry and governments have underestimated the noise from the new, larger, taller turbines which are increasingly common. Work by Frits (G. P.) van den Berg, a physicist at the University of Groningen in the Netherlands, has shown that the method used to predict noise from the large turbines is flawed (van den Berg, 2004). He challenges the assumption that wind speeds measured at a height of 10m are representative of wind speeds at the greater heights of modern turbines (often 100m and above) – because the wind speeds can be markedly greater than at 10m. This is the problem known as 'wind shear' (there are different wind speeds at different heights – the higher the turbine mast, the more exposure to wind shear).

Van den Berg argues that this is particularly the case at night when wind speeds may fall at ground level to near zero but remain fast enough at a greater height to turn the blades of the turbine. His measurements show that wind speeds at night are 2.6 times higher than would be expected. The result can increase the noise experienced by residents at ground level by 10dB in areas where there is limited background noise to mask it (van den Berg, 2004).

He is supported by other acousticians. Paul Botha (2005) wrote:

> *The historical use of 10m high wind speed measurements for the acoustic assessment of both wind turbines and wind farms has the ability to create inaccuracies and sometimes confusion around sound power levels, noise predictions and even demonstration of wind farm compliance. The use of 10m high wind speed measurements appear to be largely historic and there are advantages in using hub height wind speeds throughout the noise assessment process.*

Pedersen also acknowledges van den Berg's work: 'Common hub height of the operating wind turbines today in Sweden is 40–50 meters. The new larger turbines are often placed on towers of 80–90 meters. The wind speed at this height compared to the wind speed at the ground might (up to now) have been underestimated' (Pederson and Halmstad, 2003).

Future of on-shore wind power

Keizer wrote that, while future debates regarding matters such as air travel are likely to revolve around carbon, not noise, in debates over wind energy 'noise will be front and centre' (Keizer, 2010). The noise problem is not going to go away. In the UK, a succession of planning applications for wind farms have been refused on noise grounds. And, at present, there is no sign of the technology to remedy the situation. The only answer at present is careful siting of the wind turbines. Stewart (2006) recommended that, as general rule, 'it would be prudent that no wind turbines should be sited closer than one mile away from the nearest dwelling'. This is the distance also favoured by the Academy of Medicine in Paris, certainly for the larger turbines. Other studies recommend at least 1.24 miles. Noise need not be a 'show-stopper' in the development of onshore wind farms, but unless it is seriously addressed, it will harm many people and may curb the growth of wind power.

Off-shore wind farms

Are off-shore wind farms the answer? While the undersea noise and vibration that occurs in the course of building offshore wind farms has identifiable effects on fish (Thomsen, 2009) and marine mammals (Tougaard et al, 2003, 2005), there is less certainty about the extent to which marine creatures are affected by wind farms once they have become operational.

The pile driving during construction can damage the hearing of marine mammals and their behaviour can be disrupted at a considerable distance from the construction site. Thomsen et al (2006) reported that: 'For porpoises and harbour seals, the zone of audibility for pile-driving will most certainly extend well beyond 80kms and "masking" (the obliteration of low frequency signals) might occur in harbour seals at least up to 80kms.' Thomsen also thought it possible that pelagic fish such as cod and herring might perceive piling noise at similar distances. Other scientists believe that pile driving near spawning grounds might cause fish to move away thus reducing their range and fragmenting their breeding populations. The Scottish government, in its strategic environmental assessment of off-shore turbines identified potentially noticeable effects on a large variety of whales, dolphins and seals (Scottish Government, 2005).

So far as operational noise is concerned, scientists find it difficult to predict what effect this type of noise might have on fish as there are so many variables involved including turbine size, the nature of the sea bottom and the species of fish that are being studied. In summary, scientists working in this area do not believe that they have enough information to make any firm predictions regarding the effect of operational wind farms on fish but on present information they do not believe that offshore turbines present a serious threat.

What about the impact of operational noise on mammals? Data from Betke et al (2004) found that noise from the smaller wind turbines was audible to porpoises and harbour seals at a distance of 100m but usually not at 1000m. Masking of other sounds important to the porpoises and seals only seemed to occur close to the turbines. The evidence suggests the same to be true for dolphins. A major concern would arise if the frequency used by a dolphin, or another mammal, was the same as, or similar to, the frequency of wind turbine noise. Thomsen et al (2006) found that 'we can't rule out at this point that ... operational noise of wind-turbines will interfere with biologically relevant signals of the species in question. But the bigger mammals such a whales, which are most likely to be affected in this way, would not normally come as close to the shore as the sites of the wind farms'.

The impact of off-shore turbines may be less than those on-shore. The concern at present is that permission is being given for large wind farms at sea when there may be insufficient evidence available about the noise impacts they have on fish and mammals.

Concluding remarks

Workplace noise is still a huge problem in the industrializing world where 75 per cent of working people are. The biggest barriers to getting improvements are not technical, however, but political. The 'race to the bottom', so much a feature of the globalized economy, has meant employers tend to be reluctant to spend money on quieter machinery.

Although there have been real advances in dealing with industrial and construction noise in the richer countries, it still remains a significant problem, particularly for blue-collar workers.

Wind farms stand out as an area where the noise climate has been deteriorating. But noise need not be a 'show-stopper' in the development of wind power if they are carefully located.

References

Alves-Pereira, M. and Branco, N. (1999) 'Vibroacoustic disease: The need for a new attitude towards noise', *Proceedings of the International Conference on Public Participation and Information Technologies*, Portugal

Betke, K., Schultz-von Glahn, M. and Matuschek, R. (2004) 'Underwater noise emissions from offshore wind turbines', *Proceedings of Joint Meetings of the German and French Acoustical Societies*, France

Botha, P. (2005) 'The use of 10 metre wind speed measurements in the assessment of wind farm developments', *Proceedings of Wind Turbine Noise*, Germany

Concha-Barrientos, M., Campbell-Lendrum, O. and Steenland, K. (2004) *Occupational Noise: Assessing the Burden of Disease from Work-related Hearing Impairment at National and Local Levels*, World Health Organization, Bern, Switzerland

Dajani, D. (2007) 'Study paints disturbing picture of child labour in Jordan', *Jordan Times*, Landmark Media Enterprises, LLC, 25 April, *HighBeam Research*, 26 February 2011 www.highbeam.com

De Crespigny, F. (2009) *National Hazard Exposure Worker Surveillance: Noise Exposure and the Provision of Noise Control measures in Australian Workplaces*, Safe Work Australia, Canberra

Dias, A. and Cordeiro, R. (2008) 'Fraction of work-related accidents attributable to occupational noise in the city of Botucatu, São Paulo, Brazil', *Noise & Health*, vol 10, no 40, pp69–73

Ezzati, M., Lopez, A., Rodgers, A. and Murray, C. (2004) *Comparative Quantification of Health Risks: Global and Regional Burden of Disease Attributable to Selected Major Risk Factors*, World Health Organization, Switzerland

Hamoda, M. F. (2008) 'Modeling of construction noise for environmental impact assessment', *Journal of Construction in Developing Countries*, vol 13, no 1, pp79–89

Hughson, G. W., Mulholland, R. E. and Cowie, H. A. (2002) *Behavioural Studies of People's Attitudes to Wearing Hearing Protection and How These Might Be Changed*, Health and Safety Executive, London

Keizer, G. (2010) *The Unwanted Sound of Everything We Want*, PublicAffairs Books, New York

Nelson, D. I., Nelson, R. Y. and Concha-Barrientos, M. (2006) 'The global burden of occupational noise-induced hearing loss', *Noise & Health*, vol 8, no 30, p60

NIOSH (National Institute for Occupational Safety and Health) (1990) *National Occupational Exposure Survey Report 29*, National Institute for Occupational Safety and Health, Atlanta, GA

Nissenbaum, M. (2009), *Mars Hill Wind Turbine Project Health Effects – Preliminary Findings*, Maine Medical Association, www.wind-watch.org/documents/mars-hill-wind-turbine-project-health-effects-preliminary-symptoms-survey-results/, March

Patel, V. S. and Ingle, S. T. (2008) 'Occupational noise exposure and hearing loss among pulse processing workers', *The Environmentalist*, vol 28, no 4, pp358–365

Pedersen, E. and Halmstad, H. (2003) 'Noise annoyance from wind turbines – a review', Report 5308, Swedish Environmental Protection Agency, Sweden

Pederson, E. and Persson Waye, K. (2002) Storiningar fran Vindkraft, Sweden

Pederson, E. and Persson Waye, K. (2005) 'Human responses to wind farm noise – annoyance and moderating factors', Proceedings of Wind Turbine Noise, Germany

Pierpont, N. (2009) *Wind Turbine Syndrome: A Report on a Natural Experiment*, K-Selected Books, Santa Fe, NM

Schneider, E., Paoli, P. and Brun, E. (2005) *Noise in Figures*, European Agency for Safety and Health at Work, Luxembourg

Scottish Government (2005) *Strategic Environmental Assessment of Draft Plan for Offshore Wind Energy in Scottish Territorial Waters: Volume 2: Appendices*, Scottish Government, Edinburgh

Siddiqui, I. A. and Siddiqui, R. A. (2008) 'The effect of excessive noise exposure on the hearing thresholds of aviation workers in Karachi', *Pakistan Journal of Medical Sciences*, vol 24, no 4, pp525–530

Sinclair, J. and Haflidson, W. (1995) 'Construction noise in Ontario', *Applied Occupational and Environmental Hygiene*, vol 10, pp457–460

Stewart, J. (2006) *Location, Location, Location: An Investigation into Wind Farms and Noise*, UK Noise Association, London, www.countryguardian.net/location

Thompsons Solicitors (2010a) 'Ferry workers warned about hearing risks', news release, 26 March, www.tuc.org.uk/h_and_s/tuc-17762-f0.cfm

Thompsons Solicitors (2010b) 'Teenage work noise led to deafness', news release, 2 April, www.tuc.org.uk/h_and_s/tuc-17762-f0.cfm

Thomsen, F. (2009) 'Assessment of the environmental impact of underwater noise', OSPAR Commission, http://qsr2010.ospar.org/media/assessments/p00436_JAMP_Assessment_Noise.pdf

Thomsen, F., Lüdemann, K., Kafemann, R. and Piper, W. (2006) *Effects of Offshore Wind Farm Noise on Marine Mammals and Fish*, Biola on behalf of COWRIE Ltd, Hamburg, Germany

Tougaard, J., Carstensen, J., Hendriksen, O., Skov, H. and Teilman, J. (2003) *Short-term Effects of the Construction of Wind Turbines on Harbour Porpoises at Horns Reef*, technical report to TechWise A/S, HME/362-02662, Hedeselskabet, Roskilde

Tougaard, J., Carstensen, J., Teilman, J. and Beck, N. (2005) *Effects of Nysted Offshore Wind Farm on Harbour Porpoises*, technical report to Energie E2 A/S, National Environmental Research Institute, Ministry of Environment, Denmark

Trompette, W. and Trompette, W. (2009) *Exposure of Call Centre Operators and Prevention Solution*, French National Research and Safety Institute, France

Utley, W. and Miller, L. (1985) 'Occupational noise exposure on construction sites', *Applied Acoustics*, vol 18, pp293–303

van den Berg, G. P. (2004) 'Effects of the wind profile at night on wind turbine sound', *Journal of Sound and Vibration*, vol 277, nos 4–5, pp955–970

WHO (World Health Organization) (2001) 'Occupational and community noise', factsheet, World Health Organization, Bern, Switzerland

CHAPTER 6

Transport Noise

Transport noise has become all-pervasive.

W e are a more mobile society than ever before. Trains, cars and planes have transformed the way we get about. New opportunities and new horizons have been opened up for many people. But this new-found mobility has come with its downsides: notably, an increase in noise, emissions, air pollution and road deaths, along with a fracturing of many communities and the disappearance of local facilities.

Governments have been reluctant to tackle these downsides as vigorously as they might. There are a number of reasons for this. They recognize that people like being mobile. For many people, the car – and perhaps now the cheap flight – has come to symbolize convenience, freedom, personal choice and status. And governments tend to view this increased mobility as an inevitable and welcome consequence of greater prosperity. Many politicians, too, defend the 'right' of people to drive or fly on equity grounds. The Labour government of Tony Blair and Gordon Brown, for example, vociferously argued in favour of subsidized cheap flights because they believed they enabled 'hard-working British families' to take a holiday in the sun.

This hypermobility, however, is not spread equally. Professor John Whitelegg (1993) pointed out in his book *Transport for a Sustainable Future* that 'the "action space" for a poor black resident of Los Angeles or a poor white resident of Montgomery Alabama is no greater now than that of an urban resident 100 years ago'. And for most people in the poorer world, the mobile society remains just an aspiration. Only about 5 per cent of the world's population, for example, has ever flown (Worldwatch Institute, 2006/2007). This chapter considers the impact of mobility on noise.

The impact of transport noise

It is worth reminding ourselves just how all-pervasive transport noise has become. In 2000, more than 44 per cent of the population of the European Union (EU), that is about 210 million people, were regularly exposed to road traffic noise averaging out at more than 55dB, the level the World Health Organization (WHO) considers to be unacceptably high (den Boer and

Schroten, 2007). Fewer people were affected by rail noise: 35 million people, about 7 per cent of the population, were exposed to levels above 55dB (den Boer and Schroten, 2007). The figures for aircraft noise are less certain as the way in which they are collected is disputed (this is explained later in the chapter) but runs into millions. The aviation industry, for example, admits well over 3.5 million people in Europe are affected by night flights alone (European Commission, 2005).

Figures 6.1 and 6.2, taken with permission from den Boer and Schroten (2007), illustrate the numbers affected by road, rail and aircraft noise.

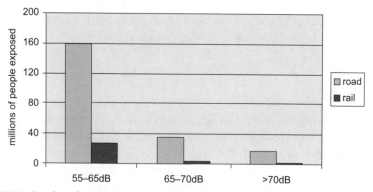

FIGURE 6.1 Number of people exposed to road and rail traffic noise in 25 EU countries in 2000

Note: This figure covers the EU27 except Cyprus and Malta.
Source: INFRAS/IWW (2004), OECD/INFRAS/Herry (2002), calculations by C.E. Delft (for Estonia, Latvia, Lithuania)

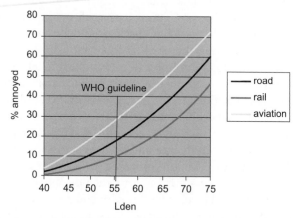

FIGURE 6.2 Percentage of people annoyed as a function of noise exposure of dwellings (Lden in dB(A))

Source: Miedema & Oudshoorn (2001)

Although the greatest numbers of people are exposed to traffic noise, there is evidence to show that people become disturbed more quickly by aircraft noise. We explore the reasons for this later in the chapter.

The monetary costs

The social and monetary costs of transport noise are enormous. Den Boer and Schroten (2007) found that 'road traffic noise in the EU is estimated to be at least 38 (30–46) billion euros per year, approximately 0.4% of total (gross domestic product) GDP'. They put the annual cost of rail noise at around €2.4 billion (about 0.02 per cent of total EU GDP), stressing that this took into account only the effects related to noise levels above 55dB(A), so was likely to be an underestimate. Aviation costs also run into billions.

Traffic noise

We turn first to traffic noise. Though all-pervasive, it is not a problem without solutions. The most cost-effective measures to cut traffic noise are those that reduce it at its source; from the vehicle, its tyres and engines. Traffic noise is created by a combination of rolling noise (arising from the tyres inter-acting with the road) and propulsion noise (comprising engine noise, exhaust systems, transmissions and brakes). As a rule of thumb, tyre-road interaction is the main source of noise above 55kph for most cars and above 70kph for lorries, with engine noise predominating at lower speeds.

Over the past 30 years or so, new cars have become quieter but that has been largely due to a reduction in engine noise. Tyre noise has not decreased significantly. Indeed, with trends to bigger, heavier cars and wider tyres, it has probably increased. The most immediate challenge, then, is to cut tyre noise. The techniques for doing so have been around for more than ten years. Effective measures have been thwarted by lobbying from the tyre industry. But its resistance is starting to crumble. For example, in 2009, the European Commission was able to introduce new regulations that, over time, will require quieter tyres to be fitted to vehicles. The frustration is that it has taken so long to agree what will become a very cost-effective measure. The Forum of European National Highway Research Laboratories (FEHRL) report (FEHRL, 2006) put the benefits of introducing quieter tyres across the EU at anything between €48 billion and €123 billion compared with costs of only €1.2 billion. In general, the benefits of at-source noise reduction measures exceed their costs by 2–4 times (Nijland et al, 2003). And, of course, these costs are borne by the owner of the vehicle not the state, as research and development costs get incorporated into prices.

Cutting speed limits

The second key way to cut noise is through lower speeds, together with improved acceleration and braking. Cutting the urban speed limit from 30mph to 20mph could reduce traffic noise by at least an average of 6dB – the equivalent of cutting the noise by more than 50 per cent. At higher speeds, the impact is less dramatic but still significant: a reduction from 70mph or 60mph to 40mph could cut noise by more than 25 per cent (Mitchell, 2009).

Acceleration and braking are also important. Noise events caused by aggressive or heavy-footed driving stand out from the anonymous background, and so can have a disproportionate effect on the perception of noisiness. Acceleration is more significant than braking in this respect and its importance is greater at lower speeds. Aggressive use of acceleration has been shown to increase noise by as much as 6dB (Ellebjerg, 2008).

According to Paige Mitchell, one of the UK's leading authorities on speed, reducing speed is the most immediate and equitable way of cutting traffic noise. It also has the advantage of being the fastest and fairest way of cutting climate change emissions (Mitchell, 2009). Transport planning consultants Steer Davies Gleave argued in their report on road transport emissions that 'better enforcement or reduction of speed limits would provide a very effective and cost-efficient means of managing carbon emissions from road transport' (Steer 2006). The report found that 'reducing the speed limit to 60mph [from 70mph] and enforcing it would reduce road transport emissions by 5.4%. These savings represent between 15% and 29% of the total savings expected from the transport sector by 2010'. The impact on emissions at much lower speed limits, though, is more complex. Some motoring pressure groups have argued that a 20mph limit, particularly if enforced by road humps, would cause so much stop-start driving that it would increase emissions, but Mitchell and others maintain that this would be off-set by a potential reduction in car use as the lower speeds make the roads less threatening for cyclists and pedestrians.

The obvious question is this: if lower speeds bring so many benefits, why are governments so reluctant to take action? They are under some pressure from business and industry who argue that lower speeds will mean longer journey times and cost them money. That may or may not be the case (it may depend on how many people switch to other modes and so cut congestion) but lower speeds would certainly benefit the economy in the round: the costs associated with noise, emissions and road deaths would fall. The latter would represent a considerable saving. According to a study cited by the WHO, a reduction in average speed of 3km/h would save 5000–6000 lives each year in Europe, and would avoid 120,000–140,000 crashes, producing a saving of €20billion (Racioppi et al, 2004).

The deeper reason for the politicians' reluctance to reduce speed limits appears to lie in the fear of a public backlash. In countries such as the UK, key

---

BOX 6.1 The importance of slow

We live in the age of speed. Fast food, faster cars, high-speed trains, jet aeroplanes. They bring us mobility, opportunities and experiences many of our parents could only dream of. The rich nations speed across a shrinking world, living life at a pace that was inconceivable just 50 years ago. And we live it out to a background of constant noise.

The Slow Movement suggests a different way of doing things. Its founder, Carl Honoré, writes on his website www.carlhonore.com: 'The Slow philosophy is not about doing everything at a snail's pace. It's about seeking to do everything at the right speed. Savouring the hours and minutes rather than just counting them. Doing everything as well as possible, instead of as fast as possible. It's about quality over quantity in everything from work to food to parenting'. The Slow Movement envisages a world where we walk and cycle around our towns and cities a lot more, mingling with our neighbours, where we take our time eating our meals, where we see the journey as part of the holiday rather than simply a way of reaching our destination. It now has supporters across the world.

In such a world there would still be noise. We referred in our opening chapter to the noise in ancient Rome or on the streets of medieval Europe – when life was lived at a slow pace. But speed does encourage noise. Two of the machines – cars and aeroplanes – that have enabled us to move around at increasing speed create more unwanted noise than just about anything else.

I think it goes a bit deeper than this, though. Because we move at speed through areas rather than linger in them, we do not identify with those areas. We feel no affinity with them or responsibility for them. Therefore it does not matter to us what impact the car, aeroplane or train we are travelling in has on those areas. We are at one remove from the consequences of our behaviour. When we speed through the countryside we do not think of the noise experienced by the villages we pass through. When we jet off to foreign parts, we rarely give a thought to the people living under the flight paths. Perhaps the starkest example of this is the drive-through, fast-food takeaway where you speed up in your car to grab a quick meal before rushing off again, creating a hard mechanical noise in a community where you do not intend to linger and in which you have little interest. This is the antithesis of this leisurely mingling. Slowing down will not eliminate noise. But, unless we do slow down, it will make it much more difficult to conquer it.

---

sections of the popular press would seek to stir up emotions by claiming the government had declared a war on motorists. However, the public's reaction to lower speeds limits is more complex than much of the media would have us believe. Studies consistently show that people support either the enforcement of the existing speed limit or the introduction of a lower one in areas where they live (Davis, 2001). The same people, of course, often like to speed through other people's neighbourhoods! But this is hardly the picture of a populace in revolt against lower speed limits.

Other measures to cut traffic noise

Other ways of cutting noise from traffic are less cost-effective. The best of the rest is the use of quieter road surfaces such as porous asphalt which can cut noise by 4–8dB, the equivalent of almost a subjective halving of it. According to a Danish study, it is 3–10 times more cost-effective than mitigation measures such as home insulation or the construction of noise barriers (Danish Environmental Protection Agency, 2003). It would also maximize the benefits of any quieter tyres that came on the market.

Good acoustic barriers or suitable vegetation, though, have a role to play at selected locations. They can cut noise levels by 5–15dB. Sound insulation of properties, too, can cut the impact of noise and can be particularly important for people living close to busy main roads. But these mitigation measures, while essential to give the worst affected communities immediate relief, are expensive. Much better in the longer term to concentrate on at-source measures: the Dutch Noise Innovation Programme calculated that every decibel reduced at-source would save €100 million in national expenditure on noise barriers and sound insulation (Dutch Ministry of Transport, 2002).

Looking forward

New opportunities to cut noise will open up with the introduction of all-electric or hybrid-electric vehicles. It is important that these opportunities are taken. It would be a mistake, though, to automatically assume that these new vehicles will glide along the streets in virtual silence. The big and powerful electrics that they will contain risk creating new and disturbing noises. Milk floats they will not be! Governments need to turn their attention to ensuring the necessary features are incorporated at the design stage to turn what could be problem vehicles into the silent knights of the road. Regulation is required to set the basic standards required from the motor manufacturing industry.

Blind and hard-of-hearing people have legitimate concerns regarding silent or near-silent vehicles. These concerns must be taken account of. It is important, though, that, when assessing these concerns, the wider context is looked at. For example, measures such as lower speed limits or vehicles fitted with pedestrian-friendly bumpers should be considered as part of the package to ensure their needs are met.

BOX 6.2 Escaping traffic noise

FOR SALE

A one-bedroom flat, sizeable rooms, modern kitchen, recently refurbished, central location, convenient for shops and local buses: £80,000

FOR SALE

A one-bedroom flat, sizeable rooms, modern kitchen, recently refurbished, secluded area, 10-minute walk to rail station: £110,000

Do not rush to buy these properties! The adverts are not for real but similar ones can be found in the windows of most estate agents. Why are the prices so different? Read between the lines and almost certainly the first flat is on a busy main road and the second one is not. The different prices reflect *the* big difference between the two flats: noise from traffic.

A lot of people, particularly in the richer world, can escape from traffic noise if they can afford to buy a property away from a busy main road. As we argued in Chapter 2, traffic noise these days is largely a main road problem. The policy in the UK, and in many other European countries, has been to direct through traffic away from the so-called 'residential' roads on to the 'main' roads. I would suggest that this is deeply inequitable, made more so by the fact that it is the people living on main roads who are less likely to own and drive cars or be able to move away. They are victims of other people's noise.

The equitable solution would be to reverse the policy of concentrating traffic on the main roads; to encourage rat-runs; to direct traffic along residential roads once the noise levels on the main roads have exceeded the recommended WHO levels. It is not likely to happen! But what is practicable (and necessary) is for efforts to cut traffic noise to be focused on the main roads where people live.

In conclusion, there is a raft of measures that could cut traffic noise significantly. Indeed, it is estimated that, with the right measures in place, annoyance caused by traffic noise could be cut by 70 per cent (den Boer and Schroten, 2007). The frustration has been the general reluctance to put them in place: none of the measures are impossible, or in some cases even difficult, to implement.

Rail noise

We now turn to rail noise. The figures are clear. Rail noise disturbs far fewer people than noise from aircraft or motor vehicles. But it does remain a problem. We showed in Chapter 3 how rail noise can affect children's education. And, as we outlined in Chapter 2, it can have a particularly disturbing impact on the poorest communities in poor countries who may be living in shanty town conditions adjacent to busy railway lines with noisy trains on poor quality tracks racing by.

Moreover, noise from freight and high-speed trains remains a particular concern in most countries of the world. In Germany and the Netherlands, for example, there have been several campaigns against rail freight noise. In the UK at present there is a vocal campaign to try and stop a high-speed rail line going through the Chilterns, which contain some of the finest landscapes in England.

Most of the noise from trains comes from the wheels rolling over the rails. It is the roughness of the rails and the wheels that causes the noise. The more roughness there is, the more disturbing the noise. The roughness is caused by wear and tear. A European Commission study found that roughness may cause noise levels to rise by up to 5dB(A) (Rust, 2003).

The noise from rails can be reduced by 'polishing'. The vibrations that cause noise can be minimized with rail dampers, which are lengths of elastic material fixed to the rails. But the big gains can come from cutting the noise of the wheels by replacing the brake pads used. A change from cast iron to composite material (the so-called K and LL blocks) could cut the noise by as much as 50 per cent (UIC/CER, 2008). It would also reduce the vibration from freight trains, which is the source of much disturbance.

There is little difficulty in fitting new vehicles with the new technology. The problem is the cost of retrofitting existing stock. There are, for example, 600,000 freight wagons, and many more passenger carriages, in use in the EU (AEA Technology, 2004). According to the International Union of Railways, it would cost around €2–3 billion to retrofit them (Oertli and Huebrer, 2006). The savings, though, would be considerable. The Dutch infrastructure company, ProRail, has calculated that the retrofitting of rolling stock with quiet brakes would result in cost savings of 500 million to €1 billion in the Netherlands alone (UIC, 2007). Much of these savings would come from the reduced need for noise walls and the insulation of neighbouring buildings.

High speed rail

There are particular problems with high speed trains. Not, though, when they are travelling at lower speeds, not much faster than conventional trains. At those speeds, they are likely to make less noise than the conventional ones because they will be fitted with all the latest noise-reducing features. The problem arises at speeds of more than 250/300km/h. That is where aerodynamic noise starts to kick in in a big way. Travel at these speeds can also generate ground vibrations, similar to the sonic boom associated with supersonic aircraft. And there is the problem of brake screech as the trains slow down or come to a halt.

There is a lot of technical work being done to examine ways of reducing the noise and vibration from high-speed trains but there is no escaping the fact that they are noisy. In overall environmental terms, they score more highly than air travel but decision-makers would do well to think through each proposed scheme very carefully indeed before proceeding, given the noise they make, the amount they cost and the far from negligible levels of carbon dioxide they produce. If a high-speed line is built, tunnels, noise barriers and insulation programmes need to be integral to the proposal. Also a cap should be imposed on the number of trains that will be operated: it would be very difficult, in noise terms, to justify a frequent high-speed service on any line.

The overall conclusion must be that there is a lot which can be done to reduce rail noise significantly but that some of the problems associated with freight and high-speed trains may prove more intractable.

Aircraft noise

Finally we turn to aircraft noise. It is estimated that more than 30 million people worldwide are exposed to disturbing levels of aircraft noise (Ollerhead and Sharp, 2001). If aviation continues to grow at its current rate – around 6 per cent a year worldwide – still more people will be affected as the introduction of quieter aircraft will be offset by the sheer growth in the number of planes. The aviation industry admits 'there are no "silver bullets" on the horizon in terms of new technology or operating procedures' (Ollerhead and Sharp, 2001).

Over the past 30 years, a step-change in the use of quieter aircraft has been cancelled out by the phenomenal surge in flying, particularly in rich countries. It has resulted in protests against aircraft noise across the world. Some have turned violent, such as the long-running battle that took place at Narita International Airport in Japan. A small number of the protestors have held back the tide of growth. The recent campaign to stop a third runway at Heathrow, the UK's premier airport, perhaps rates as their most spectacular success. The intensity of these campaigns reveals how much people dislike and fear aircraft noise.

Although a lot of people do appear to get used to it, it is undeniable that noise from planes is blighting millions of lives across the globe, particularly those experiencing it for the first time. The debate as to why people can get so disturbed by aircraft noise is ongoing but it could be to do with the high level of low-frequency content it contains. Wherever noise has a stronger than average low-frequency component – such as powerful stereo-systems, wind turbines, heavy lorries, high-speed trains – it seems to become particularly problematic.

Many in the aviation industry seem to fail to appreciate the depth of the problem aircraft noise can cause certain people. I do not think this is just an industry trying to defend itself. There appears to be a genuine failure to understand that aircraft noise can be a very real problem for people. I remember a senior person working for BAA, the owners of Heathrow Airport, saying to me that she had never thought people were really complaining about the noise; she assumed their noise complaints were just a front to cover their dislike of aviation in general and Heathrow in particular. Another senior aviation lobbyist once asked me if the noise complaints were less about noise and more about the fear of aircraft crashing. When senior figures in the industry do not understand there may be a problem, it makes it so much harder to arrive at a solution.

The situation is made even more difficult by the apparently random way people react to aircraft noise. A person living more than 20 miles from a busy airport can become utterly distressed by the noise while somebody close by will say that it does not bother them. This makes it more difficult for the aviation industry and governments to come up with satisfactory solutions. There are, though, some clear benchmarks for them to follow. The WHO has found that people in general start to get moderately annoyed when the noise averages out at 50dB over the day and severely annoyed when it averages out at 55dB. At

night, the WHO recommends that the average noise should not
outdoors (Berglund et al, 2000).

BOX 6.3 The way aircraft noise is measured

In Chapter 1, we outlined the way noise is usually measured: it is averaged out over a given period. We explained that this method might work for a busy main road where traffic is fairly constant throughout the day but as an average it is really not suitable for the more intermittent nature of aircraft noise. The averaging out of the noise includes the quiet periods of the day and the quiet days of the year, so underestimates the noise people actually hear. Moreover, the method of calculating the average gives too much weight to the noise of each plane and not sufficient to the number of planes – and so does not allow it to fully capture the main complaint of most residents: the huge increase in the number of planes there has been in the last couple of decades at many airports. A report produced by Heathrow Association for the Control of Aircraft Noise (HACAN), the organization that represents residents under the Heathrow flight paths, calculated that, by averaging out noise, one Concorde followed by three hours and 58 minutes of relief was said to be as disturbing as four hour's worth of non-stop noise from Boeing 757s at a rate of one every two minutes (Hendin, 2002). Clearly not a reflection of reality!

Some systems of averaging are better than others. LAeq, used in many countries of the world, averages out the noise over a 16-hour day. Another system in common usage, Lden, calculates the average for three different periods: day, evening and night. It then weights them to allow for the lower background levels in the evening and at night. The differences in the results produced by the two methods can be significant. At Heathrow, for example, fewer than 300,000 people live within the 57 LAeq contour (where noise averages out at 57dB over a 16-hour day) whereas more than 700,000 live within the 55 Lden contour. Local campaign groups believe the latter ties in much more closely with the reality of the situation. The American Federal Aviation Authority uses Day-Night Average Sound Level (DNL) – similar to LAeq but with a 10dB weighting for the period between 10pm and 7am.

Perhaps the most interesting innovation has come from Sydney in Australia, where they have developed a complementary metric way of measuring noise, which is more meaningful to the public. It is based on treating aircraft noise as a series of single events rather than a calculated average. It is much easier for people to understand because it shows the number of flights that can be expected over any given period, the number of hours with no planes and the likely noise of each plane. It has also been used at other airports in Australia as well as in Vienna and Stockholm.

The other big problem with the measurement of aircraft noise is that the techniques used do not fully capture the low-frequency content of the noise. This is because 'A' weighting, rather than 'C' weighting, is used to measure the noise. As we outlined in Chapter 1, the WHO suggests that, if the difference between 'A' weighted and 'C' weighted results is more than 10dB, the use of 'C' weighting should be considered when taking the results (Berglund et al, 2000). There is a considerable amount of low-frequency in aircraft noise. When HACAN measured noise in West London, a few miles from Heathrow Airport, the difference between the 'A' weighted and 'C' weighted measurements was 9dB (Hendin, 2002).

Our conclusion is that the methods used to measure aircraft noise underestimate the actual noise heard by people on the ground.

Ways of cutting aircraft noise at source

A lot of research is currently being undertaken into ways of cutting the noise from individual planes. The EU, Australia and New Zealand, together with a number of Asian countries, have adopted challenging goals to cut aircraft noise in their communities. The EU is aiming for a significant reduction by 2025 but, if growth is as predicted, the messages coming out of the aviation industry betray a lack of confidence that this will happen. I have yet to come across one figure from the industry who is prepared to stand up and say with any certainty that it will succeed with its plans to cut noise.

There are also operational measures that could be taken to cut noise levels. The angle at which planes come into land, known as the glideslope, is critical. At present, most airports use a three-degree glideslope. A steeper glideslope would mean planes would be higher longer, thus reducing the noise over more communities. At present the International Civil Aviation Organisation is looking at the practicability of a 4 degree glideslope.

A common technique to reduce noise used at some airports, including Heathrow, is Continuous Descent Approach (CDA). This is where planes aim for a smooth approach rather than the traditional step-by-step one that caused noise problems for communities in areas where aircraft were moving from a higher step to a lower one. However, CDA is not without its critics, who argue that it results in more noise in areas some considerable distance from the airport because, in order to achieve their smoother descent, aircraft are joining their final approach path further out than they did previously.

There is also constant debate about whether aircraft, when landing and taking off, should be dispersed or concentrated. There is probably no golden rule that can be applied to all airports. My own preference is for dispersal. It is usually more equitable and eases the biggest problem for those living under flight paths: the sheer number of planes overhead. Most people can cope with a plane every now and again; few can bear a constant stream of planes overhead.

Unlike road traffic and railways, there are no real grounds for optimism that there are solutions coming on-stream that will cut aircraft noise significantly. The projected growth in numbers is likely to nullify any advances in technology and operational procedures. It therefore does mean that governments, particularly in the richer countries where most of the flying takes place, need to look to measures to curb or reverse that growth. We look at the practicability and impact of this in this next section of this chapter. There is, though, an important point to be made here when we talk about the need to curb or reverse the growth in flight numbers. Aircraft noise only really presents a problem when aircraft approach or leave an airport. When in flight, the noise rarely has serious impacts. This means that as far as noise is concerned (it may be different for carbon dioxide emissions) it is more important to reduce the huge number of short-haul flights flying in and out of airports rather than be too concerned by the smaller number of long-distance flights.

Concluding thoughts

This chapter has shown that there are technical and operational measures that could cut noise from motor vehicles and trains quite significantly. But they may not be cost-effective in the case of motor vehicles if the number of cars continues to grow. We saw in Chapter 2 how industrializing countries such as Hong Kong are spending millions to reduce noise, particularly from road traffic, merely to stand still as thousands more vehicles pour onto the streets each year. This is likely to continue to be the case unless these vehicles can be replaced in the near future by near-silent electric or hybrid vehicles.

We concluded that real progress on cutting aircraft noise is unlikely unless the growth of short-distance flights, in particular, is curbed or reduced. We have not covered shipping in this chapter but in Chapter 4 we found that there was no real evidence that technical and operational measures of themselves 'would be sufficient to significantly reduce the tumult of noises that reverberate across the oceans'.

Is it practicable to curb or reverse the growth in transport? What would be its impact on the economy?

It was assumed for many years that increased levels of mobility (with the resultant growth in the number of cars, trains, aircraft and ships) were an inevitable consequence of increased economic prosperity. There is no question the two are linked but the evidence that has now emerged from the mature economies of the industrialized world shows that, once a country reaches a certain level of development, the performance of its economy is not dependent on ever-increasing mobility (SACTRA, 1999). In other words, once the basic transport infrastructure is in place (roads, railways, airports), the economy does not require ever more traffic on the roads or more aircraft in the sky to remain healthy. Indeed the evidence indicates than an excess of cars or planes can impose serious costs on an economy. The hidden costs of air pollution, emissions, congestion, road crashes and noise can run into billions. This would indicate that curbing the number of trips made, particularly by car or plane (the two modes which impose the greatest costs on society), could have positive gains for the economy.

Reducing car and aircraft use is not as difficult as it may appear. The key is to concentrate on short journeys. In the UK, 75 per cent of all trips are less than five miles long. Most of these could be done by public transport, walking or cycling rather than by car. In the case of air travel, 45 per cent of trips within Europe are 500km or less in length. Many of these are potentially transferable to rail.

It is a question of incentivizing people to change their habits. The introduction of reliable, affordable, accessible buses and trains and safe and convenient conditions for walking and cycling, probably accompanied by a bit of a 'stick' such as some form of road pricing or higher taxes on petrol, would result in modal shift. For aviation, a progressive elimination of the tax-breaks it enjoys – tax-free fuel and no payment of VAT – would make air trips more expensive and less attractive. (Currently these tax-breaks are both acting as an artificial stimulus to demand and costing nation states millions in lost revenue.) If this was accompanied by investment in fast, affordable rail services, then modal shift would take place. There are then ways to cut the number of short journeys we make by car or plane. The evidence suggests that to do so would save countries money rather than damage their economies.

If continuing problems with noise – or emissions – forced governments to significantly curb intercontinental travel, that would, of course, require a more fundamental rejigging of the economy. Certainly there are some long-distance air journeys that could be cut out without hurting the economy: certain leisure journeys or those trips to business meetings and conferences that could be replaced by (increasingly sophisticated) video-conferencing facilities, for example. We argued in this chapter that as far as noise was concerned, but not emissions, big reductions could be achieved through curbing short-haul flights while taking a more relaxed attitude towards long-distance ones. But, in reality, it is too simplistic to separate them out as neatly as that. One of the features of the globalized economy is its connectivity. Business people – and international freight – do not just make international long-haul flights. Those flights are often followed by a short-haul flight to take them to their final destination. If flying became more expensive as a result of the removal of the generous tax-breaks it enjoys, many business people would still fly as business is less price-sensitive than leisure, but there would be an overall economic cost, certainly in the short-term, until business adjusted to the new reality.

The twin threat of climate change and rising oil prices might force up the cost of long-distance travel. It could become more profitable for businesses to operate and trade more locally. That would curb the number of international planes in the air and ships on the oceans. It would also cut noise levels appreciably.

References

AEA Technology (2004) 'Status and options for the reduction of noise emissions from the existing European rail freight wagon fleet', AEA Technology Rail BV, 10 January, Netherlands

Berglund, B., Lindvall, T., Schwela, D. and Goh, K. (2000) *Guidelines for Community Noise*, World Health Organization, Bern, Switzerland

Danish Environmental Protection Agency (2003) *The Danish Road Noise Strategy*, Danish Environmental Protection Agency, Denmark

Davis, A. (2001) *Killing Speed: A Good Practice Guide to Speed Management*, Slower Speeds Initiative, Hereford

den Boer, L. and Schroten, A. (2007) *Traffic Noise Reduction in Europe*, C. E. Delft, Netherlands

Dutch Ministry of Transport (2002) *Dutch Noise Innovation Programme*, Dutch Ministry of Transport, Netherlands

Ellebjerg, L. (2008) *Noise Reduction in Urban Areas from Traffic and Driver Management – A Toolkit for City Authorities*, SILENCE, Europe

European Commission (2005) *Assessing the Economic Costs of Night Flight Restrictions*, MPD Group Limited, London

FEHRL (Forum of European National Highway Research Laboratories) (2006) *Study S12.408210*, European Commission Enterprise and Industry Directorate

Hendin, R. (2002) *The Quiet Con*, Heathrow Association for the Control of Aircraft Noise, London

INFRAS/1WWW (2004) *External Costs of Transport, Update Study*, INFRAS/IWW, Zurich/Karlsruhe

Miedema, H. and Oudshoorn, C. (2001) 'Annoyance from transportation noise: Relationships with exposure DNL and DENL and their confidence intervals', *Environmental Health Perspectives*, pp409–416

Mitchell, P. (2009) *Speed and Road Traffic Noise*, UK Noise Association, London

Nijland, H., Van Kempen, E., Van Wee, G. and Jabben, J. (2003) 'Cost and benefits of noise abatement measures', *Transport Policy*, vol 10, no 2, pp131–140

OECD/INFRAS/Herry (2002), *External costs of transport in Eastern Europe*, Zurich/Vienna

Oertli, J. and Huebner, P. (2006) *Rail Freight Noise Abatement: A Report on the State of the Art*, International Union of Railways and Community of European Railway Infrastructure Companies, France

Ollerhead, J. and Sharp, B. (2001) 'Computer model highlights the various noise reduction', *ICAO Journal*, vol 56, no 4, pp18–19, 32–33

Racioppi, F., Eriksson, L., Tingvall, C. and Villaveces, A. (2004) *Preventing Road Traffic Injury: A Public Health Perspective for Europe*, World Health Organization, Denmark

Rust, A. (2003) *Technology Report*, CALM, Europe

SACTRA (Standing Advisory Committee on Trunk Road Assessment Transport and the Economy) (1999) Her Majesty's Stationery Office, London

Steer, J. (2006) *Driving Up Carbon Dioxide Emissions from Road Transport*, Steer Davies Gleave, London

UIC (International Union of Railways) (2007) 'Noise abatement on European railway infrastructure', International Union of Railways, Paris

UIC/CER (International Union of Railways and Community of European Railway Infrastructure Companies) (2008) *Rail Transport and the Environment: Facts and Figures*, International Union of Railways and Community of European Railway Infrastructure Companies, France

Whitelegg, J. (1993) *Transport for a Sustainable Future*, Belhaven Press, London

Worldwatch Institute (2006/2007) *Vital Signs*, Worldwatch Institute, Washington, DC

CHAPTER 7

Neighbour/Neighbourhood Noise

VAL WEEDON

*Neighbourhood noise complaints have been increasing
dramatically in recent decades.*

Everyone likes to have good neighbours but for a growing number of people there is a lack of harmony across the garden fence because of conflict with their neighbours regarding noise. In modern times, neighbour noise has been described as the most common source of annoyance for individuals, taking over from traffic and aircraft noise (NSCA, 1990) with complaints rising five-fold in the last decade (Office for National Statistics, 2007).

A pilot study carried out in 1991 by the Right to Peace and Quiet Campaign (RPQC), a campaign and support group for people with domestic noise problems, revealed that noise from neighbours caused stress, ill health, lack of sleep and bad temper (Austen Associates, 1991). A further study by RPQC in 1994 uncovered the alarming fact that at least five people a year had died in noise-related conflicts between neighbours. Some of them had committed suicide due to the stress of living with a noise problem, others had been killed following violent confrontations with their neighbours (RPQC, 1994). In the pilot study, the main causes of neighbour noise were cited as anti-social behaviour, a lack of a deterrent and poor sound insulation in properties.

An increase in population in the 1960s and 1970s fuelled the need to build more homes. To cope with the demand, high-rise flats were built. Then throughout the 1980s and 1990s the demand for smaller units for single people or couples without children resulted in many older, larger family-size houses being converted into flats. Building regulations at the time did not require the testing of sound insulation in properties, so standards were often not adequate to protect people from everyday sounds their neighbours made. A report published by the UK Noise Association (Weedon et al, 2002) revealed that an estimated 2.5 million people were living in homes with bad sound insulation. In more recent times, largely fed by popular DIY television programmes, there has been a trend to install laminate wood flooring. The removal of carpeting has created huge noise problems, causing conflict between neighbours.

Since the 1960s, the rise in the standard of living has allowed people to purchase more gadgets for the home. Most of us now have household items such as vacuum cleaners, washing machines and even dishwashers. There has been a boom in DIY activities. Power drills and electrical garden equipment such as lawnmowers and hedge-trimmers have all contributed to the increasing amount of noise we make in our homes and gardens. The introduction of amplified sound for home entertainment, such as ever more sophisticated and powerful music systems and televisions, has helped fuel a dramatic increase in complaints. Add to this unreasonable behaviour and you have a lethal cocktail for annoyance!

There is a maxim that an Englishman's home is his castle. It was established in common law by politician and lawyer Sir Edward Coke in 1628 and later endorsed in 1763 by William Pitt, the first Earl of Chatham, also known as Pitt the Elder, who declared: 'The poorest man may in his cottage bid defiance to all the forces of the crown. It may be frail – its roof may shake – the wind may blow through it – the storm may enter – the rain may enter – but the King of England cannot enter' (www.phrases.org.uk/meanings/an-englishmans-home-is-his-castle.html). Whilst this dictum largely refers to the protection of anyone coming into your home without prior invitation, some have interpreted it to cover other aspects of life at home. In common law nuisance, it is generally accepted that a balance has to be struck between the right of an occupier to do as he likes in his own home and the rights of his neighbours for peaceful enjoyment of their property, but this balanced approach can lead to conflict between neighbours when it comes to noise.

The importance of campaigns

Over the years, the increasing amount of noise in our neighbourhoods has resulted in the setting up of anti-noise campaigns. The first recorded campaign against noise in the UK was the Noise Abatement League, set up in 1939. Founding member and chairman Lord Horder of Ashford, a clinician and member of the Royal College of Physicians, was 'intent on bringing home to the community how they might escape from the nervous wear and tear caused by needless noise' (British Medical Association, 1955). The league's work was disrupted with the onset of World War II and, following the death of Lord Horder in 1955, the league was disbanded.

It was in the summer of 1959 that businessman John Connell was sitting in his office in Old Bond Street in London when he came across a number of letters in a national newspaper from people complaining about noise and asking what 'they' were going to do about it? Intrigued, he followed this up with his own letter asking if people felt as annoyed by noise in 1959 as they did in 1939. The result was more than 4000 replies. This spurred Connell to set up the Noise Abatement Society (NAS). He was appointed honorary secretary, becoming chairman in 1965 when the NAS became a registered charity (Moore, undated). Campaign work carried out by the NAS led to the passing of the first Noise Abatement Law in 1960. This was followed in 1974 by the introduction of the Control of Pollution Act allowing statutory nuisance action to be taken by local authorities. The NAS dealt with a whole range of noise issues, but it found the most common complaint was noisy neighbours. In response to this, the NAS spearheaded a scheme encouraging good behaviour. This was done by distributing colourful leaflets using the slogan 'love thy neighbour'.

Throughout the 1970s and 1980s the number of domestic noise problems continued to rise. In May 1991, the RPQC was launched in response to the growing number of complaints about domestic noise. The campaign felt there was a lack of sympathy for people suffering domestic noise problems. The campaign's initial strategy was to make use of the media as a way of highlighting how domestic noise problems were affecting lives and explain why people were unable to find a solution. The campaign did this by encouraging members to tell their stories to the press. Human interest stories, in particular, were very popular in many of the women's magazines, so coverage was easily secured. Stories were also covered by national and local newspapers but it was after neighbour noise featured on the national television documentary programme *World in Action*, broadcast in January 1992, and watched by an estimated 9 million viewers, that interest was shown at government level.

Following the programme, members of the RPQC were contacted by government advisers and were invited to meet with Lord Strathclyde, the minister responsible for noise reduction. At the meeting Lord Strathclyde suggested the setting up of a Noise Forum, made up of key organizations and noise experts, with the aim of looking at ways of dealing with the growing neighbour noise problems. Campaigners had told him they felt the approach to neighbourhood noise was too passive and just tinkered at the edges of the problem. There was some criticism of the environmental health profession too. The regular complaints were that councils would either not investigate complaints or it took far too long for investigations to take place. Often it was the police people called to deal with noisy neighbours and not their local councils. This was mainly because many noise problems occurred in the evening and very few local councils had out-of-hours services to deal with night-time noise complaints, whereas the police were more accessible and on call 24 hours a day. Through the Noise Forum, campaigners were able to air their concerns, which led to new regulations and some improvements to services that local authorities offered, including more operating out-of-hours services.

The problem of people playing excessively loud music in their homes and at late-night parties was greatly reduced because of improvements to legislation such as the introduction of the Noise Act 1996. The threats of confiscation of hi-fi equipment and court action were great deterrents. Alongside this there had been a number of high-profile awareness campaigns, such as the production of a Good Neighbour leaflet. Media interest continued to grow, with debates taking place on television and radio programmes. Campaigners in the UK joined forces with campaigners abroad for the first International Noise Awareness Day which took place on 21 April 1999.

Early progress stalls

By the end of the 1990s, campaigners felt that noise was slipping down the political agenda once again. So, the year 2000 saw the launch of the UK Noise Association, a collaboration of noise campaigns, including those with concerns about community and domestic noise issues. Neighbour noise complaints continued to rise, partly due to a combination of poor sound insulation and growing anti-social behaviour problems in the home and in the wider community. In response to these concerns, the first anti-social behaviour legislation was introduced in 1999 (updated in 2003) and new housing regulations were introduced in the Housing Act 2004 to deal with the problem of poor-quality sound insulation. New building regulations for sound insulation were introduced, bringing in the option of testing standards or using Robust Details Standards (Building Regulations Approved Document E 2003, incorporating 2004 amendments), although these regulations only applied to new-build, converted or change-of-use properties. There was still the problem of dealing with poor sound insulation retrospectively.

The introduction of Anti-Social Behaviour Orders (ASBOs) was welcomed by campaigners, but government figures showed that between 2000 and 2008, more than half of ASBOs in England and Wales were breached. A BBC news report stated that 'Ministry of Justice figures show 55 per cent of the almost 17,000 ASBOs issued between June 2000 and December 2008 were breached, leading to an immediate custodial sentence in more than half of the cases' (BBC News, 2010).

At the time of writing the coalition government are consulting on more effective responses to anti-social behaviour, which some believe could see the end to the ASBO. Similar anti-social behaviour laws in Scotland were introduced and did seem to be more effective than in the rest of the UK, possibly because of their more strategic approach to the problem (Scottish Executive, 2004).

Private sector involvement

Noisedirect was set up in 2006. It was the first dedicated independent noise abatement service run by professionally qualified environmental health officers, who had previously worked for local authorities and recognized a need for an alternative service for individuals with noise problems.

Noisedirect is the only service which provides a professional assessment of cases of noise nuisance and impacts to public health. The service includes telephone advice, casework, acoustic monitoring, subjective assessments and advice on the range of legal remedies. The service is not just aimed at noise sufferers but provides independent advice to those carrying out noisy activities (employers or commercial premises) or those who may inadvertently be causing a noise nuisance with the aim of mitigating the potential for future noise problems.

As a privately run company, Noisedirect is independent of restrictions, such as budget cuts or political influence, that may prevent some local authorities from taking action. Noisedirect's sole objective is to serve clients, who, after all, pay for its services. Under the Environmental Protection Act, Section 82, you can go directly to court yourself, but having bodies such as Noisedirect means you can do so with the guidance of professionally qualified officers.

Much of Noisedirect's work also highlights the failures of some local authorities when dealing with statutory nuisance cases and a lot of councils' lack of willingness to use legislation, such as the Housing Act 2004, which allows them to deal with issues such as poor sound insulation, one of the biggest sources for complaint about domestic noise this century. It is not suggested that the statutory duty to tackle noise should be removed from local authorities; we see it more as offering an alternative choice for those people who are happy to pay for the services of qualified officers working in the private sector. We would like to see this sort of service become available to everybody regardless of income.

Government activity

At government level, the first major report into noise was published in 1963 (Wilson Committee, 1963). The report acknowledged that noise in the community was linked to bad behaviour. It was suggested that local authorities should undertake publicity campaigns both in schools and among the public generally to show that unnecessary noise is inconsiderate and ill-mannered. Towards the end of the 1964–1970 Labour government, Anthony Crosland, Minister for Housing and Local Government formed the Noise Advisory Council. When Peter Walker created the new Department of the Environment after the Conservatives came into office in 1970, he took over the chairmanship, and frequently took the chair. Membership was a mixture of expert and lay people, from Geoffrey Lilley, professor of aeronautics at the Institute of Sound and Vibration Research (ISVR) at the University of Southampton and Professor Elfyn Richards also from the ISVR, to representatives of organizations such as the Civic Trust, airport consultative committees, senior lawyers and prominent acoustics experts from government institutions such as the Building Research Establishment and the National Physical Laboratory (Thorneley-Taylor, 2010).

In 1974, the Noise Advisory Council published their report, *Noise in the Next Ten Years*, in which they recommended a Quiet Town experiment, selecting one town to investigate how noise could be reduced. Darlington was chosen as it represented a 'typical' town (Gloag, 1980). The Noise Advisory Council oversaw the project which ran for two years from 1976 to 1978. The objective of the project was 'to illustrate by practical example the scope for the reduction of noise nuisance at home and in public places by means of education, publicity and experimental schemes'. While the Noise Advisory Council had intended to look at ways of tackling ambient noise, a Working Group set up in Darlington felt that it was better to concentrate efforts on noise nuisance from individual sources. Schools in the town were heavily involved too by having talks on noise and running competitions to design posters. One primary school devoted their end-of-term concerts to a number of playlets on noise. Much of the publicity to promote the experiment was done with the help of local papers, radio and television.

In a report outlining the experiment and its outcomes, W. C. B. Robson, the chief environmental health officer for Darlington Borough Council, concluded that the experiment had made people more aware of noise, but such a scheme required a high level of resources for continued success. He felt that 'public opinion must be continually stimulated to recognize the importance of noise and the possibilities for its alleviation'. Although the main objective to raise awareness had largely been achieved, the scheme was unable to continue due to limited funding and the organizers felt there was a loss of credibility with the slogan 'Quiet Town', which some felt was misleading and restricted the projects achievements (Gloag, 1980).

New legislation

Domestic noise complaints continued to increase over the following two decades, with complaints to local authorities about noisy neighbours rising from more than 24,000 in 1979 to more than 62,000 in 1989. In 1990, the government published *This Common Inheritance: Britain's Environmental Strategy*, with promises that standards on noise would be kept up-to-date, consistent and effectively controlled. It pointed out that noise is controlled in three ways: 'Setting limits on the emission of noise at source, keeping noise and people apart and ensuring that adequate controls exist over noise nuisance.'

The same year also saw the publication of the *Noise Review Working Party Report* (Batho, 1990), which made a number of recommendations for controlling neighbour noise. The working party was chaired by W. J. S. Batho. Other members included representatives from local government, industry and voluntary bodies. In the same year, the Environmental Protection Act replaced the Control of Pollution Act 1974. It sought to clarify the basic duties of local authorities (Blatch, 1990).

One of the recommendations of the Batho Report was the setting up of a government-sponsored quiet neighbourhood pilot scheme to raise more awareness on neighbour noise problems and help reduce the number of complaints being made. The Neighbourhood Noise Awareness Scheme was launched in Forest Hill in South London in May 1991 and ran for about six months. It differed greatly from the Darlington Quiet Town project mainly because it covered a much smaller geographical area and would solely concentrate on the problem of noisy neighbours. The area included a wide variety of accommo-dation: high-rise flats, terraced housing and larger semi-detached properties, along with houses of multiple occupation. A steering committee was set up and the scheme relied heavily on a partnership with members from the local residents' association, local authority officers and community police.

One of the key components of the scheme was a Community Code leaflet that set out a number of 'do's' and 'don'ts'. This was sent out to every house-hold in the area, together with a survey form and letter from the mayor of the borough. Information collected from the survey included the numbers of people who had heard of the scheme and from what source; the numbers of people who had been disturbed by noise since the scheme commenced, what steps they took and their reasons for these; plus respondents' general attitude to the scheme. Although more than 1000 forms were sent out, only 124 were returned. But the steering committee was still able to glean some useful infor-mation about the project.

A report published (Leventhall, 1992) concluded there had been some success in raising awareness. It also recognized 'the importance of continuing publicity' for such a scheme to succeed, along with continued commitment from residents and the support of agencies such as neighbourhood council officials and the police, and the need for people with training in counselling, arbitration and mediation techniques. A final suggestion was to link it into Neighbourhood Watch schemes, which often had established networks of volunteers and a system in place. But the Forest Hill Neighbourhood Noise Awareness Scheme was disbanded once government-sponsored support came to an end.

In 1993, the Noise and Statutory Nuisance Act was introduced to deal with noise on the street such as vehicles, machinery and equipment. This was to complement the Environmental Protection Act 1990, which excluded noise complaints outside the boundaries of the home. One of the growing sources of complaint was from car alarms and the Noise and Statutory Nuisance Act allowed local authorities to deal with this more effectively. The Noise Act was introduced in 1996 and allowed local authorities to confiscate noise-producing equipment.

In 2006, the government announced it intended to produce a consultation for a national noise strategy. Year-on-year it kept promising its publication. In March 2008, the question of when it planned to publish it was raised in Parliament. Jonathan Shaw, the minister responsible for noise at the time, said 'The government plans to publish for consultation a combined national noise strategy for England, covering ambient and neighbourhood noise, later this year' (Shaw, 2008). The consultation was never published.

Mediation

Mediation became a huge focus of attention for government and local author-ities throughout the 1990s. They were wooed by the idea of resolving disputes

---

BOX 7.1 The limits of mediation

The RPQC expressed concerns following the broadcast of a television documentary in 1992 highlighting a case of a woman who had complained to her council about a rock band practising in a terraced house next door to her (*Nature Programme*, 1993). The council would not take action and instead she was left with no real alternative but to seek mediation to resolve the problem. During the television interview, the woman was clearly distressed as she explained what she had to endure, and that is why she had agreed to participate in a mediation session. The outcome was an agreement to set hours for the band to practice, even though the complainant was not happy. She felt it was preferable to have some agreement in place rather than not knowing when the band would start playing and when it would end. The campaign felt this case high-lighted how mediation was being wrongly applied and that formal action was needed where it was clear a noise nuisance existed.

---

without taking formal action. Mediation (sometimes referred to as Alternative Dispute Resolution) is about bringing two opposing parties together using the mediator as an impartial observer. The object is to find a workable agreement between the two parties and avoid going to court, which would have cost implications. In 1992, the government funded a mediation project in South London, Southwark Council's Environmental Services Mediation Project, with the intention of diverting a substantial number of noise pollution cases in the direction of mediation. Initially campaigners were supportive of the principles of mediation but became concerned when it emerged that councils were using mediation services instead of serving noise abatement notices for complaints where a clear noise nuisance existed.

Enforcement

There has always been a disparity between the number of complaints being made to local authorities and the number of noise abatement notices being served. In 1988, despite more than 14,000 complaints being identified as statutory nuisances by environmental health officers, only 2636 abatement notices were issued, with just 164 people convicted (NSCA, 1990). A survey carried out by the Chartered Institute of Environmental Health between 2008 and 2009 logged 246,370 domestic noise incidents, with 84,226 of them recorded as a statutory nuisance. The survey also claimed that more than 74 per cent of noise nuisance cases were resolved without serving a noise abatement notice (Willis, 2010).

The number of serious incidents involving noisy neighbours came to a head back in 1994 when the RPQC highlighted that between 1991 and 1994, 16 people had lost their lives in neighbour noise disputes. That worked out at an average of five people a year. Following a press conference at the House of Commons on 5 September 1994, *The Mail on Sunday*, a national news-paper, ran its own campaign to petition government for improvements to the law. This led to a further Government Working Party being set up to explore new ways of dealing with the problem. In 1996 The Noise Act was passed to deal with late night noise problems, in particular, the playing of loud ampli-fied music, which, at the time, was one of the biggest sources of complaint. Included in the Bill was the right of local authorities to seize and confiscate noise producing equipment.

The Chartered Institute for Environmental Health has monitored noise control activity by local authorities since 1966, but they have only been collecting information and statistics on noise complaints since the late 1970s. Their annual Noise Survey is the only real indicator the UK has to prove that noise has been getting worse. The data collected from every individual local authority on a yearly basis has proved an invaluable source of information. The consistent sources of complaint have been amplified music, barking dogs, DIY, followed by other anti-social behaviour such as shouting, raised voices, slamming doors and children playing noisily. There have been other types of neighbourhood noise complaints that have materialized following various trends. For example, during the late 1980s and through the 1990s a rise in what was labelled 'organized pay parties' became a huge problem. This was during a period well before mobile phones or the popularity of the internet and social network sites such as Facebook were in existence. Parties would be advertised by word of mouth and people would pay an entrance fee when arriving at the house where a party was being held. Gatherings such as 'raves' were also popular. These were often illegal as formal permission was rarely obtained to hold them. They normally took place in open fields or disused warehouses. Rave music had a particular type of style with a prominence in the bass beat and people could be affected in their homes miles away from the location where the party was taking place. This presented a problem for local authorities trying to detect where these parties were taking place, as complain-ants could hear the music but would not know the location of the rave. It was also a problem for the police who had to deal with the dispersal of party-goers. The rave movement reached a peak in the late 1980s and early 1990s, but then declined after new laws – the Criminal Justice and Public Order Act 1994, Section 58 of the Antisocial Behaviour Act 2003 and Section 1(c) of the Licensing Act 2003 – gave the police stronger powers to tackle them.

Another problem arising during the same period was car alarms and house alarms. It was popular for car owners to install alarms to protect their cars from theft. Similarly, house owners were keen to protect their homes from burglars. Both car and house alarms often became a huge problem, causing annoyance to a whole neighbourhood, especially if they sounded in the middle of the night. New regulations in 1993 – the Noise and Statutory Nuisance Act – enabled local authorities to take action against owners of vehi-cles, which allowed them to have cars towed away if the owner could not be traced to disarm the vehicle. Similarly, house alarms were becoming a problem either because they were set off accidently or through technical faults. The police have now adopted their own policy to ensure that only genuine calls are responded to. The policy requires you to have the correct system installed. It will also take account of the number of false activations there have been over a 12-month period – a high number will result in further call-outs receiving a lower priority (Association of Chief Police Officers, 2006). Some councils also run schemes for home-owners to register key holders with them so they can be contacted to de-activate alarms when the owners are away from home.

Fireworks became a huge problem following the Millennium celebrations at the beginning of 2000. The widespread use of fireworks throughout the world triggered their popular use for all sorts of celebrations. Prior to this, fireworks in the UK were mostly confined to celebrate Guy Fawkes Night on 5 November although there had been additional use for some religious festivals such as Divali and the Chinese New Year. However, misuse of fireworks following the Millennium celebrations in the year 2000 led to a number of serious incidents reported in the press where fireworks were being used maliciously as weapons to destroy property such as phone boxes and even police cars. In addition to this, more and more people were using fireworks to celebrate religious festivals, special birthdays or anniversaries. The increasing anti-social use of fireworks led to a strong campaign by animal rights organizations along with anti-noise campaigners. It became one of the biggest sources of complaints to members of parliament from constituents and so new firework regulations were introduced in 2005. The import, storage, licensing and end use was tightened up. The result has meant a vast improvement in the noise climate, especially during the autumn months between September and December each year.

Conclusions

It is clear, when looking back over the past 50 years or so in the UK and assessing what has happened, that neighbourhood noise nuisance will always be an issue. But to avoid problems getting out of hand, we need a national programme of investment in good sound insulation in homes and to constantly look at ways to change attitudes and improve behaviour. It is interesting that the most significant changes have happened at a national level when there has been real public pressure, usually coordinated by lobby and campaign organizations. We also need strong deterrents, and to ensure that enforcement is closely monitored. There is no doubt that, where tough action has been taken, the noise climate and people's behaviour has improved. In order for this to happen on a consistent basis, there needs to be a shift in attitudes towards emphasizing responsibility rather than the overemphasis on rights that has become dominant over the past 50 years.

References

Association of Chief Police Officers (2006) *Intruder Alarm Policy*, Association of Chief Police Officers, London

Austen Associates (1991) *Pilot Study Findings*, Right to Peace and Quiet Campaign, London

Batho, W. (1990) *Noise Review Working Party Report*, Her Majesty's Stationery Office, London

BBC News (2010) 'Time to *move beyond* Asbos, says Home Secretary May', 28 July, www.bbc.co.uk/news/uk-10784060

Blatch, E. (1990) *Hansard*, vol 522, 18 October

British Medical Association (1955) 'Obituary: Lord Horder of Ashford', *British Medical Journal*, vol 2, no 4937, pp493–497

CIEH (Chartered Institute of Environmental Health Officers) (2006) *Noise Nuisance 2005-06 for England, Wales and Northern Ireland*, Chartered Institute of Environmental Health Officers, London

Gloag, D. (1980) 'Noise and health: public and private responsibility', *British Medical Journal*, vol 281, no2652, pp1404–1406

Leventhall, H. G. (1992) *Forest Hill Neighbourhood Noise Awareness Scheme: Report to the Department of Environment*, Department of Environment, London

Moore, N. (undated) *Quiet Please: The Quiet Man – John Connell Interview*, source unknown

Nature Programme (1993) BBC, 20 July

NSCA (National Society for Clean Air) (1990) *Controlling Neighbour Noise*, National Society for Clean Air, Brighton

Office for National Statistics (2007) *Social Trends Survey*, www.statistics.gov.uk/social-trends37

RPQC (Right to Peace and Quiet Campaign) (1994) Press Release, 5 September, Right to Peace and Quiet Campaign, London

Scottish Executive (2004) *Guidance on Antisocial Behaviour Strategies*, Scottish Executive, Edinburgh

Shaw, J. (2008) *Hansard*, Column 2282W, 4 March

Thorneley-Taylor, R. (2010) verbal interview, Noise and Vibration Consultant

Weedon, V., Stewart, J. and Manley, D. (2002) *A Sound Solution*, UK Noise Association, London

Willis, K. (2010) *Noise Survey*, Chartered Institute of Environmental Health Officers, London

Wilson Committee (1963) *Final Report*, cmnd 2053, Her Majesty's Stationery Office, London

CHAPTER 8

Piped Music:
The Music You Cannot Turn Off

Nigel Rodgers

'Piped water, piped gas, piped electricity – but NEVER piped music!'
Stephen Fry

Piped music, also known as 'muzak' or elevator music: a nagging irritant to some people some of the time, maybe, but as a *major* problem, on a par with aircraft or traffic noise, surely it hardly registers? It can be avoided easily enough by shunning the particular pub, restaurant, hotel or shop that has it. Most people, after all, *like* music. Protestors against piped music must be grumpy old men or women, the sort of people who become enraged over the misplacing of apostrophes. They may need to be humoured, like members of the Campaign against Metric Signage, but never, *never* heeded.

This is still how some people in positions of power think, preferring to dismiss piped music as a non-issue. Such attitudes are as commonly found in the headquarters of companies such as HSBC and Marks & Spencer – two of the worst offenders in the UK vis-à-vis piped music – as in the corridors of Whitehall or the BBC. Disdain, or lack of concern, at the top filters down to the shop, bar or restaurant floor, where people who protest about piped music can indeed be made to feel like aged cranks or tone-deaf killjoys. And yet all they are asking is for the freedom to go about in public without being battered by someone else's choice of music.

There is an irony here, although hardly a joke. It is musicians who particularly dislike music being forced on them, being by their training and profession unable *not* to listen to it. (Many musicians and music teachers in consequence support Pipedown, the UK organization that campaigns for freedom from piped music.) But there is no need to be a musician to object to piped music. If the few genuinely impartial opinion polls that have been conducted are correct, 34 per cent of people in the UK dislike piped music. Among those with hearing problems – one person in seven, according to the Royal National Institute for the Deaf (RNID) – that proportion rises to 86 per cent. Objectors to piped music, while not in an absolute majority, outnumber those liking it, who form about 30% of the general population (RNID, 1998). We are not talking here about a tiny cantankerous minority.

The definition of piped music

First things first: a definition of 'piped music'. Piped music – also known as canned music, elevator music, wallpaper music, widely called muzak (a trademark) but by Pipedowners, *muzac* – does not refer to a particular type of music. It means any music relayed, transmitted or piped around a room or building, or a street or square, where people have come for purposes other than listening to music. People who face inescapable music when out shopping, eating, drink, travel, visiting the doctor or swimming pool, are experiencing piped music, whether it is the latest boy band or J. S. Bach.

Piped music also generally means only recorded music because, although live music can be very noisy, it seldom goes on continuously. The performers, being human, require rest. And they require paying. This means that live music tends to be the exception rather than the rule, and usually advertised to attract those who actually want to listen to it, so warning off those who do not want it. (Pipedown does not object to live music for precisely these reasons.)

The ubiquitousness of piped music

When asked to name a place or chain with particularly bad piped music, I point out that, as most places now have muzac, you simply need to walk down any high street. Piped music – often far too loud to be called background music – pulsates out of pubs, restaurants, hotels and shops. Theoretically these are places you could avoid – if, that is, you are prepared to become a near-hermit and do all your shopping online. But unwanted music also comes pouring down the telephone when one is placed on hold, on television and radio programmes where it can drown out speech, in hospitals and doctors' surgeries, on aircraft, in airports, even on some trains and buses. In short, it is ubiquitous.

And yet, paradoxically or perhaps consequentially, it is widely hated. According to one particular survey it is the 'third most hated thing in modern life' (*Sunday Times*, 1997). Interestingly, the first two most hated things noted by that survey were other sorts of noise. A graphic manifestation of this hatred came in February 2005 on commuter trains running from Essex into Liverpool Street Station in London. The train company, c2c, had signed a contract with TNX to broadcast a mixture of news, sport, music and, most significantly, commercials from television sets installed in all the coaches of these trains. TNX paid c2c (aka 'Commitment to Customers') trains for this privilege. There were a couple of 'quiet zones' in each train, as regulations require, but these were small, hard to locate in a rush-hour scrum and not insulated from the television sets anyway. As the trains are mainly used by commuters, most travellers crushing into the coaches at peak hours had no choice once on board but to listen and watch. They were the perfect captive audience.

Or so TNX and c2c presumably believed. Irate passengers thought otherwise. They organized protests that culminated in a near-riot, some passengers locking themselves into the toilets to make their point about the hell of inescapable piped television. Their newsworthy action made the news and led the BBC while covering the story to conduct a straw poll. Of the passengers questioned, 67 per cent objected to being forced to listen to – and watch – this piped television. Wisely, c2c trains dropped the plan and TNX soon after experienced financial problems. Attempts to pipe television on Central Railways in the area around Birmingham, the UK's second largest city, have so far also come to nothing. (Some train companies such as Virgin Trains offer passengers the option of television and music in each seat, but this is *optional*.)

If piped music can provoke such rage, it seems reasonable to ask: What is the point of it? The piped music industry, which has a turnover in excess of £120 million, is well able to afford convincing spin doctors. They produce plausible-sounding arguments to support the product, quoting extensively – and usually exclusively – from their own findings. But before examining their claims, it is worth looking at the history of what has become a major, if under-recognized, form of noise pollution.

The origins of piped music

Piped music in the UK began during World War II with 'Music while you work'. This broadcast a non-stop mixture of popular light tunes into armaments factories. The rationale was that it would boost productivity among those doing dull repetitive jobs on production lines and keep morale up. ('Music while you work' continued for a time after the war on the Light Programme, the forerunner of Radio 2.) Whether or not the music piped really worked – it can only have been audible on quieter shop floors with no heavy machinery clattering away – it was never used at Bletchley Park, where the best brains in Britain were cracking the Enigma code.

From the start, therefore, it seems to have been tacitly accepted that piped music helped only with mindless jobs. However, all commuters arriving at Waterloo Station in London just after 1945 were met with marching music broadcast (tinnily, no doubt) over the tannoy system. As many commuters at the time were recently demobilized soldiers accustomed to marching, it may have helped some of them quicken their pace, which was the idea. While the war may have made the British temporarily willing to tolerate attempted mood-conditioning music, it was not generally piped through public places and the trend died out – at the time.

The real origins, though, of piped music lie in the US. Major-General Squier is regarded as its inventor, being the first to pipe music to restaurants in New York in 1936. He also coined the term *muzak*, now the trademark of Muzak Holdings. Early technological restraints – the need to change gramophone records constantly, for example – for a while limited piped music's growth, but bracing radio programmes were piped to encourage American factory workers during the war too.

After the war, instead of demobilizing, the American piped music industry went on the offensive. It was helped by new technology that allowed it to be diffused more easily: first via tapes, then radio stations. Soon it was spreading throughout bars, hotels, restaurants and even into the White House under President Eisenhower in the 1950s. It finally went into space, NASA piping music into some Apollo moon missions to try to tranquillize astronauts.

The blandness of the typical 'piped music', commonly called muzak, is no accident but the result of careful selection by skilled teams who edit out potentially alarming highs and lows to lull listeners. This makes such muzak semi-audible in the background, noticeable only in unusually quiet spaces such as lifts – hence the name 'elevator music'. Its spread across American life – into streets, beaches, parks, even into mortuaries – finally created a reaction. In 1989, the maverick rock star Ted Nugent labelled muzak 'terminally uncool' and offered to buy up the entire stock for $10 million. His offer was declined, probably because $10 million was not enough for the already huge industry. Since then piped music has continued to spread around the world 'like an insidious cancer' in the words of Julian Lloyd Webber, an ardent supporter of Pipedown, who hates it as much as any musician.

Back in the early 1960s, the British actress Joyce Grenfell was among the first to protest about piped music. Now almost every week, some celebrity or journalist lambasts it in print or on air. But their discrete, uncoordinated complaints seem to have absolutely no impact. The piped music industry has caught the ear of those it wants: restaurateurs, hoteliers, publicans, those running department stores, public transport and hospitals. Customers, it seems to think, will simply have to accept its products – and pay for them. Piped music adds a small but real extra cost to every item. It was assumed that customers – especially the British – were too polite or timid to complain about, let alone unite against, piped music.

The origins of Pipedown

But even the polite British have their limits. One evening in 1992, I was with some friends – all aged 30-something – in Bistro 190, a small restaurant in west London. The food was good, so was the service. But suddenly we all agreed that the restaurant was *intolerable*: we could not hear each other speak because of the loud music smashing against our ears – not background muzak but in-your-face rock. Requests to the waiter to have the music turned off or at least down met with sympathy – he did not seem to be enjoying it either – but the confession that it was beyond his powers to do so. Apparently it was ordained from on high. We asked fellow-diners at nearby tables what they felt about the music. Without exception, they said they disliked it. We quickly paid the bill and left for somewhere where we could talk in peace. What we talked about was piped music.

That evening saw the start of Pipedown, a campaign which has since gone global. The US, Canada, Germany, Austria, Switzerland, Holland and South Africa now have branches or chapters of Pipedown. At first it was an almost light-hearted campaign. Naïvely we thought that by pointing out the obvious – that many people dislike piped music, and often do so strongly, their feelings about it being almost invariably stronger than those who like it – retailers and others – would pause, rethink and offer quiet alternatives. Pipedown organized (and still organizes) coordinated letter-writing campaigns to this effect. We have helped persuade Tesco, for example, not to install piped music in its supermarkets (except, alas, at Christmas.) We also thought that, once those in power had had the situation explained to them in a clear and calm way, they would accept the need for some very modest regulations. Unfortunately, Pipedown had reckoned without the cemented mindset of those who have succumbed to the blandishments of the piped music PR industry and their surveys. The value of such surveys is highly debatable.

How to prove (almost) anything you want

Foremost among studies quoted in support of piped music are those by Adrian North. He is currently professor of psychology at Herriot-Watt University, Edinburgh, but most of his research in this field was done when he was at Leicester University. There he 'discovered' that playing German music (type unspecified – was it oompah oompah music? Or Wagner?) in supermarkets resulted in shoppers buying German food and wine. Likewise playing French music (type also unspecified – accordion music?) apparently led shoppers to buy French products (North et al, 1999). Professor North's similar papers – he has written many – suggest that piped music has almost Svengali-like effects on people. Pipe classical music to diners in restaurants, for example, and they will ineluctably spend far more. This is exactly what the purveyors of piped music want to hear.

Professor North – with whom I debated in person once at Trinity College of Music in London – is an amiable man, with nothing of Dr Strangelove about him. He clearly believes his own findings (www.le.ac.uk/psychology/acn5). But it is not unduly sceptical to question the rigour and value of research based on tiny numbers – often five or six shops or restaurants – and without any 'controls' to check whether the supermarkets concerned saw any increases in sales of German/French food during promotions of such product *without* playing German/French music. (A true test would be to play *German* music when *French* food was being promoted. If shoppers then turned away from camembert and baguettes and demanded *Wurst* and black bread, Professor North would have made his point indisputably. There is no mention of such an experiment.)

A glance at commercial reality indicates a situation markedly different from that claimed by piped music's proponents. Large national chains as varied as John Lewis/Waitrose, Primark and Wetherspoons (the pub group) flourish without muzac. In Primark's case, where price is all-important, piped music is avoided simply because it is a waste of money. Royalties, chiefly payable to the Performing Rights Society, can amount to £1 million a year for a large supermarket chain. Alternatively, an in-store radio station has to be set up and run. Primark shrewdly regards both as money down the drain.

Piped music to a captive audience

This focus on shops and restaurants might make Pipedown appear a consumer organization rather like the hugely successful Campaign for Real Ale (CAMRA). (Pipedown did co-sponsor *The Quiet Pint*, a guide to muzac-free pubs compiled by Derek Dempster, which went into six editions. It is now out of print but a new website lists quiet places of all sorts, www.quietcorners. org.uk.) But it soon became obvious that piped music is far more than just a consumer issue. By spreading so pervasively, it has become both a serious health problem and a cause of concern for civil liberties, although few people as yet recognize it as either. The two – health and civil liberties – at times coincide. They do so most notably in hospitals.

Heaven please hear me and let my end come without music or TV!

This cry of anguish comes not from someone being tortured by loud music in a Guantanamo or Abu Ghraib-like prison but from a patient in a National Health Service (NHS) hospital in the UK. So wrote Ray after his experiences as a patient at St James University Hospital, Leeds. (His surname, like those of other patients, has been withheld in case he ever needs to return to the hospital.) Ray went on to say: 'What I dread is not any of the mechanical or biological parts of the treatment; it is the music and bloody TV soundtracks' (UKNA and Pipedown, 2005).

His experience in muzac-filled wards is distressingly typical. Sheila said of the Western General Hospital in Edinburgh: 'The breast clinic which I attended on many occasions had muzac. Also as an in-patient I found Ward 1 had a communal TV set. The chemotherapy Ward 6 had a noisy radio or piped music … Chemotherapy is bad enough without the blood-boiling irritation of muzac!' Michael recently had to endure the competing noise of *five* other television sets all broadcasting different programmes in his ward in New Hall Hospital near Salisbury in Southern England. (This is a private hospital that takes many NHS patients.)

A television set or a music centre is the problem in hospitals more often than piped music per se. For patients lying immobilized in beds or on stretchers, or waiting long hours to see a doctor in outpatients, even a single television playing all the time can be a torment. Patients of course are unusually vulnerable. They are often in no condition, physically or psychologically, to protest at all, being a captive audience indeed, dependent on the very nurses and other health workers who may be causing the noise (from nurses' radios, for example). Equally, if the noise comes from neighbouring patients they may not wish to antagonize them.

The normal ill-effects of noise – that it raises adrenalin and other stress hormone levels and puts up the blood pressure – apply even more strongly when dealing with the acutely sick. No informed person disputes that calm and quiet are essential parts of the healing process, so it is bizarre that such additional noise is considered acceptable.

Some people do like to watch television while in hospital. They can easily do so by using headphones plugged into the relevant television or music centre at the bedside. The best hospitals already practice such a policy but far too many do not. A survey carried out jointly by the UK Noise Association and Pipedown (2002), found that less than half of hospitals across the UK could be called 'quiet' in the sense that they are free of inescapable television or music.

The survey merely confirmed stories that had been coming in for years. Because of them, I approached Robert Key, then MP for Salisbury (my constituency) about ten years ago about the need for a new law. Luckily, he was enthusiastic and tried for a slot for a Private Member's Bill. Unfortunately, he failed to win such a slot (there is keen competition). He did, however, introduce a Ten-Minute Bill in March 2000 to ban piped music and televisions in hospitals and similar places. Like most such bills it was never passed but it served to raise the issue for the first time in the House of Commons.

Six years later, in June 2006, Tim Beaumont, the only representative of the Green Party in the House of Lords to date, proposed a bill along similar lines to 'draw up a plan to prohibit piped music and the showing of television programmes in the public areas of hospitals and on public transport; and to require the wearing of headphones by persons listening to music in the public areas of hospitals and on public transport'. This finally passed the House of Lords in 2008, but Lord Beaumont's death that year meant that the bill was not presented to the House of Commons and has now lapsed.

Such a bill remains one of Pipedown's chief goals. With so many fresh MPs in the new House of Commons, we are hopeful that members of the present parliament will prove more open to recognizing the need to curtail piped music in hospitals and a few similar places that people are forced to attend.

The previous government was markedly uninterested in noise pollution in any form and it chose not to regard piped music as a serious issue at all; the new coalition government might conceivably prove more sympathetic.

Jingle hells or music while you work

One of the most annoying things about piped music is its repetitiveness. This affects shoppers far less than those who work in shops, for obvious reasons. The problem is particularly bad in the run-up to Christmas when, according to the RNID's (1998) survey, some sales assistants will have to listen to 'Jingle Bells' 320 times. This is indeed torture.

Over the years, Pipedown has received many appeals for help from people working in muzac-polluted premises as varied as Waterstone's in Hereford, a factory in Swindon, Marks & Spencer in Epsom and a duty-free shop at Terminal 4, Heathrow Airport. What united them were feelings of despair and powerlessness if they tried to complain about piped music, coupled with a reluctance to stand up and be counted. Fears that any protests could harm their careers and relationships with colleagues – who might label them as eccentric killjoys, ancient has-beens, and so on – were probably justified. Certainly USDAW, the relevant union for workers in shops, has simply not wanted to know about their problems – so I have been forced to conclude after years of getting no replies to letters. But sufferers' reticence makes it hard to help them effectively.

And then Doug Perry came on the scene. Doug Perry was, until very recently, working in the sorting office of Royal Mail's Hull Centre in the North of England. Along with several colleagues he was tormented by the loud music piped throughout the premises. 'Two major concerns are to be addressed', he wrote in an early letter of 15 September 2006. 'First is the volume, set at a level where music became the dominant sound ... to a point where it exceeded machinery noise ... The other [concern] is the all-pervasive nature of the music from which there is no escape.' A survey by the management found, however, that most of the workers concerned wanted the music (a commercial radio station) to continue. Doug and those who felt like him found themselves in a harassed minority.

Minorities have their rights too, however, and sometimes they have their voices. Doug and his friends did not despair or give up. He pointed out that, while the decibel level was below that officially deemed injurious to hearing (85dB), far lower levels of music can cause long-term stress, according to the World Health Organization (WHO). The pleasure the majority working in Hull's sorting office derived from their piped music was at the expense of the ill-health of the minority.

Doug Perry took his complaint further to the appropriate people, the Communication Workers' Union (CWU) and the Health and Safety Executive

(HSE). Both responded with masterly obfuscation, presumably masking indifference. Then he had a stroke of luck. In January 2007, he met his MP Alan Johnson. Johnson, a former General Secretary of the CWU (and once a player in a rock band), proved very sympathetic to his plight – and to Pipedown's arguments in general when I wrote to him later. Johnson wrote pointed letters to Geoffrey Podger, chief executive of the HSE, receiving the routine stuff about the decibel level being under 85dB and so no threat to health (a deeply misleading statement from a psychological viewpoint but within the letter of the current inadequate laws).

Johnson also wrote to Jonathan Shaw, then the relevant minister at the Department for Environment, Food and Rural Affairs (Defra, the UK's environment department, responsible for noise policy) and a man with a reasonable track record on noise, saying that Perry was being 'bombarded with inane disc-jockey chatter at high volume every day of the week … his employer has done virtually nothing to help'. He added that 'there appears to be *a lacuna in our legislative system*' (my italics). Correspondence then followed inconclusively. When Johnson became Minister for Health, he found himself almost in the position of a gamekeeper turned poacher, he had to excuse or overlook offences he had earlier condemned. But in so doing he has effectively proved his earlier point: there *is* a lacuna in our laws.

Perry took early retirement at the beginning of 2010, partly because of the muzac-fouled environment in which he worked. He is now out of the fight but the battle goes on and not just in the UK. At Christmas 2007, some Austrian shop workers sought compensation for suffering from the 'psychological terror' of piped music – 'Silent Night' was a particular unfavourite. The city of Linz, Austria's fourth largest city, has recently declared itself *Beschallungsfrei*, meaning free of unwanted music. Linz gives awards to the best quiet places while naming and shaming the noisiest. Its example is being copied by other Austrian and German cities. It should be emulated across the world.

A recent survey from a British university, the University of Cardiff (Parham and Vizard, 2010) explodes the whole concept of 'music while you work' boosting productivity. Their summary stated that 'results [of their studies] revealed performance to be poorer for both music conditions and the changing-state speech compared to quiet and steady-state speech conditions', silence stimulates real productivity more than piped music.

Yob deterrent and brave new world

Classical music is being played as 'yob deterrent' in a number of public places such as train stations or shopping malls. The music of Bach or Mozart wafting over deserted night-time platforms is said to strike terror into the hearts of potential thugs. It was reputedly first deployed for this purpose in the Netherlands and has since been used in Newcastle and other UK cities. The attractions behind using Mozart's music as an acoustic scarecrow are obvious: the method is relatively cheap; it is unlikely to offend those benefiting from it, whether or not they actually like Mozart; and it *seems* to work.

In the short-term it may work, but not because there is anything magically civilizing or 'deyobbing' about Mozart. (He is a superb composer but he lacks the powers of Orpheus, whose songs charmed wild beasts and even rocks and trees, according to ancient legend.) Classical music is clearly so alien to the experience of potential vandals or muggers that they feel disorientated and threatened by it. But, just as birds soon grow accustomed to scarecrows, sooner or later yobs will discover that piped Mozart does not actually affect them at all. As with many claims for piped music, this rests on a very slender factual basis. And, although it seems an unusually benign use of piped music, it raises issues that go much deeper and have far more sinister implications.

Two of the great dystopian novels of English literature, Aldous Huxley's *Brave New World* (1932) and George Orwell's *1984* (1949) take very different views of how human liberty will be crushed in the future. Huxley foresaw early (indeed prenatal) conditioning, soft-drugs and casual sex reducing even the most intelligent people to doped acquiescence, stupefied by piped music. Orwell, more grimly, foresaw a 'boot stamping on a human face – forever' finally having the same effect to the crunch of breaking bones and cartilage. On one point they were equally prophetic, however: the incessant background noise produced by televisions that can *never be turned off*. (In *1984* television sets spy on the viewers, a sophistication yet to come). This helps to intimidate or befuddle the cowed inhabitants yet further.

In *Clockwork Orange* (1962), Anthony Burgess's remarkable dystopian novel (later filmed by Stanley Kubrick), the psychopathically violent but intelligent narrator Alex has one potentially redeeming feature in his life: his love of music, especially Beethoven's Ninth Symphony. This very music is then used, as part of the 'Ludovico Technique', to help condition Alex so that he can no longer commit acts of violence. The misuse of great music is, of course, a common feature of some of the worst totalitarian regimes.

Conclusion

'Music has charms to sooth a savage breast', wrote the playwright Congreve 300 years ago, and the piped music industry is certainly not alone in agreeing with him. The muzac-purveyors may genuinely see their products as making people happier, or at least tranquillizing them in an agreeable way. No one disputes that music has unique powers, appeal and benefits that other sounds, even the most pleasing, generally lack for humanity. For this very reason music *when misused* has also unique powers to harm and to distress people even at relatively low volumes.

Unwanted music – loud, inescapable, unwanted, unceasing music – is now a notorious form of torture in the world's worst prisons. The music so viciously used is not composed and played by special bands of musical torturers but is simply particularly aggressive music played extremely loudly, inescapably and non-stop – these are definitions also of piped music. Garret Keizer (2010) in his recent book on noise points out that there are echoes of the fascistic Ubermensch about some rock stars who ram their music into the bodies of listeners, willing or otherwise.

This particular parallel may be thought contentious, but it is recognized that it is the powerless in society who suffer the most from noise in any form. In 1969, the International Music Council of the United Nations Educational, Scientific and Cultural Organization (UNESCO) passed unanimously a resolution upholding the 'right of everyone to silence, because of the abusive use, in private and public places, of recorded or broadcast music' which constitutes 'an intolerable infringement of individual freedom' (Schafer, 1970).

These are fine ennobling sentiments, but more than 40 years on they remain simply that. What is needed, in the UK and around the world, is legislation to protect workers – in department stores, post offices or on aircraft, where cabin crew can be even more maddened by repetitive in flight music than passengers – as well as patients immobilized and powerless in beds or on stretchers. There is no question here of consumer choice but of civil liberties being repeatedly abused and of the health of the public being imperilled – for no real reason other than to please a vocal yet relatively small industry. The fact that in some places at some times more people may like the music being piped than dislike it – as in Hull postal sorting office – in no way invalidates UNESCO's points. Headphones exist, after all, and can be used by those who cannot live without a constant stream of music. (Some people are now effectively addicted to non-stop music – a problem, perhaps, but quite another issue.)

One last survey sums the situation up. According to a study of 115 blood donors at Nottingham Medical School Hospital (British Psychological Association, 1995), playing piped music made donors *more* nervous before giving blood and *more* depressed afterwards than silence. What the donors (who are all volunteers in the UK) objected to most, the survey found, was *their utter lack of control* over the music being played. The problem of piped music in a nutshell.

References

British Psychological Association (1995) 'Proceedings', January, British Psychological Association, London

Keizer, G. *(2010) The Unwanted Sound of Everything We Want: A Book About Noise,* PublicAffairs Books, New York

North, A., Hargreaves, D. and McKendrick, J. (1999) 'The influence of in-store music on wine selections', *Journal of Applied Psychology*, vol 84, pp271–276

Parham, N. and Vizard, J. (2010) 'Can preference for background music mediate the irrelevant sound effect?' published online *Applied Cognitive Psychology*, http://onlinelibrary.wiley.com/doi/10.1002/acp.1731/full

RNID (Royal National Institute for the Deaf) (1998) *Musak: Music to Whose Ears?*, Royal National Institute for the Deaf, London

Schafer, M. (1970) *The Book of Noise*, Arcana, Ontario

Sunday Times (1997) 15 February

UKNA (UK Noise Association) and Pipedown (2005) *Whose Choice is it Anyway? Piped Music and Freedom*, UKNA/Pipedown, London

CHAPTER 9

Noise and the Law

FRANCIS MCMANUS

*Some of the laws are useful; others do not seem to be adequate.
But all law is only as good as its enforcement.*

In this chapter, we look at noise law. The main focus is on the UK, but the
chapter also has sections on noise law in Europe, including European Human
Rights law, Australia and the US. The purpose of this chapter is to show what
role law can perform in noise policy. We felt that this could be best done by
concentrating in some detail on a few countries rather than attempting a more
superficial look at noise law across many nations. We have not tried to make
any assessment of whether noise law in the countries we have chosen to highlight is better or worse than in other countries.

The chapter looks at the law as it applies to neighbourhood, transport
and industrial noise (including construction noise). Each section starts with
a summary of the key points. This should be particularly useful to the general
reader as the more detailed arguments are principally aimed at those people
more closely involved with noise law.

We start with the UK.

Neighbour and neighbourhood noise

Summary

The key piece of legislation is the Environmental Protection Act 1990. It requires
a local authority officer to investigate a noise complaint. If the officer decides
the noise is a nuisance, as defined by the Act, the local authority can take the
noise-maker to court. Individuals can also use the Act to take the noise-maker
to court without going through a local authority. The weakness in the Act is
its very tight definition of 'nuisance'. It means many cases are never taken to
court. However, there are other laws which can be used to get round this. The
Crime and Disorder Act 1998[1] allows a local authority to lodge a complaint to a
magistrate's court if it believes that a person has acted in an anti-social manner.

If the noise occurs at night, the Noise Act 1996, which lays down strict rules of conduct, can be used. Before 1960, the only way to take action on noise was through the common law of nuisance, but it is used much less frequently now as it has been largely overtaken by legislation. Local authorities also have powers to control noise through the planning system – they can refuse a planning application on noise grounds or can impose conditions when granting an application. They may, for example, limit the opening hours of licensed premises.

Statutory nuisance

In the UK, the vast majority of neighbour and neighbourhood noise complaints are dealt with by a local authority using the statutory nuisance provisions under the Environmental Protection Act 1990. Under this Act,[2] noise (which includes vibration) ranks as a statutory nuisance. This is the key piece of legislation. It largely excludes noise from industrial activities that fall under the Pollution Prevention and Control Act 1999 regime. It also excludes transport noise. The Environmental Protection Act places a mandatory duty on a local authority to investigate a noise complaint that it receives.[3] If a local authority is of the opinion that a noise nuisance exists, it must serve an abatement notice on the responsible person. It has no discretion.[4] The person on whom the notice is served can appeal against the notice either to the magistrates court or to the sheriff in Scotland.[5] If the person on whom the notice is served, without reasonable excuse, contravenes or fails to comply with the notice he commits an offence.[6] The Environmental Protection Act also allows a private individual to take summary action in the magistrates' court or before the sheriff.[7] This, though, can turn out to be costly.

We now look at other legislation which can be used to tackle neighbour or neighbourhood noise.

Noise Act 1996

An attempt to break away from nuisance-based law was made by the Noise Act 1996, which covers England and Wales. The Noise Act gives local authorities additional powers to deal with night-time noise, defined as the period from 11pm–7am.[8] In summary, the Noise Act[9] allows a warning notice to be served on a person who is responsible for noise (or in the case of licensed premises, the licensee[10]), which exceeds the permitted level, that is to say, a predetermined level that has been set by central government, currently 35dB(A). It is an offence for a person on whom a warning notice has been served to exceed the permitted level of noise without reasonable excuse. An important feature of the Noise Act is that it allows fixed penalty notices to be served on the relevant person if the officer has reason to believe that the person is committing or has just committed an offence.[11] In Scotland, Part 5 of the Antisocial Behaviour (Scotland) Act 2004 contains similar provisions.

Anti-social behaviour legislation

The Crime and Disorder Act (1998)[12] allows a local authority to lodge a complaint to a magistrates court if it believes that any person has acted in an anti-social manner, that is to say, in a manner that caused or was likely to cause harassment, alarm or distress or was likely to cause alarm or distress to one or more persons not of the same household as himself. Noise would clearly be included in this definition of 'anti-social'. The magistrates court may, if it believes that anti-social behaviour has taken place, make an anti-social behaviour order (ASBO). The Antisocial Behaviour Act (Part 6) also allows a local authority to close noisy licensed premises. The Act has been recently amended to allow the police to close premises where a person has engaged in anti-social behaviour or the use of the premises is associated with significant and persistent disorder or persistent serious nuisance to members of the public.[13]

Control of Pollution Act 1974

As far as street noise is concerned, the Control of Pollution Act 1974[14] makes it an offence to operate a loudspeaker between 2100 and 0800hrs for any purpose and at any other time for the purpose of advertising any entertainment, trade or business. There are some exceptions to this, such as loudspeakers that are used by the emergency services.

Using planning law

Town and Country Planning law has an important role to play in controlling noise. Most new developments require planning permission. When a planning authority is considering an application the relevant planning authority must take into account the potential for the development to generate noise as well as the extent to which the development will be affected by noise. It can reject the application on noise grounds or it can impose conditions that regulate noise from the development. If the individual who has been granted planning permission flouts a planning condition, the planning authority can take action against him.

Licensed premises

Licensed premises are perennially a potential source of noise. In order to attract custom, licensed premises are increasingly providing entertainment for their patrons ranging from live music, karaoke and discotheques to simple jukeboxes. Licensing authorities have the power under licensing laws to impose conditions on the grant of a license. Such conditions can be used to control noise from the premises. For example, a condition could be imposed to the effect that no noise is discernible at the boundary of the premises.

Local authority bylaws

Local authorities in the UK have the power[15] to make bylaws for the good rule and government, and for the suppression of nuisances in its area. Bylaws could be used, therefore, to proscribe certain types of conduct that generate noise, for example, busking. In Scotland, the Civic Government (Scotland) Act[16] 1982 gives the police the power to deal with specific types of noise.

Common law

Before 1960, the only way to take action on noise was through the common law of nuisance, but it is used much less frequently now as it has been largely overtaken by other legislation. But over the years, a number of noise nuisance cases have been decided by the courts where a wide variety of noise sources have been held to constitute nuisance at common law. The list includes noise from printworks,[17] building works,[18] domestic birds,[19] cattle,[20] an oil refinery,[21] an unruly family,[22] a go-kart track,[23] pigeons[24] and a nursery.[25] This list is by no means exhaustive but gives the reader some idea of the wide variety of sources of noise pollution that can rank as a nuisance in law. In time more factors may be added to the list. (In English law there is no need to prove fault to establish a nuisance,[26] but in Scottish law it must be proven that the defender is at fault in some way.[27])

What constitutes a nuisance under common law?

For noise to rank as a nuisance in law, the activity that generates the noise must be deemed unreasonable. It needs to be more than the everyday noise of people going about their normal business as was illustrated in the House of Lords case *Baxter v Camden LBC*.[28]

The courts take a variety of factors into account when deciding if a noise ranks as a nuisance. However, all of the factors listed below are not automatically applied in every nuisance case. Rather, the courts have tended to emphasize several factors to the exclusion of others. Furthermore, it is possible that each factor may be accorded different weighting in the judicial scales. The factors courts will typically take into account are:

1. *The sensitivity of the claimant.* The courts are unwilling to assist people who are oversensitive to noise. In the leading case of *Heath v Brighton Corporation*[29] it was held by the court that the claimant who said that he was adversely affected by the low frequency noise from the defendants' electricity generating station had no remedy in law because he possessed hyper-sensitive hearing.
2. *Whether the nuisance could have been avoided by the claimant doing something about it.* For example, if somebody was affected by the noise from a

go-kart track near their house, the courts would not take into account the fact that the noise from the track could be mitigated by the installation of double-glazing. The courts are reluctant to put the person bringing a noise nuisance case under any legal obligation to either avoid completely or simply mitigate the effects of a nuisance.[30]

3. *The usefulness of the activity.* The more socially useful an activity is, the less likely will the court be willing to rule that it constitutes a nuisance.[31] For example, noise which is caused by a house party is more likely to rank as a nuisance than noise from (say) a factory or wind-farm since the two latter activities are deemed more useful.

4. *The motive of the defendant.* If the noise is being made simply to annoy the claimant, the courts lean heavily towards the view that it is a nuisance in law. The leading case is *Christie v Davey.*[32]

5. *The type of area where the noise occurs.* The basic rule is that the more typical the alleged noise is of the area, the less likely will the court regard it as a nuisance on the grounds that those who live in the area will have become used to it and, therefore, less likely to be annoyed by it. However, this does not give the maker of the noise carte blanche to create a nuisance.[33]

6. *The duration and intensity of the noise.* The longer the noise persists and the louder it is the more likely it is to be deemed a nuisance.[34]

7. *The time it occurs.* Noise which takes place during the night is more likely to constitute a nuisance than if it takes place during the day.[35]

8. *Whether it is typical of modern life.* There is some authority to the effect that, if an adverse state of affairs is caused by something that is typical of modern life, for example, tall buildings[36] or perhaps aeroplanes, the state of affairs is less likely to rank as a nuisance.

9. *How long the claimant has put up with the noise.* The claimant will not succeed in a nuisance action if he has put up with the noise for more than 20 years. However, for the defence to succeed, it must be shown that the nuisance has remained substantially constant[37] over the prescriptive period and also an actionable nuisance during the same period.[38]

10. *Whether the noise has been authorized by a statutory authority.* If the nuisance has been caused by activity, which has been authorized by an Act of Parliament, the claimant has no remedy under the law of nuisance.[39]

11. *Whether the claimant moved to the noise.* It is *no* defence that the claimant has come to the nuisance.[40] For example, if one decides to live in close proximity to a noisy pub one can still avail oneself of the law of nuisance.

Noise from industry

Summary

This section deals with using the law to control the impact of noise from industry on 'outsiders'. It does not look at the affect noise has on the workforce.

Noise pollution from industrial activities is regulated by the Pollution Prevention and Control Act 1999, which in turn implements European Union (EU) Directive 96/61/EC that requires member states to set up a licensing system for the activities that are listed in the Directive. Essentially, this is done by imposing conditions when granting a permit. If the conditions are breached, remedial action can be taken. Under the earlier Control of Pollution Act 1974 local authorities can designate areas noise abatement zones. The *raison d'être* of a noise abatement zone is to prevent 'creeping noise', that is noise that gradually increases with the passage of time. Local authorities have also got wide powers under the Control of Pollution Act 1974[41] to deal with construction noise.

Industrial activities

Pollution, including noise pollution, from many industrial activities is now regulated under the integrated pollution regime that was instituted by the Pollution Prevention and Control Act 1999, which, in turn, implements Directive 96/61/EC that requires member states to set up a command and control licensing system in relation to the activities that are listed in the Directive. A variety of installations are included in the new regime. The appropriate regulatory authority (the Environment Agency and local authorities in England and Wales and the Scottish Environment Protection in Scotland) is required to impose conditions on the granting of a permit. If a condition is breached the enforcing authority can take appropriate remedial action.

Construction site noise

Local authorities have got wide powers under the Control of Pollution Act 1974[42] to deal with construction noise. A local authority can serve a notice imposing requirements as to the way in which the works have to be carried out. The notice, which can be served on the builder or other person having control over the carrying out of the works, for example, the owner of the premises, may *inter alia* specify the plant or machinery that is to be used. It may also specify the hours during which the works may be carried out and the level of noise that may be emitted from the premises. The person who intends to carry out construction works can also apply to the relevant local authority for consent. The local authority may attach conditions to the consent. If they are complied with, the local authority is excluded from taking statutory action against the builder but private individuals are not.

Noise abatement zones

The most innovative provisions of the Control of Pollution Act 1974 are those that deal with noise abatement zones. Such zones are made by a local authority order. The Act allows a local authority to designate all or part of it a noise abatement zone.[43] Wide discretion is given to local authorities as to which premises are included in the order. In practice, local authorities have tended to confine relevant noise abatement orders to industrial and commercial premises or places of entertainment but need not do so. The procedure for setting up a noise abatement zone is set out in Schedule 1 to the Act. The *raison d'être* of a noise abatement zone is to prevent 'creeping noise', that is noise that gradually increases with the passage of time. After the noise abatement zone has been established the local authority is required to measure the level of noise that emanates from the premises to which the order relates, and then record the measurements in a register which must be kept by the authority.[44] The Act gives the local authorities powers to reduce noise if the noise levels are not acceptable for the purposes for which the order was made. About 60 noise abatement zones thus far have been established in England, but none in Scotland.

Transport noise

Summary

There is a large body of law covering transport noise but a lot of it is of limited use to people disturbed by aircraft, traffic or rail noise. Section 76(1) of the Civil Aviation Act 1982 makes it very difficult to take legal action against noise from aircraft. It is similar in the case of rail. Since the power to construct a railway derives from an Act of Parliament, it is most likely that any legal action against either Network Rail or the various train companies would fail by virtue of the defence of statutory authority,[45] since the activity from which the noise is coming has been authorized by an Act of Parliament. It may be possible, though, to take action against the growing problem of train horns. There is no legal provision to take action against increased levels of road noise. It is this lack of legal remedy to deal with aircraft, rail and traffic noise that has forced people to turn to the European Court of Human Rights. That is dealt with in the next section of this chapter. This section outlines transport noise law in the UK. Most of the law concerns the regulations that the manufacturers of vehicles and aircraft are required by law to follow.

Noise from aircraft

Aircraft can annoy the community either while the aircraft is in flight or after the aircraft is preparing to take off or has landed at an airport. The relevant statutory controls over aircraft noise can be roughly divided into those that relate to the control of noise from the flight of the aircraft, and those that specifically relate to the control of noise from aerodromes.

Flight noise

Section 76(1) of the Civil Aviation Act 1982 makes it very difficult to take legal action against noise from aircraft. However, some legislation does apply specifically to aviation. Annex 16 of the Chicago Convention on International Civil Aviation, signed in 1944, deals specifically with aircraft noise. More recently, the European Commission (EC) has introduced a number of directives that are based on agreements made under the aegis of the International Civil Aviation Organization. As far as the UK is concerned, the relevant provisions of both the Chicago Convention and the appropriate EC Directives are implemented by orders which are made under s60(3)(r) of the Civil Aviation Act 1982. The general aim of this legislation is to gradually phase out the use of noisier aircraft. Additionally, the Air Navigation (Environmental Standards) Order 2002[46] states that certain types of aircraft, namely, supersonic, microlight aeroplanes and helicopters, may not land or take off in the UK unless a noise certificate has been issued by the Civil Aviation Authority (CAA).

Noise certification (for all subsonic aircraft) is governed by the Aeroplane Noise Regulations 1999.[47] All civil propeller-driven aeroplanes which are registered in the UK and fall within the categories which are set out in Volume 1 of Annex 16/1981 of the International Civil Aviation Convention are required to be in possession of a noise certificate, which is granted by the CAA.[48] Similar requirements apply to civil subsonic jets which are registered in the UK.[49] The CAA must grant a noise certificate if it is satisfied that the aeroplane complies with the standard which is specified in the regulations.[50]

Under the Air Navigation Order 2009,[51] the Secretary of State may make Rules of the Air that regulate the manner in which aircraft may move or fly over the country. It is an offence to fail to comply with the rules. The current rules of the air are the Rules of the Air Regulations 2007.[52] The regulations[53] prohibit low flying. The main aim of the regulations is to protect those on the ground from planes crashing but the provision has also some relevance as far as the impact of noise on communities is concerned. Of further relevance is the provision that aircraft may not take off or land within an aerodrome traffic zone unless the aircraft has obtained the permission of the air traffic control unit.[54] In practice, this power is often used to regulate the flight of aircraft in such a way as to reduce the noise from aircraft to those living in the vicinity of the aerodrome.

Airport noise

Under Section 77 of the Civil Aviation Act 1982, provision can be made by way of an Air Navigation Order for regulating the conditions under which noise and vibration may be caused by aircraft on aerodromes. As long as the provisions of the order are complied with, no action in respect of nuisance can be taken. The Air Navigation Order 2009[55] allows the Secretary of State to prescribe the conditions under which noise from aircraft may be caused on aerodromes. The Order also provides that Section 77 of the 1982 Act applies to any aerodrome in relation to which the Secretary of State has prescribed appropriate conditions regulating noise. Therefore, no action lies in the law of nuisance in relation to such airports if the requisite conditions have been complied with.

An important control over noise from aerodromes was introduced by the Aerodromes (Noise Restrictions) (Rules and Procedures) Regulations 2003,[56] which implements EU Directive 2002/30 that relates to the introduction of noise-related operating restrictions at UK airports. The regulations apply to city airports and also to civil airports that have more than 50,000 take-offs and landings of civil subsonic jet aeroplanes per calendar year.[57] In summary, the regulations allow the relevant competent authority[58] to operate flight operating restrictions in order to reduce noise. The competent authority is required to adopt a balanced and proportionate approach in dealing with noise problems. Economic incentives may also be used.[59]

Planning law also has an important role to play in relation to noise from aerodromes. Planning authorities can impose conditions on the granting of planning permission in relation to a new aerodrome, or, when a new aerodrome is constructed, or an existing aerodrome is extended or a new terminal is constructed.

Military aircraft

Noise from military aircraft, airfields, ground-running and testing of engines and low flying aircraft presents a particular problem.[60] The problem is compounded by the fact that the design of military aircraft is such that military aircraft have more capacity to create noise than civil aircraft. The legal controls that relate to noise from civil aircraft are inapplicable to military aircraft. The Crown is generally immune from civil action in respect of noise from military aircraft.[61] However, the Ministry of Defence (MoD) keeps noise from military aircraft under constant review through its Noise Panel, which has no statutory status. Since 1985, the MoD has provided noise compensation schemes for those living in the vicinity of military airfields. These *ex gratia* compensation schemes are comparable to those that are in operation at Heathrow and Gatwick. Furthermore, the MoD is also prepared to financially compensate owners of dwellings that have depreciated in value as a result of noise and other physical factors resulting either from the creation of new airfields or the extension of existing airfields.

Railway noise

As in the case of aircraft noise, it is difficult to take legal action against noise from trains. Since the power to construct a railway derives from an Act of

Parliament and not under normal planning procedures, it is most likely that any action either by way of common law or statutory nuisance against either Network Rail or the various train companies would fail by virtue of the defence of statutory authority,[62] the activity from which the noise is coming has been authorized by an Act of Parliament. The Noise Insulation (Railways and Other Guided Transport Systems) Regulations[63] impose a duty on the authority which is responsible for constructing *inter alia* railways under statute to provide certain buildings with insulation against noise or to pay for insulation work to be carried out to such buildings.

It may be possible, though, to take action against train horns. The use of horns is governed by the provisions of a document, known as the Master Rule Book. It has no statutory force. However, train drivers must comply with it.

Road traffic noise

The Road Traffic Act 1988[64] allows the Secretary of State to make regulations that, *inter alia*, govern the use of motor vehicles on roads and the conditions under which they can be used, and give him the power to make regulations that relate to the construction and use of vehicles. The main regulations presently governing the construction and use of vehicles are the Road Vehicles (Construction and Use) Regulations 1986.[65] The regulations make provision for every vehicle that is propelled by an internal combustion engine to be fitted with an exhaust system including a silencer, both of which are required to be maintained in good and efficient working order.[66] The regulations also make provision in relation to noise limits that must not be exceeded.[67] Furthermore, no motor vehicle may be used in such a manner as to cause excessive noise that could have been avoided by the exercise of reasonable care on the part of the driver.[68] The Motor Vehicles (Type Approval)(Great Britain) Regulations 1984[69] make provision for both noise and also silencers in respect of vehicles.

Brief mention should be made of the Noise Insulation Regulations 1975.[70] Under these regulations, where the use of a highway that opened to the public after 1972 or an additional carriageway has been or is about to be constructed since that date causes or is expected to cause noise at a level that is specified in the regulations, then the appropriate authority (for example, a roads authority) is required to carry out insulation work itself or make the appropriate grant in respect of carrying out the insulation work. Grants, though, are only available, subject to certain exceptions, in respect of dwellings and other buildings which are used for residential purposes. But it is near impossible to take legal action simply against traffic noise as such.

Noise and human rights

Summary

It is now possible for people who are affected by noise to take action under the European Convention of Human Rights (ECHR). Key sections of the ECHR, in particular Article 8, guarantee the right to peaceful enjoyment of property and possessions. The human rights legislation on noise has still to be fully tested but there have been some major cases that have begun to clarify matters.

The key cases, outlined below, show that:

- excessive noise that the authorities allow to continue for years can breach Article 8 (*Oluic v Croatia*);
- seriously disturbing traffic noise can infringe Article 8 (*Andrews v Reading Borough Council*);
- significant compensation can be awarded to residents who had to endure noise from military aircraft (*Dennis v Ministry of Defence*);
- but noise only infringes Article 8 in particular circumstances: other factors need to be taken into account – such as rights of aircraft passengers or airlines to make a profit (*Hatton v The United Kingdom*);
- the intensity and duration of the nuisance, its physical or mental effects, the general context and whether the noise complained of was negligible in comparison to the environmental hazards inherent to life in every modern city (*Fadeyeva v Russia* and *Galev v Bulgaria*);
- Article 8 has a subsidiary role – national authorities are, in principle, better placed than an international court to evaluate local needs and conditions (*Galev v Bulgaria* and *Greenpeace EV v Germany*). These decisions suggest that, for the court to rule that Article 8 has been breached, the noise annoyance must be at least as great as would be deemed a noise nuisance under UK law.

The ECHR

Until recently individuals who have been affected by noise pollution have either had to resort to the common law of nuisance in order to obtain redress or, alternatively, persuade the relevant local authority or other regulatory agency such as the Environment Agency to take appropriate action under statute. It is now possible for people who are affected by noise to take action under the ECHR. Article 8 and Article 1 of Protocol No 1 of the ECHR guarantee respect for family life and home as well as the right to peaceful enjoyment of property and possessions. The human rights legislation on noise has still to be fully tested but there have been some major cases which have begun to clarify matters.

The most recent case under Article 8 of the ECHR is *Oluic v Croatia*.[71] In this case, the applicant had been subjected to excessive noise. The national authorities allowed this state of affairs to persist for almost eight years. The court held that the state had failed to discharge its positive obligation to guarantee the applicant's right to respect for her home and family life. Therefore, there had been a violation of Article 8.

In *Andrews v Reading Borough Council* [72] it was held that an increase in traffic noise that seriously affects an individual may engage Article 8. Collins, J. went on to state that whether an increased level of noise crossed the threshold was a question of fact.

In *Dennis v Ministry of* Defence,[73] the claimants lived on a huge private estate, overflown by very noisy jets from the nearby Royal Air Force Wittering base. The noise proved unbearable for the residents. The court ruled the noise from the jets amounted to both a nuisance at common law and also breached both Articles 8 and 1 of Protocol No 1 of the ECHR. However, the judge thought it inappropriate to grant an injunction against the MoD from flying the jets over the estate, given its national importance to the defence of the country. Instead, the claimant was granted considerable damages. There is some doubt as to whether *Dennis* would be followed in Scotland.[74]

In *Hatton v The United Kingdom* [75] an action was brought against the UK government by a group of residents who lived under the flight path of Heathrow Airport. They claimed the noise from the aircraft at night flouted Article 8 of the ECHR. The court found there is no explicit right to a clean and quiet environment[76] but it held that, where an individual was both directly and also seriously affected by noise or some other form of pollution, it was possible that Article 8 could be contravened. It went on to state that Article 8 could be contravened equally by either a positive act on the part of the state or, as was the case here, by the failure of the government to protect citizens from noise, however, it found that, in the latter situation, the court enjoys a wide margin of appreciation in determining which steps are required to be taken in order to secure compliance with the ECHR.[77] In the last analysis, the court was of the view that, in this case, a fair balance had been struck by the government between the competing interests of individuals who had been affected by the noise and the community as a whole.[78]

In *Fadeyeva v Russia*,[79] which concerned pollution, including noise, from a steel plant, the court held that the adverse effects of environmental pollution must attain a minimum level if Article 8 is to be engaged. Furthermore, the assessment of that minimum level is relative and depends upon all the circumstances of the case, such as the intensity and duration of the nuisance, as well as its physical and mental effects. The general environmental context should also be taken into account.

In *Gomez v Spain*,[80] the applicant lived in a flat in a residential quarter of Valencia. Since 1974, the Valencia City council had allowed licensed premises such as bars, pubs and discotheques to open in the vicinity of her home, thereby making it very difficult for people who lived in the area to sleep. The applicant claimed that this state of affairs amounted to a breach under Article

8 on the grounds that, whereas the council was not the direct source of the noise pollution, it had caused the adverse state of affairs in question by issuing an unlimited number of licences without taking the requisite measures to reduce the noise. Gomez claimed that, in sharp contrast to the circumstances in *Hatton,* her home was neither in nor adjacent to an area that was relevant to a strategic transport or communications infrastructure. The court found that, whereas the object of Article 8 is essentially to protect the individual against arbitrary interference by public authorities, it may also place an affirmative duty on authorities to secure compliance with Article 8 in terms of relations between individuals themselves. In the last analysis, on the facts of the case Article 8 had been infringed.

In *Galev v Bulgaria,*[81] it was claimed that *inter alia* the noise and smell from a newly established dental surgery in a block of flats breached Article 8. The court held that it would have to be shown that the alleged nuisance attained a minimum level of severity. In determining this issue, one was required to take into account the intensity and duration of the nuisance, its physical or mental effects, the general context and also whether the detriment complained of was negligible in comparison to the environmental hazards inherent to life in every modern city. In the court's view, the noise which emanated from the dentist's surgery did not contravene Article 8 of the ECHR.[82] Of fundamental importance is the fact that the ECHR has a subsidiary role and that national authorities are, in principle, better placed than an international court to evaluate local needs and conditions.

In *Greenpeace EV v Germany,*[83] the court, after reiterating this point, stated that the complexity of issues regarding environmental protection renders the court's role a subsidiary one and its power of review is necessarily limited. These decisions suggest that, for the court to rule that Article 8 has been breached, the noise annoyance must be at least as great as would be deemed a noise nuisance under UK law.

The EU and Noise

Summary

Until the early 1990s, the EU regarded noise as a local issue and, therefore, did not get involved. That changed when it became clear that noise could have an impact on people's health. The Fifth Environment Action Programme, published in 1993, said nobody should be exposed to noise levels which endanger health and quality of life. It was followed by a Green Paper in 1996 and the Sixth Environment Action Programme in 2001, which set targets to cut noise. Much of the Action Programme, but not the targets, were embedded in EU Noise Directive (2002), which requires member states to produce noise maps and noise action plans.

Action by the EU

In 1985, Rehbinder and Stewart scathingly described the EU's approach to noise as, 'no more than a regulatory patchwork'.[84] Tacitly, noise was treated as a local matter which was best dealt with by individual member states. Noise did not warrant special attention on the part of the EU. A possible explanation for such a 'hands-off' approach to noise on the part of the EU is that, until recently, noise was not really associated with harm to human health.

However, a change of direction was seen in the Fifth Environment Action Programme, published in 1993,[85] which dealt with the problem of urban noise. Under the programme, a general environmental objective was established, to the effect that no person should be exposed to noise levels that endanger health and quality of life. This approach to noise was somewhat revolutionary, certainly in terms of the traditional UK approach to noise control, in that the programme expressly recognized an environmental right, as it were, in relation to noise pollution. Targets for reduced exposure to noise were set out in the programme. It was of importance that a link was drawn between environmental noise and human health.

The Fifth Environment Action Programme was followed in 1996 by the EC Green Paper, *Future Noise Policy*.[86] The EC accepted the view that, whereas the *impact* of noise is, essentially, a local responsibility and therefore best dealt with by member states themselves, the *sources* of noise problems are not of local origin and are therefore best dealt with at EU level. However, it is not really useful to make a sharp distinction between the source of noise and its impact, since they are often inextricably intermeshed. For example, the manner in which a particular product impacts on the local community depends not only on the capacity of the product to generate noise but, of course, also on the manner in which the product is used by its owner. But the Green Paper was nevertheless very important in that it recognized noise pollution as a human health problem. It also identified that the lack of available data on noise was a fundamental drawback to the formulation of a coherent noise policy. This unfortunate situation was compounded by the lack of uniform noise assessment methods that, in turn, led to poor data on the extent of environmental noise as well as the exchange of information on the subject of noise exposure between states.

The Sixth Environment Action Programme was published in 2001.[87] It expressly recognized that noise was a growing problem in the community that affected both the health and also the quality of life of at least 25 per cent of the EU population. The EC also acknowledged that noise raises stress levels and increases the risk of heart disease. Much of the noise problem was associated with transport noise. The programme set an objective to reduce the number of people regularly affected by noise – an estimated 100 million in 2000 – by around 10 per cent by 2010, and around 20 per cent by 2020. Furthermore, the EC re-emphasized that a uniform system of noise assessment should be introduced by way of legislation in order to achieve a common understanding and language on noise. The production of noise maps was considered to be a valuable means of informing the public about environmental noise.

The policy that was embedded in the Sixth Environment Action Programme found expression in 2002 in an EU Directive entitled, 'The assessment and management of environmental noise',[88] commonly known as the Environmental Noise Directive (END).

The Environmental Noise Directive

The general aim of END is to reduce people's exposure to noise that is emitted from major sources, in particular, roads and railways. END also seeks to harmonize noise indicators and assessment methods. Its objective is to establish a common EU framework for the assessment and management of exposure to environmental noise[89] by using common methods of noise measurement and furthermore, and importantly, ensuring that such information is made available to the public.[90] The scope of END is wide-ranging and applies to environmental noise to which humans are exposed, particularly in built-up areas, in public parks or other quiet areas in an agglomeration (in effect, towns with a population of more than 100,000),[91] in quiet areas in the open country, near schools, hospitals and other noise-sensitive buildings and areas. END does not cover domestic noise.

Noise maps and action plans

END requires member states to draw up noise maps for agglomerations, major roads, major railways and major airports.[92] The noise maps, which are required to use common indicators and assessment methods, cover agglomerations with more than 250,000 people, major roads with more than 6 million vehicle movements per year, major railways and major civil airports. Noise maps relating to smaller agglomerations and roads with fewer vehicle movements will follow.

Action plans

By 18 July 2008,[93] action plans should have been drawn up to indicate how the EU countries were going to deal with the noisiest areas identified in the maps and to protect quiet areas. The production of the action plans is behind schedule. After the noise maps and relevant action plans are prepared, the information must be sent to the EC, which is required to set up a data bank of information on noise maps. The EC is also required to publish a summary report on noise maps and action plans every five years and is required to submit to the European Parliament and the Council of the EU a report on the implementation of END.

The US

We now turn, briefly, to the US. In 1972, the US Congress passed the Noise Control Act in which it declared that it was the policy of the US to promote an environment for all Americans that would free them from noise that could jeopardize their health and well-being. This Act was not rescinded and from a legal perspective is still the law. At the time it passed this Act, Congress gave the Office of Noise Abatement and Control (ONAC) in the Department of Environmental Protection the obligation to enforce this act. During its early years, the ONAC published many documents highlighting the dangers of noise to our mental and physical health, established noise emission standards for certain categories of construction and transportation equipment, provided the Federal Aviation Administration (FAA) with scientific and technical information on noise and reached out to state environmental agencies to assist them in passing and carrying out activities to lessen noise.

However, when President Ronald Reagan came into office in 1981, ONAC lost most of its funding with Reagan declaring that noise abatement was best dealt with at the local level. However, the local levels were being assisted in their noise efforts by the federal government and so when the federal office eliminated their funding, the local offices essentially dropped their noise programmes. It should be pointed out, however, that the federal government does oversee some noise programmes: the Department of Transportation develops noise standards for highway construction, the Occupational Safety and Health Administration oversees noise in the workplace, the FAA controls aircraft noise. The Environmental Protection Agency (EPA) has limited noise control abilities, for example, regulating noise of motorcycles, and information on their activities can be accessed by going to its website (www.epa.gov). However, for the most part, the federal government largely curtailed its efforts to protect its citizens, despite the fact that the law obligating them to do so is still in force.

The increase in studies linking noise to health and the appearance of anti-noise groups, which have been able to interact among themselves as the result of the internet, has resulted in citizens pressuring city and state officials to pass their own noise ordinances. New York City was unique in that it had enacted a detailed Noise Code in 1972 and, recognizing the limits of this older code to adequately address growing numbers of complaints in New York City, it revised and updated its code in 2007. Information on New York City's Noise Code can be found at New York City's Department of Environmental Protection website www.nyc.gov. Information on ordinances in cities and states across the US can be found at www.noiseoff.org.

Australia

Summary

In Australia, noise is mainly, but not exclusively, regulated at state level. In this summary, we highlight some of the most interesting features from each state. South Australia, for example, has a very comprehensive planning Act that covers all its development proposals. Western Australia and Victoria also have extensive planning legislation. Western Australia has interesting regulations that categorize properties into how noise-sensitive they might be – for example, residential properties are regarded as more noise-sensitive than industrial premises. Western Australia, along with the Northern Territories, also has legislation that requires some consumer goods to use labelling to indicate the amount of noise they make. The Northern Territories has an interesting summary offence that enables action to be taken speedily against noise-makers. New South Wales has a holistic legal framework that covers all aspects of environmental pollution from industrial noise to neighbour noise. Sections of Tasmania's noise law are driven by health considerations. We will look at each state in turn.

South Australia

In South Australia, excessive noise is regulated by the Environment Protection Act 1993 and the Environment Protection (Noise) Policy 2007. It forbids activities, including noise, that pollute or might pollute the environment unless all reasonable and practical measures are taken to prevent or minimize the resulting environmental harm. Failure to comply is not an offence, but the person concerned may be liable to pay any administrative costs.[94] Anybody who pollutes the environment intentionally or recklessly and with the knowledge that an environmental nuisance will or might result is guilty of an offence and subject to a fine.[95] In extreme cases, noise pollution that has a high impact, is on a wide scale or involves actual or potential harm to the health or safety of human beings can amount to material environmental harm for which the Environmental Protection Act provides heavy penalties.[96]

Planning law

The Development Act 1993 is the principal planning Act. It is all-embracing. It requires the appropriate minister to ensure that development plans[97] for South Australia accord with the Act[98] as part of the state's planning strategy.[99] Individual development proposals are required to be assessed against the provisions of the appropriate development plan.[100] Ministers, though, do have the power to designate, if necessary, developments of major importance[101] but they must undergo a more extensive assessment process, the details of which are prescribed by the Development Assessment Commission.[102]

The importance of the provisions of the relevant development plan in regulating noise emissions can be seen in *Edwards v District Council of Mount Barker*,[103] where an appeal was made in relation to the council's refusal of an application the conditions attached to which forbade the use of audible bird scaring devices. The appeal was refused. It was held that the operation of the devices in the proposed way in the locality was likely to impact significantly and adversely on the amenity of local residents. The proposal did not, therefore, meet the requirements of the provisions of the relevant development plan.

Western Australia

The Environmental Protection Act 1986 is the principal Act that deals with noise. The key issue is whether or not noise is 'unreasonable'.[104] For example, the occupier of any premises who does not comply with a prescribed standard for noise emissions[105] and does not take all reasonable and practical measures to prevent or minimise noise from the premises, commits an offence.[106]

The Environmental Protection (Noise) Regulations 1997, which are made under the 1986 Act,[107] set out the law in relation to premises. The regulations divide premises into those that are noise-sensitive (such as residencies) and commercial and industrial premises, with permitted levels assigned for each category. There are also 'prescribed premises'.[108] These are premises, listed in Schedule 1 of the Environmental Protection (Noise) Regulations 1997, where any works that might cause, increase or alter the nature of pollution, require a works approval[109] and a pollution licence.[110]

Western Australia also requires certain goods, such as air conditioners, which can cause noise problems, only to be sold with a label indicating the noise level permitted, under the 1985 Noise Abatement (Noise Labelling of Equipment Regulations (No 2)) Act.

As in the UK, common law nuisance also plays an important role in the suppression of noise. A good example of a nuisance action is *Painter v Reed*[111] where it was held that both the movement and also the stamping of a milk vendor's horses was a nuisance in law. Also in *Haddon v Lynch*[112] it was held that the ringing of church bells in a residential suburb for two minutes at 7.30am and for three minutes at 8am on Sundays and also public holidays constituted a nuisance. However, *Cohen v City of Perth*[113] provides a good example of a case where a successful action was brought for breach of statutory duty as opposed to nuisance.

Planning law

Planning law plays an important role in controlling noise. Any planning proposal[114] that is likely, if implemented, to have a significant effect on the environment, may be referred to the Environmental Protection Authority for assessment.[115] The results of the assessment are published in a report and then distributed to any relevant decision-making authority.[116] The minister for the environment may decide, after consultation, that the proposal should not be implemented.[117] Legislation that relates to land use planning in Western Australia is consolidated in the Planning and Development Act 2005. Below are examples of how it has been used in case law.

Huachong Development Pty Ltd and Western Australian Planning Commission[118] concerned a development application for 139 grouped dwellings that were approximately 6.3km from the east-west cross runaway at Perth Airport. The principal issues in the case were whether the proposed development was inconsistent with State Planning Policy (SPP) no 5.1 (Land Use Planning in the Vicinity of Perth Airport) and, if so, whether that SPP should be departed from in this case. The SPP aimed to protect Perth Airport from unreasonable encroachment by incompatible noise sensitive development, and also to minimize the noise impact of aircraft operations on both existing and future communities. The tribunal determined that the proposed development was materially inconsistent with the SPP because, by virtue of the scale of the proposed development, 80 per cent of the dwellings would be subject to unacceptable aircraft noise. This applied even if the development was permitted subject to the condition that the construction of the houses would achieve acceptable indoor sound levels when the windows of the dwellings in question were closed, as this would reduce the enjoyment of outdoor areas in the proposed development. The tribunal held that, while people do not 'live' in their private open space, they should be able to use that area and enjoy a reasonable level of amenity while doing so. To allow the development to proceed would be contrary to the intent of the Residential Design Codes of Western Australia (2008) in relation to open space and outdoor living areas. In the last analysis, there was no cogent reason to depart from the SPP.

Driscoll and Shire of Augusta-Margaret River[119] involved an application for review of the refusal of a development application for a day-care centre for children. The issues for review were whether the proposed development was acceptable having regard to development standards, traffic, noise and amenity in any planning application. The tribunal determined that planning approval be granted for the proposed day-care centre. In assessing whether the proposal was acceptable having regard to noise, the tribunal was mindful of the provisions of the relevant Town Planning Scheme (TPS)[120] that ultimately required consideration of amenity. The tribunal also considered the provisions of Planning Bulletin 72 (Childcare Centres) that *inter alia* sets out noise objectives to limit the impact of the child-care centre on adjacent properties. The tribunal placed weight on the requirement that the intention was not to ensure no impact of noise, but, rather to limit the impact. The levels of noise that were projected in the Noise Impact Assessment were sufficiently low in comparison with the standards which were set out in the Environmental Protection (Noise) Regulations 1997. The tribunal, therefore, granted planning permission.

Victoria

The Environment Protection Act 1970 provides for the promulgation of state environment protection policies, including noise,[121] on the recommendation of the Environment Protection Authority.[122] Such policies establish the basis for maintaining environmental quality including, where appropriate, maximum environmental noise levels.[123] If the Environment Protection Authority is satisfied that they do not, it may serve a pollution abatement notice on the occupier of those premises or on the person who is responsible for the process or activity. A person who contravenes the requirements of a notice is guilty of an indictable offence and is liable to a penalty. The Act also sets noise stand-ards motor vehicles,[124] boats,[125] tools and equipment and allows for directions to be given regarding noise from entertainment venues.[126]

The Environment Protection (Residential Noise) Regulations 2008 that are made under the Environment Protection Act 1970,[127] deal with noise from existing residential premises and residential premises which are under construction and list specific types of equipment and their prohibited times. Noise is unreasonable if certain items are audible inside a neighbouring residence during the prohibited times but noise can still be unreasonable even outside the hours that are listed in the Regulations.

Planning law

The Environment Effects Act 1978 establishes a system for assessing the envi-ronmental effect of a proposed development. It provides for an Environment Effects Statement (EES) to be undertaken for public works and certain private works and for the EES to be submitted to the minister for assessment by a planning panel. Projects which could reasonably be considered either to have or to be capable of having a significant effect on the environment may be declared to be public works for the purposes of the Act.[128] Noise is usually a consideration in this process.[129]

The Planning and Environment Act 1987 establishes a system of plan-ning schemes which regulate the use and also the development of land in Victoria. A planning scheme may make provision which relates to the use, development, protection or conservation of any land in the area.[130] The Act distinguishes between the Victoria Planning Provisions (VPP) and a plan-ning scheme. The VPP set out standard planning provisions for Victoria.[131] It includes provisions which are mandatory in all planning schemes in Victoria. In relation to noise the VPP[132] states that:

> *Planning and responsible authorities should ensure that development is not prejudiced and community amenity is not reduced by noise emissions, using a range of building design, urban design and land use separation techniques, as appropriate to the land use function and character of the area.*

The VPP also requires the development of a Local Planning Policy Framework that sets a local and regional strategic statement and also specific local planning policies. The following is an example of the interaction between state and local policies.

Berrybank wind energy facility (May 2010): a panel was appointed under the Planning and Environment Act 1987 to consider submissions and make recommendations to the minister regarding the construction of a 100-turbine wind energy facility. The policy and planning guidelines for development of wind energy facilities in Victoria required that wind farms comply with a relevant standard relating to the assessment and measurement of sound from wind turbine generators. The panel was of the opinion that a plan to manage construction site noise was an essential part of the environmental management plan for the development. It was noted that the Environment Protection Authority could take action for unreasonable construction noise. Draft conditions were recommended for the development that required the development of a complaints system including that for noise complaints.

New South Wales

The main statute is the Protection of the Environment Operations Act 1997 no 156. It set out the legal framework for environmental protection policies for New South Wales.[133] Any relevant policies must be taken into account by the Environment Protection Agency and other regulatory authorities when they are granting licences, issuing environment protection notices, and so on. Examples of environmental policies include the industrial noise policy (the overall aim of which is to allow the need for industrial activity to be balanced with the desire for quiet in the community[134]), environmental criteria for road traffic noise (which aims to provide for the consideration of road traffic noise mitigation early in the road development process and also the promotion of a range of noise reduction strategies and assessment of noise impacts from roads). Certain activities listed in the Act require an environmental licence.

Part 8.6 of the Act makes special provision for the problems associated with noise. It gives the appropriate regulatory authority powers to deal with

residential noise,[135] including restricting the times of day at which a specified level of noise can be emitted.[136] The occupier of any premises affected by
offensive noise may also apply to the local court for an order. The court may
direct the respondent to abate the noise within a specified time, or to prevent
a recurrence of the noise.[137] It is an offence to contravene a noise abatement
order.[138] However, noise abatement orders are not effective against the activities of public authorities.[139] Authorized persons may also issue noise abatement
directions.[140] The police are also given powers in some circumstances to seize
equipment which is being used to contravene a noise abatement direction.[141]

Planning Law

Under the Environmental Planning and Assessment Act 1979, either the
governor or minister may make environmental planning instruments.[142] An
environmental planning instrument may make provision for, among other
things, protecting, improving or utilizing to the best advantage, the environment[143] and controlling development.[144] When a consent authority is considering a development application, it is required to take into account the likely
environmental impacts of the development on both the natural and also the
built environments.[145]

Queensland

The main statute that deals with noise in Queensland is the Environmental
Protection Act 1994. It defines 'environment' in a broad way. The Act provides
that any unreasonable interference, or likely interference, with an environmental
value that is caused by, among other things, noise, ranks as an 'environmental
nuisance'.[146] If the environmental harm which is caused by noise nuisance is
not trivial or negligible,[147] or causes irreversible or widespread environmental
impact[148] or more than a threshold amount of loss,[149] such harm may amount to
material environmental harm or serious environmental harm.

Chapter 2 of the Act provides for the making of environment protection policies by the relevant minister. The Environmental Protection (Noise)
Policy 2008, which is made under the Act, aims to protect the qualities of the
acoustic environment.[150] The policy sets out acoustic quality objectives for
sensitive receptors,[151] a noise management hierarchy[152] and also measures for
preventing 'background creep'.[153] Certain activities, such as mining, greenhouse
gas storage and petroleum extraction, require environmental authority.[154] The
requisite authority may require the preparation of an environmental impact
statement as part of the environmental assessment process.[155]

A person must not carry out any activity that causes or is likely to cause,
environmental harm (including noise-related environmental nuisance) unless
the person takes all reasonable and practicable measures to either prevent or

minimize the harm. This is termed 'the general environmental duty' under the Act.[156] It is an offence to cause serious[157] or material[158] environmental harm. There is also a lesser offence of unlawfully causing an environmental nuisance, which is perhaps more likely to be applicable in the case of noise pollution.[159]

Planning law

The main planning act in Queensland is the Sustainable Planning Act 2009. Its aims include 'applying standards of amenity ... in the built environment that are cost-effective and for the public benefit'.[160] The relevant minister may make state planning policies.[161] State planning policies prevail over local planning instruments.[162] The state planning policies set out state policy on matters of state interest.[163] In terms of noise, the most relevant state planning instrument is State Policy 5/10 Air, Noise and Hazardous Materials. It seeks to ensure that local planning instruments, structure plans and master plans 'protect the health, well-being, amenity and safety of communities and individuals from the impact *inter alia* of noise'.

Australian Capital Territories

Noise can constitute an environmental nuisance or pollutant under the Environment Protection Act 1997. A pollutant causes environmental harm if it exceeds the prescribed limit.[164] The Environment Protection Authority may serve an environment protection order,[165] which may mandate that an activity ceases or be conducted in a different manner.[166] It is an offence to contravene an environment protection order.[167] If the Supreme Court is satisfied that contravention is likely to cause serious environmental harm, an injunction may be granted. There are also offences of knowingly or recklessly causing environmental harm[168] where increased penalties for causing serious or material harm apply.[169] Furthermore, a person must not sell a prescribed article that, when in operation, emits noise that exceeds the prescribed level.[170] The Act also mandates the preparation of environment protection policies by the Environment Protection Authority.[171] Its policies relating to noise include the *The Noise Environment Protection Policy, Outdoor Concert Noise* and *Motor Sports Noise*.

Planning

The Noise Management Guidelines 1996[172] set out objectives that aim to minimize the impact of planning decisions on noise-sensitive areas, and also guidelines for acceptable and maximum desirable background noise levels in respect of various land classes. The planning regime should aim to separate new noise-generating land uses from existing noise-sensitive land uses, and vice versa.[173] Where this is not possible, the use of acoustic barriers and/or building design measures in order to minimize noise impact should be considered. Other planning guidelines also deal with the issue of noise.

Northern Territory

Noise is dealt with under the Waste Management and Pollution Control Act 1998.[174] One means by which its objectives are achieved is through the imposition of a general environmental duty. A person whose activities or actions either cause or are likely to cause pollution that results in environmental harm must take all measures that are reasonable and practicable, as defined by the Act, to prevent or minimize the pollution or the environmental harm.[175] Where an incident causes or may threaten to cause pollution that results in material or serious environmental harm, the person conducting the activity must notify the Administering Agency[176] as soon as practicable (and within 24 hours). It is an offence to fail to comply with the duty of notification[177] unless a person can prove to have exercised due diligence.[178]

The Northern Territory also has the Summary Offences Act. A member of the police force may, in response to a noise complaint, order the noise to stop or abate the noise.[179] Such directions may specify times when the noise is to be abated and remains in force for up to 48 hours.[180] After a ten-minute grace period, it becomes an offence to contravene such a direction.[181] Where a person who is occupying premises makes a noise complaint to a justice, the justice has powers to ask the noise-maker to abate the noise.[182] The court may restrict the hours that the noise generating activity may be permitted or impose such other conditions as it thinks fit.[183] It is an offence to contravene a noise abatement order.[184] Undue noise is also often prohibited by local by-laws.[185]

Planning law

The main aim of the Planning Act 1999 is to minimize the adverse impact of development on existing amenity.[186] It provides for a Northern Territory Planning Scheme[187] that sets out policies and plans for the use and development of land across the territory.[188] The scheme includes provisions to minimize noise impact upon vulnerable areas, for example, those close to airports and under flight paths.[189] If a noise-generating development is likely to have a significant environmental impact it may be subject to an environmental impact assessment in terms of the Environmental Assessment Act 1982, the object of which is to ensure to the greatest extent practicable that matters that are capable of having a significant effect on the environment are fully examined and also taken into account *inter alia* in the formulation of proposals and carrying out of works.[190]

Tasmania

Pollution is dealt with by the Environmental Management and Pollution and Control Act 1994. Any person who wilfully and or unlawfully causes an environmental nuisance is guilty of an offence.[191] The Environment Protection Policy (Noise) 2009, which is made under the Act, sets a strategic framework for noise management in Tasmania. As with the EU, much of the noise legislation is driven by health considerations. Restrictions on neighbourhood noise are prescribed in the Environmental Management and Pollution Control (Miscellaneous Noise) Regulations 2004. They define the operating conditions for neighbourhood noise sources such as lawn mowers, chainsaws, power tools, heat pumps, car and building alarms. Planning legislation[192] does not deal specifically with noise. However, projects of 'regional significance' may require to be assessed for their environmental impact, including noise.

Conclusions

There is a lot of noise law! We noted in earlier chapters that many recently industrialized and industrializing countries – places such as China, Hong Kong, Japan, South Korea and India – also have a large body of noise law. Some of the laws are useful; others do not seem to be adequate. Sometimes the interests of the noise sufferer can lose out to other interests, particularly those of an economic nature. But all law is only as good as its enforcement. No matter how all-embracing and substantively worthy of praise, unless such noise laws are effectively enforced they remain quite meaningless. The challenge for governments and other regulatory bodies will not only be to assess the adequacy of their noise laws but to ensure they are enforced effectively.

Notes

1   Crime and Disorder Act 1998 s1.
2   Environmental Protection Act 1990 s79(1)(g) and (ga).
3   Environmental Protection Act 1990 s79(1).
4   Environmental Protection Act 1990 s80(1).
5   Environmental Protection Act 1990 s80(3).
6   Environmental Protection Act 1990 s80(4).
7   Environmental Protection Act 1990 s82.
8   Noise Act 1996 s2(6).
9   Noise Act 1996 s3.
10 Noise Act 1996 s3(6).
11 Noise Act 1996 s8(1).
12 Crime and Disorder Act 1998 s1.
13 Anti-Social Behaviour Act 2003 Part 1.

14 Control of Pollution Act 1974 s62(1).
15 Local Government Act 1972 s235 and Local Government (Scotland) Act 1973 s201.
16 Civic Government (Scotland) Act 1982 s54(1).
17 *Rushmer v Polsue and Alfieri* [1906] 1 Ch 234.
18 *Andrea v Selfridge and Co Ltd* [1938] Ch 1.
19 *Leeman v Montague* [1936] 2 All ER 167.
20 *London, Brighton and South Coast Railway v Truman* (1886) 11 App Cas 45.
21 *Allen v Gulf Oil Refinery Ltd* [1981] AC 1001.
22 *Smith v Scott* [1973] Ch 314.
23 *Tetley v Chitty* [1986] 1 All ER 663.
24 *Fraser v Booth* (1949) 50 SR(NSW) 113.
25 *Moy v Stoop* (1909) 25 TLR 262.
26 *Cambridge Water Co v Eastern Counties Leather plc* [1994] 2 WLR 53.
27 *RHM Bakeries (Scotland) Ltd v Strathclyde Regional Council* 1985 SC (HL) 17.
28 *Baxter v Camden LBC* [1999] 4 All ER 449.
29 *Heath v Brighton Corporation* (1908) 24 TLR 414.
30 *Webster v Lord Advocate* 1984 SLT 13.
31 *Harrison v Southwark and Vauxhall Water Co* [1891] 2 Ch 409.
32 *Christie v Davie* [1893] 1 Ch 316.
33 *Rushmer v Polsue & Alfieri, Limited* [1906] 1 Ch 234.
34 *Harrison v Southwark Water Co* [1891] 2 Ch 409.
35 *Bramford v Turnley* (1862) 31 LJQB 286.
36 *Hunter v Canary Wharf Ltd* [1997] EnvLR 488, for example.
37 *Webster v Lord Advocate* 1984 SLT 13.
38 *Sturges v Bridgman* (1879) 11 ChD 22.
39 *Allen v Gulf Oil Refining Ltd* [1981] AC 1001.
40 *Webster v Lord Advocate* 1984 SLT 13.
41 Control of Pollution Act 1974 Ss 60–61 incl.
42 Control of Pollution Act 1974 Ss 60–61 incl.
43 Control of Pollution Act 1974 S63.
44 Control of Pollution Act 1974 S64(2).
45 *Hammersmith and City Rly. v Brand Rly* [1869] LR HL 171, for example, which concerned the issue as to whether the plaintiffs who were affected by vibration from a newly built railway that had been built under permission that had been granted by a private Act of Parliament were entitled to statutory compensation. The House of Lords held that if the inevitable consequence of a state of affairs which Parliament has sanctioned is the creation of a nuisance then no remedy lies. The learning in *Hammersmith Rly* was approved in the modern House of Lords case of *Allen v Gulf Oil Refining Ltd.* [1981] AC 1001 that concerned liability under common law nuisance for nuisance that was caused by oil smut, noise, and so on from an oil refinery which had been established under a private Act of Parliament.
46 Air Navigation (Environmental Standards) Order 2002 SI No 798.
47 Aeroplane Noise Regulations 1999 SI No 1452.
48 Aeroplane Noise Regulations 1999 regs 4 and 5.
49 Aeroplane Noise Regulations 1999 reg 8.
50 Aeroplane Noise Regulations 1999 reg 16(1).

51   Air Navigation Order 2009 SI No 3015, art 160.

52   Rules of Air Regulations 2009 SI 2007 No 734.

53   Rules of Air Regulations 2009 reg 5.

54   Rules of Air Regulations 2009 reg 45.

55   Air Navigation Order 2009 SI 2009 No 3015, art 215.

56   Aerodromes (Noise Restrictions) Rules and Procedures/Regulations 2003 SI 2003 No 1742.

57   Aerodromes (Noise Restrictions) Rules and Procedures/Regulations 2003 reg 3.

58   In relation to the 'designated airports' namely, Heathrow, Gatwick and Stansted, the Secretary of State is the competent authority. In relation to other airports the competent authority is the airport operator.

59   Aerodromes (Noise Restrictions) Rules and Procedures/Regulations 2003 SI 2003 No 1742, reg 5.

60   Wray, R. (2004) *Aircraft Environmental Noise Report*, Ministry of Defence

61   Crown Proceedings Act 1947 s11(1). See, however, *Dennis v MoD* [2003] EWHC 793.

62   *Hammersmith and City Rly v Brand Rly* [1869] LR HL 171, for example, which concerned the issue as to whether the plaintiffs who were affected by vibration from a newly built railway that had been built under permission which had been granted by a private Act of Parliament were entitled to statutory compensation. The House of Lords held that if the inevitable consequence of a state of affairs that Parliament has sanctioned is the creation of a nuisance then no remedy lies. The learning in *Hammersmith Rly* was approved in the modern House of Lords case of *Allen v Gulf Oil Refining Ltd* [1981] AC 1001 that concerned liability under common law nuisance for nuisance which was caused by oil smut, noise, and so on from an oil refinery which had been established under a private Act of Parliament.

63   Noise Insulation (Railways and Other Guided Transport Systems) regulation 1996 SI 1996 No 428.

64   Road Traffic Act 1988 s41(1).

65   Road Vehicles (Construction Use) Regulations 1986 SI 1986 No 1078 (as amended).

66   Road Vehicles (Construction Use) Regulations 1986 reg 54.

67   Road Vehicles (Construction Use) Regulations 1986 regs 55–57 incl.

68   Road Vehicles (Construction Use) Regulations 1986 reg 54.

69   Motor Vehicles (Type Approval) (Great Britain) Regulations 1984 SI 1984 No 981.

70   Noise Insulation Regulations 1975 SI 1975 No 1763. See also the Noise Insulation (Scotland) Regulations 1975 No 460.

71   European Convention of Human Rights [2010] ECHR 686.

72   European Convention of Human Rights [2005] EnvLR 2 at 18.

73   European Convention of Human Rights [2003] EnvLR 34.

74   *King v Advocate General for Scotland* [2009] CSOH 169.

75   (2003) 37 EHRR 28.

76   Ibid. at [96].

77   Ibid. at [98].

78   Ibid. at [119].

79   European Court of Human Rights (2005)(App. No 55723/00) judgement of June 9.

80 European Court of Human Rights (2004) (App No. 4143/02) judgement of November 16. See F McManus, '*Gomez v Spain*' (2006) 8 EnvLR 225.
81 European Court of Human Rights (2009) App No. 18324/04.
82 See also *Leon and Agnieszka Kania v Poland*.
83 [2009] ECHR 868 at [1].
84 Rehbinder, E. and Stewart, R. (1985) *Environmental Protection Policy* at 203.
85 *Official Journal* (1993) No C138/01.
86 European Commission (1996) *Future Noise Policy, Environment Fifth Action Programme*, COM(96).
87 European Commission (2001) *Future Noise Policy, Environment Sixth Action Programme*, COM (2001) 31 Final.
88 European Commission (2002) EC Directive 2002/49/EC.
89 'Environmental noise' is defined as unwanted or harmful outdoor sound created by human activities outdoors, including noise emitted by means of transport, road traffic, and from sites of industrial activity Annex 1 to Council Directive 96/61/EC of 24 September 1996 concerning integrated pollution prevention and control.
90 Article 1.
91 An agglomeration is defined as 'part of a territory, delimited by a Member State having a population in excess of 100,000 persons and a population density such that the Member State considers it to be an urbanised area'.
92 EC Directive 2002/49/EC Article 4.
93 EC Directive 2002/49/EC Article 8.
94 Environment Protection Act 1993 s135.
95 Environment Protection Act 1993 s82.
96 Environment Protection Act 1993 s80.
97 Environment Protection Act 1993 'Development' is defined in S4 of the Act and includes building work, a change in use of land, the division of allotments and the construction of roads and streets.
98 Environment Protection Act 1993 s32.
99 Environment Protection Act 1993 s22(2).
100 Environment Protection Act 1993 s33(1)(a).
101 Environment Protection Act 1993 s46(1).
102 Environment Protection Act 1993 s46(7) Criteria for this are determined by the Development Regulations 2008 under s46(8) of the Act.
103 *Edwards v District Council of Mount Barker* [2010] SAERDC 19. See also *MacGillivray v District Council of Mount Barker* [2000] SAERDC 11.
104 Environment Protection Act 1986 s49(5).
105 Environmental Protection (Noise) Regulations 1997 sets them out.
106 Environment Protection Act 1993 s51.
107 Environment Protection Act 1986 s123 and Sch 2.
108 Environmental Protection (Noise) Regulations 1997 sets them out Defined in s3(1) of the Act as premises prescribed for the purposes of Part V of the Act.
109 Environmental Protection (Noise) Regulations 1997 sets them out s53.
110 Environmental Protection (Noise) Regulations 1997 sets them out s56.
111 *Painter v Reed* [1930] SASR 295.
112 *Haddon v Lynch* [1911] VLR 332.

113 Cohen v City of Perth [2000] WASC 306.

114 Environment Protection Act 1986 – under s3 of the Act a proposal is defined as a project, plan, programme, policy, operation, undertaking or development or change of use of land that is not a scheme.

115 Environmental Protection Act 1986 ss37b and 38.

116 Environment Protection Act 1986 s44.

117 Environment Protection Act 1986 s45.

118 *Huachong Development Pty Ltd and Western Australian Planning Commission* [2008] WASAT 188.

119 *Driscoll and Shire of Augusta-Margaret River* [2008] WASAT 219.

120 Town Planning Scheme (undated), paras 69 and 70.

121 Environment Protection Act 1970 s46.

122 Environment Protection Act 1970 s16.

123 Environment Protection Act 1970 s18. Thus far, State Environment Protection Policies have been made in relation to the control of noise from commerce, industry and trade, the control of music noise from public premises. Noise Control Guidelines (TG302/92) have been made in order to assist municipal officers resolving complaints or averting a possible noise nuisance. The Modified Vehicle Guidelines provide a practical guide to vehicle modifications which comply with the Environment Protection Act 1970. The Interim Gunshot Noise Guidelines (N6/91) establish standards for the consideration of noise complaints and as a basis for advice in planning matters. The Interim Guidelines for Control of Noise from Industry in Country Victoria (N3/89) provides maximum allowable noise levels at sensitive receptors outside Metropolitan Melbourne. There are separate limits for both day, evening and night periods.

124 Environment Protection Act 1970 s48B.

125 Environment Protection Act 1970 s48B.

126 Environment Protection Act 1970 s48AB.

127 Environment Protection Act 1970 ss48A(5) and 71.

128 Environment Effects Act 1978 s3(2).

129 See, for example, the panel report relating to a proposed expansion of the New Bedigo Gold Project at the Carshalton mine Site.

130 Environment Protection Act 1970 ss48B and 6(2)(b).

131 Environment Protection Act 1970 ss48B and 4A.

132 Environment Protection Act 1970 s48B Clause 15.05-2.

133 Protection of the Environment Operations Act 1997.

134 Protection of the Environment Operations Act 1997 para. 1.1.

135 Protection of the Environment Operations Act 1997 s264(2).

136 Protection of the Environment Operations Act 1997 s265(1)(2).

137 Protection of the Environment Operations Act 1997 s268.

138 Protection of the Environment Operations Act 1997 s269.

139 Protection of the Environment Operations Act 1997 s270.

140 Protection of the Environment Operations Act 1997 s276.

141 Protection of the Environment Operations Act 1997 s282.

142 Environmental Planning and Assessment Act 1979 s24.

143 Environmental Planning and Assessment Act 1979 s26(a).

144 Environmental Planning and Assessment Act 1979 s26(b).

145 Environmental Planning and Assessment Act 1979 s79(1)(c).

146 Environment Protection Act 1994 s15(a). Noise includes vibration of any frequency, whether emitted through air or another medium. Noise also ranks as an environmental contaminant under s11(d).

147 Environment Protection Act 1994 s16(1)(a).

148 Environment Protection Act 1994 s17(1)(a).

149 Environment Protection Act 1994 ss16(1)(b) and 17(1)(c).

150 Environment Protection Act 1994 s7.

151 Environment Protection Act 1994 s8.

152 Environment Protection Act 1994 s9.

153 Environment Protection Act 1994 s10.

154 Environment Protection Act 1994 ss426 and 426A.

155 Environment Protection Act 1994 ss37 and 309A.

156 Environment Protection Act 1994 s319(2).

157 Environment Protection Act 1994 s437.

158 Environment Protection Act 1994 s438.

159 Environment Protection Act 1994 s440.

160 Sustainable Planning Act 2009 s5(1)(f).

161 Sustainable Planning Act 2009 s44.

162 Sustainable Planning Act 2009 s43.

163 Sustainable Planning Act 2009 s54.

164 Environment Protection Act 1997 s5(a).

165 Environment Protection Act 1997 s125(1).

166 Environment Protection Act 1997 s125(4).

167 Environment Protection Act 1997 s126.

168 Environment Protection Act 1997 s139. The Environment Protection Regulations 1997 divides ACT into zones for the purpose of determining the applicable noise standard. Under Reg 27 noise which is emitted from a parcel of land in a noise zone is to be taken to cause environmental harm if the noise level exceeds the zone noise standard in respect of the period during which the noise is emitted.

169 Environment Protection Act 1997 ss137 and 138.

170 Environment Protection Act 1997 Schedule 2.2, Part 2.2.

171 Environment Protection Act 1997 s24.

172 Noise Management Guidelines 1996. These are in draft form.

173 Noise Management Guidelines 1996 O3.5.1.

174 Waste Management and Pollution Control Act 1998 s4. Noise is defined as a 'vibration of a frequency in the range of 0–20,000Hz'.

175 Waste Management and Pollution Control Act 1998 s12(1).

176 Waste Management and Pollution Control Act 1998 – this is the agency for the time being which has been allocated administration of the Act under an Administrative Arrangements Order, see s4.

177 Waste Management and Pollution Control Act 1998 s14(1).

178 Waste Management and Pollution Control Act 1998 s84(1).

179 Summary Offences Act (undated) s53B.

180 Summary Offences Act (undated) s53B(2A).

181 Summary Offences Act (undated) s53B(3).

182 Summary Offences Act (undated) s53D(1).

183 Summary Offences Act (undated) s53(D)(2).
184 Summary Offences Act (undated) s53(D)(3).
185 Summary Offences Act (undated) – see e.g. the Alice Springs (Control of Public Places) By Laws, s46 and the Tennant Creek (Control of Public Places) By Laws, s38.
186 Planning Act 1999 s2A(e).
187 Planning Act 1999 s7(1).
188 Planning Act 1999 – see generally, s9(1).
189 Planning Act 1999 Northern Territory Planning Scheme, para 6.9.
190 Planning Act 1999 s4.
191 Planning Act 1999 s53(1) and (2).
192 Land Use Planning and Approvals Act 1993 is the main statute which regulates land use in Tasmania.

CHAPTER 10

Making Change Happen

There are practical and realistic steps that can be taken
to transform the noisy world in which we live.

There are practical and realistic steps that can be taken to transform the
noisy world in which we live. They need, though, to be preceded by a
change of attitude. Without a real understanding of the impact noise is having
on millions of people, and on the planet, it is unlikely we will see the radical and
urgent action that is required. Noise will continue to be regarded as an inevitable
by-product of growth, globalization, mobility and the consumer society.

But things can be different. It is not difficult to make significant cuts in
noise levels, certainly in the richer countries of the world. Even in poorer
countries much can be done. Some noise problems, such as those caused by
international sea travel, are more challenging but they should not act as a
barrier to what could be done relatively simply.

More straightforward measures

Traffic noise annoyance could be cut by 70 per cent (den Boer and Schroten,
2007). We have the means to do it. We can manufacture quieter vehicles, introduce lower speed limits, improve road surfaces and, where necessary, put in
mitigation measures such as noise barriers. Moreover, we can be confident
that cutting the number of cars on the road will not damage the economic
performance of all but some of the least-developed economies (where vehicle
numbers in any case tend to be low). The health of mature economies is
not related to the number of vehicles on their roads (SACTRA, 1999). Once
countries have in place a basic transport infrastructure, their economy is
not dependent on ever-more vehicles on their roads. Indeed, a cut in vehicle
numbers could assist the economy as the huge cost of noise, emissions, air
pollution and road accidents would fall significantly.

A strategy to cut traffic noise should probably be centred round the
introduction of electric and hybrid vehicles. It makes sense for three reasons:
quiet vehicles are the most cost-effective solution since the noise is reduced at
source; it would allow expenditure on insulation and mitigation measures to

be cut; and it would be tapping into an already expanding market, one driven by the need to find alternatives to fossil fuels. It would be a mistake, though, to see electric vehicles as the silver bullet solution to traffic noise. There are still doubts as to how quiet the new vehicles will be and how fast they will come on to the market, particularly in poorer countries. Moreover, even if they did appear soon, the wider social problems caused by cars – road building, community destruction and road deaths – would not be solved without lower speeds, investment in public transport and a reduction in the number of cars on the roads. Quieter (and cleaner) vehicles will probably simply mean that cars numbers will need to fall less steeply than they otherwise would.

Rail noise could be cut by at least 50 per cent (UIC/CER, 2008). We know how to do it. The roughness of the rails can be reduced by 'polishing' but the big gains would come from cutting the noise of the wheels by replacing the brake pads used, changing them from cast iron to composite material. High speed trains, though, would continue to be noisy. Until and unless there is a step-change in technology, the noise implications of every proposed high-speed scheme need to be assessed very carefully. If any scheme is given the go-ahead, noise barriers and insulation programmes would need to be integral to it and a cap placed on the number of trains allowed on any one line.

Neighbour noise can be dealt with. It is largely caused by poorly insulated properties and bad behaviour by the noise-maker. Both problems can be sorted. The initial high capital cost of insulation would be recouped over time because the value of private properties would rise and the state would save money on the social and medical problems caused by noise. There are also ways of dealing with the inconsiderate or bad behaviour of noise-makers. Most people will curb their behaviour when asked. Those who will not – the people who invariably are causing the worst and most persistent problems for their neighbours – need to face the full sanction of the law. That requires us to recognize bad behaviour for what it is and to abandon the non-judgemental attitude so common in recent times. That attitude has too often penalized the victim. Tough tenancy agreements, properly enforced, do work. Anti-social behaviour and harassment orders given to persistent noise-makers will curb their behaviour. It is the political will that has been missing.

Piped music can be controlled. There is no public clamour for it. In particular, legislation is needed to protect people trapped by piped music in places such as workplaces and hospitals. This is not a question of restricting choice but one of protecting civil liberties. At present these are being repeatedly abused for no real reason other than to please a vocal yet relatively small industry.

More challenging measures

Aircraft noise is more challenging because, if growth rates rise as predicted, simply to maintain the status quo around airport communities would require reductions that the industry doubts are achievable. The number of flights needs to be reduced. If the tax-breaks the aviation industry receives, such as tax-free fuel and non-payment of VAT, were to end and if the industry was made to pay the full cost of the environmental damage it causes in terms of noise, emissions and air pollution, fares would go up and demand would fall. In particular, the demand for short-haul flights would fall. We noted in the transport chapter that this is the key to improving the noise climate since aircraft noise is only really a problem in most areas as planes approach and leave airports. Since at most airports short-haul flights make up the bulk of the traffic, if their numbers were to fall, noise would be cut considerably.

Fewer short-haul flights might not damage the overall economy as leisure travellers – who make up the big majority of people using these flights – are likely to spend their money on something else, thereby boosting other areas of the economy. The complicating factor, though, is that short-haul flights cannot be separated too easily from long-distance flights as many business people – and freight – use both to get to their destination. Higher fares may not reduce demand from business significantly but could impose a cost on the economy, certainly in the short term until business is able to adapt to the new reality.

Shipping noise, the biggest source of human noise in the oceans, can be reduced significantly. The big win would be to cut the noise from the propellers. The techniques exist to do so but may not be sufficient in themselves if the number of ships criss-crossing the oceans continues to grow. The implications of curbing growth are assessed in the next section.

Wind farm noise need not continue to be the problem it currently is. Depending on the terrain, wind turbines should be located 1–1.5 miles from residential properties if the noise problems are to be sorted out. Improved technology may, over time, allow them to be sited closer. We have, however, put wind turbine noise in the 'more challenging' section for two reasons. First, in order to deal with current noise problems, some wind farms, sited too close to properties, would need to be removed and that would not be an easy thing for any government to do or for the wind power industry to countenance. Second, there are big plans in many countries for off-shore wind farms that could cause unacceptable noise problems. As we showed in Chapter 5, the impact of wind turbine noise on sea creatures still needs further research. We suggest this is done as a matter of urgency. Big decisions will need to be taken soon regarding off-shore wind farms. We understand the contribution they could play in a low-carbon economy but, until their true impact on the natural sound rhythms of the seas and oceans is known, it would be unwise to forge ahead with large-scale projects.

Most challenging measures

Industrial noise has been reduced in richer countries over the past few decades through the introduction of quieter machinery, often as the result of pressure from the trade unions, but also because the number of people working in mines, heavy manufacturing industries and agriculture has fallen. There are still problems, though, in the richer countries – particularly for blue-collar workers, where the proportion facing noise problems remains high – but it is the situation in many industrializing countries that is critical. Quieter machinery and equipment is available and could be installed. However, we have put industrial noise in the 'most challenging' section because, under pressure to compete in the globalized market, many firms in the industrializing world are reluctant to pay for quieter equipment and mitigation measures. The situation may change if countries become richer and workers are in a position to demand more protection but, at present, the pressure to compete is working against the introduction of effective measures to cut noise.

The industrializing countries will find it challenging to reduce noise from any source. But things can change. China and Hong Kong are two countries that have made real progress. They could act as a model for much of the industrializing world. In both places, change only began to happen once their governments started to understand the need to tackle noise. That led to action: strategic plans, rigorous regulation, better planning and improved implementation. The results have been impressive.

The biggest challenge

The hardest task for both industrialized and industrializing countries will be tackling those areas where noise levels can only be brought down by challenging the travelling habits many of us enjoy or through changing current globalized trading patterns. We suggest both may be necessary. We showed how the high noise levels in places such as the US, Australia and Europe are, at least in part, down to the increased use of cars, planes and, to a lesser extent, trains by many of their citizens in recent decades. We saw that Hong Kong is spending millions on tackling traffic noise just to stand still because of the extra cars coming on to the roads each year. We noted that improved technology in ships and planes is likely to be cancelled out if their numbers grow at the predicted rate. We looked at the way the natural sound systems of the planet are being threatened by human noise, much of it the result of growth and globalized trade patterns.

To solve these problems would not require shutting down the world, more telling it to shut-up! Technology may well surprise us – it has a habit of doing so – but on the available evidence, our current patterns of growth, trade and movement are not compatible with a less noisy world. Other factors might force a change, particularly rising oil prices and the threat of climate change. If they did, it could usher in an era where peace and quiet became much more of a reality for many more people and where the natural sounds systems of the planet were given a chance to recover.

References

den Boer, L. and Schroten, A. (2007) *Traffic Noise Reduction in Europe*, C. E. Delft, Netherlands

SACTRA (Standing Advisory Committee on Trunk Road Assessment Transport and the Economy) (1999) *Transport and the Economy*, Her Majesty's Stationery Office, London

UIC/CER (International Union of Railways and Community of European Railway Infrastructure Companies, (2008) *Rail Transport and the Environment: Facts and Figures*, International Union of Railways and Community of European Railway Infrastructure Companies, France

Index

A

abatement approaches
  barriers 38, 39, 41, 99, 162, 163
  orders 115, 132, 152, 154
  organizations 109–110
  zones 136–137
Abdulali, Sumaira 38
academic success 55–56
acceleration and braking 97
acceptable behaviour 31, 32
acidification 64
acoustic barriers 99, 153
action plans 26, 44, 74–75, 145
activism 27
  see also anti-noise campaigns; campaigns
Addis Ababa, Ethiopia 35
Africa 35
aggression 50
aircraft noise
  challenge of 163–164
  children's learning 56
  Europe 25, 95
  growth 43
  Hong Kong 39–40
  law 137–139, 142, 149
  opposition to 49–50
  quality of life 54
  reducing 3, 102–104, 105–106
airguns 66
airport noise 138–139
Alternative Dispute Resolution 114–115
Alves-Pereira, Mariana 88
Andrews v Reading Borough Council 141, 142
animals 68–73
annoyance 48–49, 50, 53, 87, 102–103, 108
  see also complaints; disturbance
Antarctic and Southern Ocean Coalition (ASOC) 65
anthropony 68–69

anti-noise campaigns 7, 27, 29, 31, 32, 44, 109–112
  see also campaigns
anti-social behaviour 111, 116, 133
Argentina 36
ASOC *see* Antarctic and Southern Ocean Coalition
assessment of noise 144–145
attitudes
  change 162
  consumer society 2, 9–14, 30–32
  government 3
  new 32–33
  non-judgemental 32, 163
  sound becoming noise 6
  transport noise 24–25
Australia 22, 30, 79, 81, 147–155
authorized noise 135
averaging of noise 20–21, 103
aviation 29, 164
  see also aircraft noise
avoidance of noise 134–135
awareness 113–114
'A' weighting 19, 41, 103

B

Baguley, D. M. 52
Bangkok, Thailand 33
Bangladesh 34
bass 17–18, 48
Batho, W. J. S. 113–114
bats 71
Bayaka pygmies 74
Beaumont, Tim 125
behaviour
  acceptable 31, 32
  anti-social 111, 116, 133
  changing 105–106, 117, 163
Beijing, China 14–15

Berglund, B. 49
Berrybank wind energy facility 151
Betke, K. 90
biodiversity 69, 72–73
biophony 68
birds 70, 71, 72
bird scaring devices 148
birth defects 54
Blesser, Barry 10–11, 13
Blomberg, Les 23, 36
blood donating 129
blood pressure 53, 54, 55
Borsky, P. N. 48
Botha, Paul 89
bottlenose dolphins 65
braking 97, 101, 163
Brave New World 128
Brazil 36, 83
Bronzaft, Arline L. 47–61
Buenos Aires, Argentina 36
building regulations 108, 111
Bull, Michael 9–10, 12
Burgess, Anthony 128
business 2, 13–14, 26, 30, 34, 44, 106

C

call centres 82
campaigns
    aircraft noise 102
    neighbourhood noise 7, 109–114, 116
    organizations 117
    piped music 119, 122–123
    see also anti-noise campaigns
Capital Territories, Australian 153–154
car alarms 114, 116–117
carbon dioxide 64, 67, 70, 73
cardiovascular problems 53
cars 3, 26, 27, 96, 162
    see also traffic noise; vehicle noise
cavitations 66
CDA *see* Continuous Descent Approach
Central African Republic 74
cetaceans 63–64, 65, 90–91
Chepesiuk, R. 48–49
Chicago Convention on International Civil
        Aviation, 1944 138
children 4, 10, 24, 53–54, 55–57, 84
China 3, 14–15, 40–41, 43, 165
Christmas music 126, 127

circulatory problems 53
citizens' groups 42, 44, 146
Civil Aviation Act, 1982 137, 138
civil liberties 124, 129
classical music 127–128
classrooms 24, 56, 57
climate change 62, 67, 73, 97, 106, 165
Clinton, Bill 51
cognition 55–57
Coleman, Vernon 27, 29–30
common law 109, 132, 134–135
communication 62, 63, 64, 65, 68, 70
community level 14, 49, 50, 114
commuters 120–121
complaints
    aircraft noise 102
    annoyance 48–49
    helplessness 50
    local authorities 131, 132
    neighbourhood noise 108, 109, 111, 113,
        114, 115, 116, 117
    piped music 126–127
    wind farm noise 86, 87–88
    worldwide 23, 28, 30, 36
    see also annoyance; disturbance
Connell, John 109–110
construction noise 34, 40, 85, 90, 136
consumer goods labelling 147, 148
consumer society 2, 3, 9–14, 15, 22, 30–32
Continuous Descent Approach (CDA) 104
control 6, 12–13, 14
Control of Pollution Act, 1974 133, 136
costs
    fuel 27, 66, 106, 165
    noise reduction 3–4
    solutions 42
    sound insulation 163
    transport noise 96, 97, 99, 101, 105
    see also economics
Crime and Disorder Act, 1998 133
'C' weighting 19–20, 103

D

Dah-You, Maa 40
Darlington 112–113
day-care centres 149
deafness 4, 13, 17, 71, 82, 83
    see also hearing problems
decibels 15

defining noise 47–48
den Boer, L. 95, 96
Dennis v Ministry of Defence 141, 142
dental surgeries 143
De Silva Wijeyeratne, Gehan 71
despair 126
development 147, 149, 154
discontentment 14–15
dispersal landing and taking off 104
disturbance
  impacts 6–7
  low-frequency noise 18–19, 48
  mental well-being 49
  traffic noise 23, 25
  wind farm noise 86, 87–89
  see also annoyance; complaints
DIY activities 108, 109
dogs 8
dolphins 63–64, 65, 90–91
Dragon, Jackie 66–67
Driscoll and Shire of Augusta-Margaret
  River 149–150
duration of noise 135

E

ECHR *see* European Convention of Human
  Rights
EC *see* European Commission
economics 105, 106, 162, 164
  see also costs
ecosystems 1, 62–63
education 24, 29, 39, 50, 55–57
Edwards v District Council of Mount Barker
  148
EES *see* Environment Effects Statement
Egypt 35
electric and hybrid vehicles 99, 162–163
elephants 70, 71
elevator music *see* piped music
elitism 31, 32
emotional responses 48, 51, 73–74
END *see* Environmental Noise Directive
enforcement 41, 42, 115–117, 155
Environment Action Programmes, EU 143,
  144–145
environmental aspects
  consciousness 29–30
  health 110
  management and pollution control 155

protection 132, 143, 147, 148, 150, 151,
  152, 153
environmentalism 1, 3
Environmental Noise Directive (END) 145
Environment Effects Statement (EES) 150
Ethiopia 35
EU *see* European Union
Europe 1, 22, 24–26, 79, 81, 95
European Agency for Safety and Health at
  Work 80–81
European Commission (EC) 138, 145
European Convention of Human Rights
  (ECHR) 141–142
European Union (EU)
  aircraft noise 104, 139
  lack of action 25–26
  law 143–145
  policy 44
  transport noise 94–95, 96
  workplace noise 80–81

F

Fadeyeva v Russia 142
fear 9–10, 12, 77
federal government 27–28, 29, 146
feeling noise 86, 87, 88
ferry workers 83
festivals 34
Finegold, L. 42
fireworks 117
fish 67–68
flats 108
Fligor, Brian J. 51–52
foetus impacts 54
football noise 5–6
forests 62, 63, 68, 69–70, 74
fragmentation 72–73
France 24–25
freight trains 100
frequency 15, 17–18, 47
Fry, Stephen 119
fuel costs 66
future aspects 84, 99–100

G

Galev v Bulgaria 141, 143
gardens 76–77
gas 66, 67

gas embolisms 65
Germany 25, 79
Girdner, J. H. 8
glidescope 104
globalized economy 2, 106, 165
global noise 22–43, 79–80
Gomez v Spain 142–143
government
  aircraft noise 142
  anti-noise campaigns 44
  attitudes 3
  lack of strategies 1, 2, 25–26, 30–31
  neighbourhood noise 110, 111, 112–114
  speed limits 97–98
  transport noise 94
  wind farm noise 86
green movement 1, 62–78
Greenpeace EV v Germany 141, 143
Grenfell, Joyce 122

H

Harry, Dr Amanda 88
Hatton v The United Kingdom 141, 142
health
  law 144, 146
  natural sounds 73, 74
  overview 6, 47–61
  piped music 124, 125
  US 29, 146
  wind farm noise 87–89
  workplace noise 84
  see also hearing problems
hearing problems
  animals 71
  attitudes 13
  construction noise 85
  loud sounds 51–52
  piped music 119
  workplace noise 79, 81, 82, 83
  see also deafness; health
Heathrow airport, UK 49, 102, 103, 139,
    142
helplessness 14, 49, 50
hertz 15, 17–18
high-speed trains 3, 100, 101, 163
historical aspects 7–8, 27, 121–122
home noise 56, 57
Hong Kong 3, 38–40, 43, 105, 165
hospitals 3, 53, 124–125

house alarms 116, 117
household gadgets 30, 41, 109
housing 108, 111, 149
*Huachong Development Pty Ltd and Western
    Australian Planning Commission* 149
hum 18–19, 20, 48
human rights 141–143
humpback whales 63–64
Huxley, Aldous 128
hypermobility 94

I

identity 10
India 14, 33, 34–35, 37–38, 83
industrialization 8–9
industrialized countries 36–42, 79, 165
  see also richer countries
industrializing countries 4, 14–15, 33–43,
    79, 83–85, 91, 105, 165
industrial noise 33, 53, 135–137, 164–165
infrasound 70, 71
insulation 140, 163
  see also sound insulation
intensity of noise 19, 135
iPods 9, 12–13, 77

J

James, Oliver 10
Jasny, Michael 63, 66
Jing Tian 41
Johnson, Alan 127
Jordan 84
Jozefowicz, Chris 65

K

kangaroo rats 71
Karachi, Pakistan 33
Keizer, Garret 86, 89–90, 129
Key, Robert 125
Krause, Bernie 68, 69, 70, 73–74
Kryter, K. D. 48
Kunstler, James 27
Kuwait 85

L

labelling consumer goods 147, 148
Labour government, UK 31–32
land-use planning 42, 148
language 55–57
learned helplessness 50
learning 55–57
legal aspects
  behaviour 163
  China 40–41
  lack of 30, 57
  neighbourhood noise 110, 111, 113–114
  overview 131–161
  rights 32
  US 28–29
  workplace noise 81
  see also regulations
Levy, Steven 12
Lewis, C. S. 75–76
licensed premises 133, 142–143
Linz, Austria 127
live music 120
local level
  campaigns 110, 112
  industry noise 136, 137
  law 131, 132, 133, 134, 144, 146
long-distance flights 43, 104, 106, 164
loudness 10–11, 13, 15–21, 47–48, 51–52
loudspeaker jagrans 34–35
Lowey, Nita 29
low-frequency noise
  aircraft 102
  animals and birds 70
  description 17–19, 20
  disturbance 48
  oceans 64, 65
  sensitivity to 41
  wind turbines 88
low-noise materials 38–39

M

machine sounds 8, 9, 74–75
McManus, Francis 131–161
Maa Dah-You 40
Maitland, Sara 75, 76
mammals 90–91
mapping noise 26, 145
marine life 63–68, 90

marketing 13–14, 123–124
Mars Hill Wind Farm, Maine, US 87
Martin, Andrew 8
measuring noise 15–21, 103
mechanical noises 8, 9, 10, 74–75
media 14, 20, 35, 50, 98, 110–111, 116
mediation 114–115
meditation theories 76
mega-cities 33–34, 34–35
mental well-being 48–50
Metcalf, Kathy 67
micro-management 26, 44
military noise 65–66, 139, 142
Millennium celebrations 117
Ministry of Defence (MoD) 139
Mitchell, Paige 97
mobility 94, 105
MoD *see* Ministry of Defence
modern noise 8–9, 10–11, 135
moral bearings 31–32
Moscow, Russia 25
motivation 135
Mumbai, India 38
Munjal, M. L. 37
murder 6, 7, 108
music 3, 82, 115, 116, 119–130, 163
muzak *see* piped music

N

NAS *see* Noise Abatement Society
National Committee on Noise Pollution
    Control, India 37
national noise strategies 3, 43–44, 114
National Parks, US 74–75
natural sound systems 5, 62–63, 73, 74, 165
navigation 63
navy noise 65–66
neighbour/neighbourhood noise
  children's learning 57
  disturbance 6, 7
  overview 108–118
  reducing 3, 58, 163
  regulations 40, 132, 155
Neiman, Susan 32
neonatal intensive care units (NICUs) 53
New Labour, UK 31–32, 43
New South Wales, Australia 147, 151–152
newspapers 20, 36, 50, 109, 110, 116
New York, US 1, 9, 22, 28, 146

NICUs *see* neonatal intensive care units
night noise 55, 89, 132
noise abatement
    barriers 38, 39, 41, 99, 162, 163
    orders 115, 132, 152, 154
    organizations 109–110
    zones 136–137
Noise Advisory Council 112–113
Noise Association, UK 111
Noisedirect 111–112
noise-reduction equipment, use of 81
non-judgemental attitudes 32, 163
North, Adrian 123–124
Northern Territory, Australia 147, 154
Norway 22
Nugent, Ted 122
nuisance 131, 132, 134–135, 148, 152

O

Obama, Barack 29, 57
oceans 62, 63–68, 164
Office of Noise Abatement and Control
    (ONAC), US 28, 146
off-shore wind farms 90–91, 164
oil and gas 27, 66, 67, 106, 165
Oke, Yeshwant 14
older people 51
Oluic v Croatia 141–142
ONAC *see* Office of Noise Abatement and
    Control
on-shore wind power 89–90
organic sounds 8
organized pay parties 116
Orwell, George 128

P

Pakistan 33, 83
Paris 22
Parker Shine, Pamela 7
Pawley, Martin 10
Peace and Quiet Campaign 7
Pederson, E. 87, 89
Perry, Doug 126–127
personal stereos 9, 10, 12
Persson, Waye, K. 87
Pierpont, Nina 88
pile driving 90

piped music 3, 119–130, 163
Pipedown 119, 122–123, 126
planning
    Australia 147–148, 149–150, 150–151,
        152, 153–154
    improving 38, 42
    road 100
    UK 133
Podger, Geoffrey 127
policy 31, 33, 37, 42, 131, 144
Pollution Prevention and Control Act, 1999
    136
poverty 2, 14–15, 22, 24, 32, 36, 94
    see also industrializing countries
powerlessness 126, 129
prescribed premises 148
prisons 76, 129
private sector 4, 111–112
privatized worlds 12–13
propulsion noise 96
protected areas 67
protective equipment 81
psychological impacts 126, 127
public disorder 15
public engagement programmes 39
public spaces 11–13, 15, 125

Q

quality of life 47, 54, 144
Queensland, Australia 152–153
quieter approaches
    aircraft 29, 43, 102
    classrooms 57
    environments 27, 58, 73
    machinery 84, 91, 164–165
    products 2, 4, 26, 41, 58, 73
    road surfaces 98–99
    vehicles 24, 26, 37, 41, 44, 96, 162–163
Quiet Garden Movement 76–77
quiet neighbourhood pilot scheme
    113–114
Quiet Town experiment 112–113

R

railway noise 96, 100–101, 137, 139–140,
    163
    see also train noise

rainforests 68, 69–70, 74
raves 116
reading 56
Reagan, Ronald 3, 28, 43, 51, 146
recreational activities 51, 52
regulations
  aircraft noise 138–139
  building 108, 111
  business opposition 2
  industrialized countries 36–42
  innovation 4
  new technology 26
  railway noise 140
  traffic noise 96
  US 27–28
  see also legal aspects
Rehbinder, E. 144
religious noise 34–35, 75, 117
renewable energy 3
residential noise 150, 152, 164
richer countries
  attitudes 11, 14
  consumer society 2, 3, 9, 22
  industrial noise 164–165
  traffic noise 100
  workplace noise 79, 80–83, 91
  see also industrialized countries
rights 32, 33, 94, 129, 141–143
Right to Peace and Quiet Campaign
  (RPQC) 108, 110, 115
ringing in the ears 51, 52
Rio de Janeiro 1, 22
road noise 38–39, 41, 137, 140
  see also traffic noise; transport noise
Road Traffic Act, 1988 140
Robson, W. C. B. 113
Rodgers, Nigel 119–130
rolling noise 96
RPQC *see* Right to Peace and Quiet
  Campaign
rush hour 33

S

Sao Paulo, Brazil 36
Satan 75–76
schools 24, 28, 29, 56, 57, 113
Schroten, A. 95, 96
Schwela, D. 42
second hand noise 36

secular philosophies 76
seismic equipment 73
sensitivity 6, 41, 48, 134, 147, 152
Shaw, Jonathan 114, 127
shipping noise 3, 66–67, 73, 105, 164
shops 126, 129
short-haul flights 43, 104, 105, 106, 164
silence 74, 75–77, 129
Sim, Stuart 13–14
Skelly, Ian 74
Slabbekoorn, Hans 70, 72
Slater, Linda-Ruth 10–11
sleep disruption 55
Slow Movement 98
social justice 2, 36
sonar systems 64–65, 65–66, 73
sorting offices 126–127, 129
sound 5, 6, 47–48
sound insulation 3, 31, 99, 108, 111, 112,
  117, 163
South America 36
South Australia 147–148
South Korea 36–37
spadefoot toads 70
Spain 68
speed 66–67, 97–98
Squier, George Owen 122
standards 25–26, 39, 113
state level 28, 44, 147
statutory nuisance 132
steel plants 142
Steer Davies Gleave 97
Stewart, William H. 29, 54
Stewart, J. 42, 90, 144
Strathclyde, Lord 110
stress 50, 52–53, 72, 126
subjectivity of noise 47, 48
suicide 6, 7, 108

T

Tasmania, Australia 147, 155
tax-breaks 105–106, 164
technology
  children 10
  dependency 27
  home focus 11
  potential of new 26
  quieter 43, 44, 165
  widespread noise 23

televisions 9, 35, 53, 108, 110, 120, 125
Thailand 33
Thompson, Emily 7–8
Thomsen, F. 91
Tian, Jing 41
tinnitus 18, 52
torture 129
Town and Country Planning law 133
Townshend, Pete 52
trade unions 4, 82, 165
traffic noise
    costs 96
    disturbance by 25
    exposure 30
    industrializing countries 36, 38–39, 43
    law 137, 140, 142
    opposition to 49
    poorer communities 24
    reducing 2–3, 96–100, 162–163, 165
    rush hour 33
    see also transport noise; vehicle noise
train noise 3, 55, 120–121, 137
    see also railway noise
Train, Russell E. 29
transport noise 2, 24–25, 43, 94–107,
        137–140
tsunami 71
turbine noise 87–91
tyre noise 26, 96

U

underwater noise 1, 62, 63, 64, 90, 164
United Kingdom (UK)
    attitudes 9
    hum 20
    law 131–143
    neighbourhood noise 109–117
    piped music 119–129
    widespread noise 23–24
    wind farm noise 90
    workplace noise 81, 82
United States of America (US)
    classroom noise 57
    law 146
    National Parks 74–75
    noise recognition 54
    piped music 122

widespread noise 27–30, 43, 44
    wind farm noise 87, 88
    workplace noise 79
usefulness of the activity 135
US navy 65–66

V

VAD *see* vibroacoustic disease
van den Berg, G. P. 89
vehicle noise 37, 38–39, 41, 43
    see also traffic noise
vibration 47
vibroacoustic disease (VAD) 88
Victoria, Australia 147, 150–151
Vietnam 15
vulnerability 24, 32, 71

W

warning notices 132
wedding celebrations 34
Weedon, Val 7, 108–118
weighting noise measurements 19–20
well-being 47, 54, 73
Western Australia 147, 148–150
whales 63–64, 64–65, 91
Whitelegg, John 94
widespread noise 22–46
Wilkinson, John 69
wind farm noise 3, 17, 18, 85–91, 151,
        164
workplace noise 4, 79–93, 126–127, 129,
        165
World in Action 110

Y

yob deterrents 127–128
young people 51–52

Z

Zambia, workplace noise 83
Zaner, Annette 27
zoning approaches 40–41